WILLIAM SHAKESPEARE

JULIUS CAESAR

(*COMPLETE TEXT WITH PARAPHRASE, NOTES, EXPLANATORY COMMENTS AND IMPORTANT QUESTIONS WITH ANSWERS*)

by

R.K. Sharma
&
Har Prashad Gupta

LAXMI PUBLICATIONS (P) LTD.
INDIA • USA • GHANA • KENYA

WILLIAM SHAKESPEARE JULIUS CAESAR

Printed and bound in India
New Edition
NJC-0313-250-JULIUS CAESAR-SHA
ISBN 978-81-318-0944-0
Price: ₹ 250.00/USD 4

PUBLISHED IN INDIA BY

Laxmi Publications (P) Ltd.
113, GOLDEN HOUSE, DARYAGANJ,
NEW DELHI - 110002, INDIA
Telephone : 91-11-4353 2500, 4353 2501
Fax : 91-11-2325 2572, 4353 2528
www.laxmipublications.com
info@laxmipublications.com

Uganda Representative:
Benjamin Mpaka
✆ 0702358591
✆ 0782358591
benjampaka@gmail.com

C— 8350/014/03
Printed at: Ajit Printing Press, Delhi

CONTENTS

PART I

PART II

JULIUS CAESAR

1. ***Introduction***
2. ***Texts, its Notes and Paraphrase****—(Actwise)*

LIST OF ALL CHARACTERS
(Alphabetical)

Aeneas
Anchises
Antonius
Antony
Apollo
Artemidorus
Brutus
Caesar
Caius Cassius
Caius Ligarius
Calpurnia
Capitol
Carpenter
Casca
Cassius
Cato
Cicero
Cimber
Cinna
Cinna the Poet
Claudio
Claudius
Clitus
Cobbler
Colossus
Dardanius
Decius Brutus
Flavius
Ghost of Caesar
Julius Caesar
Laena
Lepidus
Lucillius
Lucius
Lupercal
Lupercallia
Marcus Brutus
Mark Antony
Marullus
Messala
Messenger
Metellus
Metellus Cimber
Miss
Octavius Caesar
Philippi
Pindarus
Plebeians
Poet
Pompey
Popilius Lena
Portia
Publius
Rhodes
Soothsayer
Strato
Tiber
Titinius
Trebonius
Tribunes
Triumvirate
Troy
Varro
Varrus
Volumnius
Young Cato

JULIUS CAESAR

MAIN CHARACTERS OF THE PLAY

Julius Caesar	—Roman General.
Octavious Caesar Marcus Antonius M. Aemelius Lepidus	Triumvirs after the death of Caesar.
Cicero Publius Popilius Lena	Members of the Roman Senate.
Marcus Brutus Cassius Casca Tribonius Ligarius Decius Brutus Metellus Cimber Cina	Conspirators against Caesar.
Flavius and Marullus	—Tribunes, faithful to Pompey.
A Soothsayer	
Cinna (*Helvius*)	—A Poet, killed by the mob.
Lucillius Titinius Messala Young Cato Volumnius	Friends of Brutus and Cassius.
Varro Clitus Claudius Strato Lucius Dardanius	Servants of Brutus.
Calpurnia	—Wife of Julius Caesar.
Portia	—Wife of Marcus Brutus.
Pindarus	—Servant of Cassius.

Senators, Citizens, Guards, Another Poet, Attendants, etc.

SCENE Rome ; The neighbourhood of Sardis;
The neighbourhood of Phillippi.

INTRODUCTION

1. SHAKESPEARE

Shakespeare is one of the greatest poets and dramatists of the world, and undoubtedly, the greatest of all English poets and dramatists. Though a lot of research has been done to find out facts and details about Shakespeare's life, yet very little is known about him. He was born on April 23, 1564 in the village Stratford-on-Avon. His father, John Shakespeare was a trader. Shakespeare's parents were illiterate.

It is said that Shakespeare had very little of formal education in a school or college. The world of living men and women was the school where Shakespeare got his real education. He married in 1582. In the year 1587, Shakespeare left his place and went to London. In London he worked in theatres, and came in contact with great dramatists and writers of his age. From London, he started his career as a writer.

All these details about Shakespeare's life are of no great use for us in understanding his play. The best of Shakespeare is in his plays. We can know Shakespeare, if we read his plays, become acquainted with his characters, and learn to understand and appreciate what Shakespeare has to say about life and its problems through his characters. We should feel the touch of noble passion, intense conflict of emotions and profound wisdom revealed in his plays. We will read 'Julius Caesar'. Let us be ready to meet great men and women of ancient Rome. Let us see how they live, love, suffer, enjoy and what they say and do.

2. THE PLAY "JULIUS CAESAR"

Theme of the play :

The play deals with the conspiracy hatched against Julius Caesar. It shows how some Romans thought that Caesar was becoming the all-powerful dictator of Rome. He was becoming a danger to freedom and republicanism. So believers in republicanism conspired against Caesar and murdered him in the Senate House. The supporter of Caesar, Antony, excited the fury of the mob against the conspirators. The conspirators had to fly away. Then Antony, with the help of Lepidus and Octavius Caesar, raised troops and gave a crushing defeat to the troops led by the conspirators. Cassius and Brutus, the leaders of the conspiracy committed suicide after their defeat. So we see that defeat of republicanism and victory of Caesarism is the theme of the play.

3. HISTORICAL BACK-GROUND AND BRIEF STORY OF THE PLAY

At first Rome was ruled over by strong and powerful kings. Then at a certain age the kingship was abolished. Rome became a Republic headed by a Senate. The Senate was a representative body consisting of elected members. Then came the Civil War. The Aristocrats of the Senate clashed with the republicans. The republicans were defeated. The Aristocrats became all powerful in the Senate. The Senate, headed by the first Triumvirate (*the group of three highest administrators enjoying equal rights and authority*), ruled over Rome. But after some time, there arose a conflict between Pompey and Caesar. Pompey rose up in the rebellion, and was defeated. After Pompey's death, Caesar became very powerful. He defeated Pompey's sons. Caesar returned to Rome after defeating Pompey's sons. The people of Rome were ready to take Caesar in a victory procession through the streets of Rome. They were going to offer him a crown. Thus Caesar was going to be a king wearing a crown. Some republicans were jealous of Caesar's growing power.

The play 'Julius Caesar' starts from here. Julius Caesar has returned to Rome after his victory over Pompey's sons. The common people wearing their best clothes are out in the streets to give him a thundering welcome. They are impatient to catch a glimpse of their hero as he passes in a victory procession. Caesar's statues are decorated with ribbons and coloured handkerchiefs. There is, however, a section of Senators and officials who are discontented and unhappy. They are jealous and afraid of this growing power of Caesar.

Two tribunes, Flavius and Marullus rebuke the common people, and ask them to go home. They tell them that Caesar has murdered the sons of Pompey whom once they worshipped as their hero. The tribunes move through the streets and remove decorations from Caesar's statues. Thus we see that there is strong opposition against Caesar among the higher classes and the republicans. But the common people want a strong man like Caesar. They want a hero whom they can worship.

Caesar, with his followers, reaches the place where the feast of Lupercalia is to be held. A sooth-sayer warns Caesar against the coming danger. But Caesar pays no heed to it. When Caesar and his train pass, Cassius meets Brutus. Cassius is a very clever and cunning man. He is jealous of Caesar's growing power. Very artfully Cassius tells Brutus that Caesar is in no way better than Brutus or Cassius, yet he has become the most powerful man of Rome. All other men of Rome are like his slaves. They only flatter him and bow before him.

Thus Cassius tries to win Brutus to his side. He talks to other Senators, and thus hatches a conspiracy against Caesar. At Brutus' place in the night, the conspirators decide to kill Caesar the next morning. Cassius suggests that Antony, who loves Brutus deeply, should also be killed. But Brutus, an idealist, says that there should be no unnecessary blood-shed.

Next day Caesar's wife asks Caesar not to move out, as she has had a bad dream in the night. The augurers (*foretellers*) also send a warning. Caesar agrees not to go. But Decius Brutus, one of the conspirators, gives a different interpretation to the dream of Caesar's wife, and persuades Caesar to go to the Senate House. Soon other conspirators reach Caesar's house in a group and Caesar accompanies them to the Senate House. On his way, Caesar is warned by a soothsayer, but he pays no heed to him.

In the Senate House the conspirators put a petition before him. On their knees, they ask Caesar to call the brother of Metellus Cimber back from his exile, and grant him freedom. Caesar gives them all a flat refusal. At this, Casca a conspirator, stabs Caesar and then others also strike at him. Caesar falls dead. There is a panic all around. Antony, the closest friend of Caesar runs home in great panic. After some time Antony sends his servant. The servant tells Brutus that Antony has all regard and respect for them. But he wants to be assured that no harm will be done to him. Brutus gives this assurance. Antony comes to the Senate House. He asks Brutus to give him permission to take Caesar's body out, and to speak at Caesar's funeral. Cassius, the practical man, objects to it. But, Brutus, the idealist, allows him to do that. Antony makes a moving speech. He proves to the mob that Caesar was not ambitious. He was a great servant and lover of his people. Antony's speech rouses the fury of the mob. They take the body of Caesar and run mad with anger, to kill all the conspirators and burn their houses. The conspirators run for their lives.

Antony, with the help of Octavius and Lepidus, raises a powerful army. Brutus and Cassius also raise their forces. The two forces meet on the plains of Philippi. Brutus sees the ghost of Caesar. It proves that the spirit of Caesar (*Caesarism ; imperialism*) is still alive. Before the final battle, the leaders of the two armies hold a conference which turns into an exchange of hot and bitter words. Then orders for battle are given. Brutus gains some advantage over the forces of Octavius. But forces of Cassius are surrounded and overpowered by the troops of Antony. Cassius sends Titinius to find out the fate of Brutus' forces. Soon, Cassius's slave Pindarus gives wrong information that Titinius has been caught. Fate plays a trick upon Cassius. Utterly disappointed, Cassius asks his slave Pindarus to kill him. Cassius dies. Cassius' death shocks Brutus. He makes one more attempt to push the enemy back, but now enemy is very powerful. Forces of Brutus are overpowered and defeated. Brutus also kills himself. The victors, Antony and Octavius pay their homage to Brutus. Antony rightly calls him the "noblest Roman of them all". Order is given to do all honour to Brutus' dead body. Then the victors depart to share the glory of their grand victory.

This, in short, is the story of the play "Julius Caesar".

CONTENTS OF THE PLAY (*ACT-WISE*)

ACT I

SCENE (*i*)

The streets of Rome are full of gay people wearing their best clothes. Suddenly Flavius and Marullus, two Tribunes (*officials chosen by the people*) appear on the scene. They ask the people why they are not at their respective jobs, why they are moving about gaily dressed, and in a holiday mood. Some-one from the crowd tells them that they are going to give Caesar a grand reception. Caesar, the great general, is returning home after a glorious victory over the sons of Pompey (*another great Roman who had rebelled against Caesar*). Marullus seems to have no respect for the common people. He calls them names, rebukes them and reminds them that once they loved and worshipped Pompey as their hero. He calls them ungrateful wretches who are now going to greet Caesar who is the murderer of Pompey's sons. He also asks them what great victory Caesar has won. He has brought no prisoners of war with him. He has not conquered any new territory. He has not brought any wealth to Rome. Both the tribunes ask the crowd to go back home, and weep and repent of what they have done. The people move away like chidden dogs. Then Flavius says that they should both move through the streets and remove all decorations from Caesar's statues. He says that Caesar has become very powerful. He wants to fly higher up. His feathers should be plucked. Caesar should not be allowed to become all-powerful. The Tribunes leave with these words.

[*The first scene gives us a peep into the political unrest and discontent among the higher classes. The mindless mob loves Caesar. For the mob loves hero-worship. Caesar is their hero. But the officials, like these Tribunes, are jealous as well as afraid of Caesar's growing power*]

SCENE (*ii*)

It is a public place. Caesar, with his wife and a train of his followers, appears on the scene. They are going to celebrate the feast of Lupercalia. A sooth-sayer warns Caesar against the coming danger on 15th of March. Caesar, however, pays no heed to his warning. Caesar wants that Antony who is going to run the race in the celebrations of Lupercalia should touch his wife, while he runs the race. Caesar has a superstitious belief that this touch will cure his wife of her barrenness. We see that Caesar is feared and flattered by almost all. All are silent when Caesar speaks.

While all this is going on, Cassius, a very cunning and clever man, catches hold of Brutus who is greatly respected by all the Romans very cleverly. Cassius tells Brutus that he (*Brutus*) is ignorant of his own worth.

He then says that Caesar has become the most powerful man in Rome. He gives some instances to prove that Caesar is actually a weak and worthless man. He has become powerful only because the Romans have lost all sense of self-respect and all love of freedom. Brutus assures him that he would do everything for the good of his people. While they are talking, they hear loud shouts.

Soon Caesar returns with his train. Caesar sees Cassius who is a lean and thin man. Caesar says that he fears such a man because he reads and thinks too much. Such a man is always jealous of others' power. Caesar goes away with his train. Cassius holds Casca and asks him what those three shouts were. Casca tells them that three shouts were raised by the people when three times Caesar refused to accept the crown which Antony offered him. Casca also expresses his fears about Caesar's growing power. Casca goes away. Brutus also takes leave of Cassius. Left alone, Cassius decides that he will have some letters written in different hands, thrown into the window of Brutus. In these letters Brutus will be requested to save Rome from Caesar's tyranny. Cassius also goes.

[*Scene second shows us Cassius at work. He is a very clever man. He is jealous of Caesar. Brutus, on the other hand, is a noble man, an idealist. He has no grudge against Caesar. But he is not a practical man. Caesar is physically weak, very proud and superstitious*]

SCENE (*iii*)

It is a dark stormy night. Casca and Cicero come. Casca talks about the strange and supernatural happenings. He says how he saw a slave whose hand was in flames, but he did not feel the burnt; he saw men enveloped in fire, moving up and down the streets; he saw a lion in front of the capitol. Casca says that these evil omens show that something terrible is going to happen to Rome and the Romans. Cicero goes away. Cassius comes and joins Casca. Cassius says that Caesar himself has become full of horror and monstrous power like this strange stormy night. Caesar now moves about and roars like a lion in the capitol. Cassius tells Casca that Caesar has become a wolf because he finds the Romans to be weak and mild like lambs. He has become a lion because he finds the Romans to be harmless like deer. Casca tells Cassius that the Senators are going to make Caesar a king. He will wear his crown in all the parts of the Roman empire except Italy (*Rome*). Cassius says that in that case he would make himself free by killing himself. He tells Casca that they have a very dangerous work in hand. At this point Cinna joins them. Cinna has already been won to the cause of conspiracy. Cinna suggests that Cassius should try to win Brutus' support. If noble Brutus is with them, their act of killing Caesar will not be considered an act of murder. It will be considered an act of liberation of Rome. Cassius says that Brutus is more than half with them.

Cassius gives some letters to Cinna and asks him to place them at different places in Brutus' house. He assures Casca that Brutus' support will surely be won.

[*This scene shows us the development of the conspiracy. We also see the motives of the different conspirators. All except Brutus, have some personal grudge (jealousy) against Caesar*]

ACT II

SCENE (*i*)

This scene opens in the house of Brutus. Brutus is walking in his garden. He is thinking over the plan of Caesar's proposed murder. The poison poured by Cassius into his heart and mind has started doing its work. Brutus is now torn between his love for Caesar and his love for Rome. He is trying to find out convincing reasons for Caesar's murder. He says that he has nothing against Caesar. Hitherto Caesar has been good, reasonable and just. But, then, Brutus argues in his own philosophic way. He says that Caesar is not dangerous now, but as his power grows he may become dangerous. He is like a serpent's egg which becomes dangerous as soon as it is hatched, and the snake comes out of it. Brutus thinks, that it is better to kill the serpent in the egg. So this idealist decides to kill Caesar because he fears that he may grow into a danger to Rome and the freedom of the Romans.

At this point his servant gives Brutus the letters forged by Cassius. Brutus reads them and gets convinced that Caesar should be murdered for the good of his countrymen. Soon Cassius and other conspirators came to Brutus' house. Seeing their faces partly covered with their hats and cloaks, Brutus, the idealist says that conspiracy cannot hide its ugly face even in the darkness of hell. Cassius introduces the other conspirators to Brutus. He proposes that they should take an oath in order to bind them together and to execute their plan with faithfulness and complete secrecy. Here again, the idealist Brutus does a thing which is wrong from a practical point of view. He objects to any oath-taking. He says that only liars, priests and ill intentioned persons take oath. Their sense of honour, their faith in their noble mission should be strong enough to bind them together. Then Cassius, a practical man of action proposes that Antony should also be killed along with Caesar. Here again Brutus' nobleness wins. Brutus, says that Antony is only a limb of Caesar. He will be harmless as soon as Caesar's head is cut off. For all his love for Caesar he can do no harm to them. He can harm only himself by dying of grief over Caesar's death. Brutus further says that they should sacrifice Caesar on the altar of the freedom of Rome. They should not behave like butchers. No one except

Caesar should be touched. This is one big practical mistake of Brutus, the idealist. Cassius has more practical understanding of human nature and human affairs. He proposes the right thing. But he bows before Brutus' noble character. The conspirators decide to meet in the Capitol, and take leave of Brutus.

At this point Portia, Brutus' wife enters. She wants to know why Brutus is disturbed and worried. Brutus tries to put her off, saying that he is only sick. But in the name of her love, her beauty and her right as wife, Portia asks Brutus to open his mind to her. Portia tells him that she is his wife and not his keep (रखैल) or mistress. She has a right to know his secrets. She is the daughter of great Cato and wife of noble Brutus. Though a woman, yet she has strength enough to keep his secrets. Brutus still does not want to disturb her by telling about the plan to murder Caesar. He puts her off saying that she should go to her bed now, and very soon he will disclose everything to her.

[*This scene shows that Brutus is a noble man. But he is not fit to be the leader of the conspiracy. We also see that the leadership slips from the hands of Cassius, and goes into the hands of Brutus. Cassius as leader would have been better, but Brutus' nobility of character makes Cassius submit to Brutus' wrong proposals. As a man Brutus is noble. His love and respect for his wife prove that he is a man who can respect another person's individuality*].

SCENE (*ii*)

It is Caesar's house. Caesar is ready to go to the Capitol. But, he sends a servant to ask the augurers to make sacrifice, and tell him about the result of it. He wants to be sure about the success of his day's mission. Calpurnia, Caesar's wife comes in. She asks Caesar not to go out of his house. She mentions the omens and strange happenings of the night. She says that these evil omens are a warning that something bad may happen to Caesar. Proud and boastful Caesar pays no heed to his wife's request. Caesar says that these omens are there for all. Calpurnia again argues that no omen appears to announce the death of ordinary men. But the deaths of kings and great men like Caesar are announced by gods through omens and portents. The servant also tells Caesar that the augurers advise Caesar not to leave his house. Because when they sacrificed an animal, they found that it (*the animal*) had no heart. It was an evil omen, a warning to Caesar. Caesar, however, boasts that gods want to say that if Caesar does not go to the Senate House, he is a person without a heart (*courage*), like the sacrificed animal. He boasts that he is more dangerous than danger itself. But, somehow, he is moved by the appeals of his wife and agrees to stay at home. He agrees to send Antonio to the Senate House to tell the Senators that Caesar is not coming.

Just, then, Decius Brutus, one of the conspirators comes to take Caesar to the Senate House. Caesar tells him that he will not go to the Senate House, because his wife had a bad dream last night. She saw that Caesar's statue was throwing out blood from many holes, and some healthy Romans with smiling faces were washing their hands in that blood. Decius gives a favourable interpretation to the dream. He says that the dream indicates that Caesar will fill Rome with new life-blood, and that Romans will dip their handkerchiefs in that blood to keep them as sacred relics or memorials. He further tells Caesar that his not going to the Senate on this occasion will be ridiculed. Some one may taunt–"Let the Senate disperse till Caesar's wife has a better dream." These words rouse the pride of Caesar. He at once gets ready to go. He tells his wife that her fears are foolish. At this point Brutus, along with other conspirators, comes to take Caesar to the Senate House. Antony, Caesar's great admirer and friend, also comes. Caesar greets them warmly. Brutus is moved to see this unsuspecting warmth of Caesar. He says that they all are not what they appear to be to Caesar. (*Caesar greets them as friends, but they are going to kill him very soon*). They all leave for the Senate House.

[This scene shows Caesar's character. Caesar is a proud, boastful, superstitious man suffering from mental as well as physical weakness. He has a wavering mind. He is full of fear, yet he says that he fears nothing. He boasts that he is more dangerous than danger itself. As a husband also, Caesar appears to be proud and inconsiderate. He has no regards and respect for his wife. He treats her only as a plaything, a creature to be rebuked, and sometimes to be humoured].

SCENE (*iii*)

Artemidorous, a sooth-sayer comes to know of the conspiracy against Caesar. He has written a warning on a piece of paper. He stands in the street to hand over this warning to Caesar when Caesar, on his way to the Senate House, will pass that way.

SCENE (*iv*)

Portia, the wife of Brutus, is standing outside her house. She is very much disturbed and worried about the fate of her husband and the secret plan in which he is involved in killing Caesar. She sends her servant to the Senate House. She wants to know how her husband is, and what Caesar is doing. She prays for the success of the conspirators.

ACT III

SCENE (*i*)

When Caesar approaches the Capitol to attend the meeting of the Senate, Artemidorus requests him to read the paper on which he has written the warning. Caesar just brushes him aside and enters the Senate House. There the conspirators work according to their plan. First Metellus Cimber kneels down before Caesar. He appeals to Caesar to recall his brother from his exile. Cassius also appeals to Caesar. But Caesar makes an arrogant speech. He says that Cassius' flattery and kneeling too will not move him. He says that he is firm and fixed like the Pole Star. He will never change his decision. He says even this that if Cassius crawled at his feet like a dog, he (*Caesar*) would kick him as if he (*Caesar*) were a dog. Even Brutus' appeal fails to move Caesar. Cinna and Decius also make an appeal to him. But Caesar remains unmoved. They also get a similar arrogant answer. At this point Casca stabs Caesar. Then the other conspirators also stab him. When Brutus stabs Caesar, it is too much for Caesar. He is shocked. He gives up all resistance. He cries, "You, too, Brutus"! (Ettu, Brute!)—with these words Caesar falls dead in a pool of his own blood. As soon as Caesar falls, there is wild rushing and running. Panic-stricken, Antony also rushes home for his life. After some time Antony's servant comes and tells Brutus that Antony, his master, wants to meet him.

Antony comes. He first pays homage to dead Caesar. He tells the conspirators that if they want to kill him, they should kill him at once. Their swords bathed in Caesar's blood will be the best weapon to kill Antony with. Brutus assures him that they mean no harm to him. They killed Caesar because they loved Rome more than they loved Caesar. Antony asks Brutus to allow him to take Caesar's body to the market place, and also to make a funeral speech at Caesar's funeral. Noble minded Brutus commits another fatal mistake. He allows Antony to do all that. Cassius again objects to it, but he surrenders to the stronger character of Brutus. Brutus allows Antony to speak on two conditions—(*i*) that Antony will speak after Brutus and from the same forum from which Brutus will speak. (*ii*) Antony will praise Caesar as much as he may like, but he will not blame the conspirators.

SCENE (*ii*)

This is a very important scene. A huge crowd has gathered in the market place. Brutus is standing on a public stage. The people cry that they want proper explanation for Caesar's murder. Brutus is a thinker; he knows his books, but he knows nothing about the working of the mind of the mob. He makes a philosophic speech. His arguments are too subtle for the common people to be understood.

Brutus makes an appeal to their reason. He forgets that common people are more sentimental and emotional. They have very little reason. In a mob even the most rational man becomes irrational. Brutus does not know it. "He says that he loved Caesar. He killed Caesar only because he loved Rome more than he loved Caesar. Caesar was ambitious. He longed to become a super-power. He was a danger to the freedom of Rome. He has tears for the love that Caesar had for him (*Brutus*) ; he has respect for Caesar's greatness and goodness. He was happy that Caesar was fortunate, but he killed Caesar because he was ambitious. Caesar, if living would have made all the Romans his slaves. So he had to be killed." This appeal to reason makes no deep impression on the people. But the fickle minded mob cries "Let Brutus be Caesar". It shows that all that Brutus spoke against Caesar and Caesarism fell flat on their deaf ears. Mob is always fickle minded. Mob loves to worship heroes ; freedom and honour mean little to them. Brutus requests the people to wait and listen to Antony's speech.

Brutus gets down the stage and goes out. Antony is a more practical man. He has to start with a handicap (बाधा). The mob is very much impressed with Brutus' words. They call Caesar a tyrant. So Antony has to win a mob already prejudiced against Caesar. But Antony knows how the mind of the mob works. He knows that appeal to the emotions and passions of a mob make the deepest effect. So he gives up cold logic and uses every possible trick to rouse the anger and passions of the mob. He says that he has come to bury Caesar, not to praise him. When the mob is in a mood to listen, Antony says that Brutus has called Caesar ambitious and if he was ambitious, it was a great fault in him. But, then Antony goes on to prove that Caesar was not ambitious. He was kind, just, generous and good to his people. Antony gives concrete instances. He tells the mob that on the feast of Lupercalia he himself offered Caesar a crown three times. But every time Caesar refused it. Was it an ambition of Caesar ? Strange, that an honourable man like Brutus should call Caesar ambitious ! Whenever he saw poor people suffering, he wept for them. Was it ambition ? An ambitious man can never be so kind-hearted.

Antony tells the mob that Caesar won battles and brought many prisoners. The price for release of those prisoners enriched the treasury of Rome. All this does not prove Caesar to be ambitious. Then like a master actor, Antony pauses as if he were overwhelmed with grief. His pathetic appeal, his repeated ironical reference to Brutus' honesty produce the desired effect on the mob. Then very cunningly he mentions Caesar's will, but says that he will not read it. Because if he reads the will to them, they will be moved. They are not lifeless woods and stones. Thus Antony has excited their curiosity all the more. But when they compel him to read the will, he says that he will first show them the man (*Caesar*) who had made that will.

Then he gets down the pulpit, and again like master actor, he holds the cloak of Caesar and points to the holes made by the daggers of Caesar's murderers. Movingly he describes how the wound given by Brutus was unkindest and most unnatural, because Caesar had great love and respect for Brutus. When the mob is deeply moved, Antony says that they have been only moved at the sight of Caesar's wounded cloak. He asks them now to see the wounded body of Caesar. With a dramatic gesture he uncovers the body of Caesar and says, "Here is himself, marr'd, as you see, with traitors."

The people are now furious. They cry "Revenge! seek! burn! fire! kill". It is at this point that Antony asks them to stay and hear the will read. He reads out that Caesar has left seventy five drachmas for every individual; he has left his private walks, gardens and bowers for the free use of the public. This last stroke lashes the mob into a mad fury. They lift the body of Caesar and rush to catch and kill all the conspirators, and set fire to their houses.

Antony says that he has roused the passions and fury of the mob. Now it will take its own course. At this point a servant of Octavius brings information that Octavius has returned to Rome. Antony goes to meet him.

[*This scene shows a sudden change in Antony. From a merry maker and pleasure-seeker, he becomes a shrewd man of action. The fate of the conspiracy also takes a sudden turn. We see that Cassius' fears about Antony were real. Cassius has a better understanding of human character. Brutus considers everybody to be as good as he himself is*]

SCENE (*iii*)

This short scene opens in a street in Rome. The angry mob catches hold of Cinna, the poet. They ask him where he is going, whether he is married or not and such other silly questions. They ask his name. When he tells them that his name is Cinna, they shout that he is a conspirator, he should be cut to pieces. The poor fellow says that he is not Cinna the conspirator, but Cinna the poet. At this some fool among them cries that he should be killed for his bad poems.

[*The scene shows how irrational, cruel and foolish a mob can be. The mob in 'Julius Caesar' plays an important role. Brutus fails because he does not understand the mob. Antony wins because he knows the mob. This mindless mob could not appreciate freedom. It wanted to be ruled over by a powerful man like Caesar*]

ACT IV

SCENE (*i*)

The scene opens on a room in Antony's house.

This scene is called proscription scene. Because in this scene, Antony, Octavius and Lepidus prepare a list of unwanted people who are to be killed by them. Some months have passed. Now the government of Rome is in the hands of Octavius, Antony and Lepidus. They are the highest administrators. They make the new Triumvirate. Brutus and Cassius are now in Greece.

First, these three persons decide that the brother of Lepidus, and Antony's cousin, Publius must be killed. They mark their names in the list. Then Antony sends Lepidus to bring Caesar's will. They want to reduce the amount that Caesar had left for the people in his will.

When Lepidus is away, Antony tells Octavius that he (*Lepidus*) is a fool fit to be used only as a beast of burden. He does not deserve the honour of ruling over Rome with them. Now with these honours, he shares some blames also. But when he has served their purpose, they must take away all his powers and titles. Octavius takes leave of Antony and goes.

[*This scene reveals a new side of Antony, who was till now only a masker and reveller, and then a faithful friend of Caesar. But now we see how selfish, cruel and unprincipled he can be. He can use a friend only as a beast of burden. He can tamper with* (*change*) *the sacred will of Caesar. All this proves that Antony is mad after power and he can do anything and everything to get it.*]

SCENE (*ii*)

Now we reach Sardis. Brutus' forces are camping at Sardis. Brutus stands before his tent. His servant Lucillius comes with Pindarus, a slave of Cassius. Brutus has some grievances against Cassius. He asks Lucillius how Cassius had received him. Lucillius tells him that Cassius did not show that warmth and love as he used to do in the past. Brutus feels that Cassius is now cooling down. He does not love him as he used to do.

Soon, Cassius reaches there with his forces. He openly accuses Brutus of having done a wrong to him (*Cassius*). Brutus says that they should not quarrel before their troops. So they go into Brutus's tent.

SCENE (*iii*)

Cassius is in Brutus' tent. Both, Brutus and Cassius have grievances against each other. Cassius tells Brutus that he has done a great wrong to him. Cassius says that Brutus accused Lucilius Pella of exacting bribes from the Sardinians. Cassius himself had written to Brutus that Pella should not be accused. But Brutus paid no heed to Cassius' letters. Cassius further says that in times of great crisis, such offences should not be taken seriously. Brutus tells cassius that he was wrong to defend such an act of dishonesty. He further reminds Cassius of the noble motive behind Caesar's murder. So, they who killed Caesar should not behave like robbers by exacting bribe. Brutus becomes even harsher. He tells Cassius that he himself (*Cassius*) has been exacting bribes for the promotion to higher posts. He says that Cassius sold higher posts. He appointed incompetent and worthless persons on higher posts, simply because he is greedy and wants money. This charge shocks Cassius. He tells Brutus not to provoke him any further, for, in his anger he may do some great harm to Brutus. He may even kill him. Then Brutus tells Cassius that he (*Brutus*) had asked him (*Cassius*) to send some money. But he refused to do that. Cassius, then, tells him that the messenger who brought that news to Brutus was a fool. Cassius is so sad that he takes out his dagger and asks Brutus to kill him. Then, Brutus tells him that he is sorry for having used such harsh language. He further tells Cassius that he is disturbed and ill-tempered because Portia, his wife has killed herself by swallowing burning coals. This news shocks Cassius. He says that Brutus should have killed him for being so harsh to him when he (*Brutus*) was so grief-stricken. Cassius asks Brutus to forgive him for his ill-temper which he has inherited from his mother.

Then the two friends discuss what they should do. Cassius suggests that they should wait for the enemy forces. Because in marching to them, the enemy forces will get tired and exhausted, but their forces will remain fresh and ready to meet them. Here again Brutus' impractical idealism commits a mistake. Brutus proposes that their army should march. Once again Cassius gives way, and the fate of the conspirators is sealed. Cassius goes out.

Now we see Brutus as a man with a lot of the milk of human kindness. He wants to enjoy music. But he cannot be harsh to his slave. He asks his guards to sleep on cushions in his tent. Lucius his slave plays on his harp and sings a song for Brutus. But, when he is overpowered with sleep, Brutus takes his harp and leaves him asleep. It is at this stage that Caesar's ghost appears. Brutus thinks that it is an illusion of his weak eyes. But the ghost tells Brutus that it will meet him on the plains of Philippi. Brutus rouses his guards. He asks them to go to Cassius and tell him that he should order his forces to march early in the morning.

[*This scene shows that the cause of conspiracy is cracking. It also throws some light on the character of Brutus and Cassius. Cassius is always more practical. His suggestions are better than those of Brutus. But, Cassius has a weaker character. So he always gives way to Brutus.*]

ACT V

SCENE (*i*)

The scene opens on the plains of Philippi. Octavius and Antony come with their army. Antony tells Octavius. that the enemy (*Forces of*

Brutus and Cassius) is full of great fear. But he wants to hide his fear behind a show of courage and military splendour. Just then a messenger brings the news that the enemy forces are rushing with a great show of army splendour. Their red flag is flying in the air. Soon, Brutus and Cassius reach there with their forces. The generals on the two sides hold a conference. The conference, however, changes into an exchange of taunts, hot words and challenges. Antony calls them dogs, slaves and flatterers. Cassius reminds Brutus that his suggestion to kill Antony along with Caesar was right. If Brutus had allowed that, Antony would not have lived to insult them now. Cassius also hurls abuses on Antony and Octavius. He calls Octavius a worthless school boy, and Antony, a masker and reveller. Soon the conference is over. Octavius tells them to come to the battlefield if they have courage. Octavius and Antony go away with their army. Cassius is depressed.

It is the last meeting of Brutus and Cassius. Cassius says that he will commit suicide, if they are defeated. Brutus still says that he would not commit suicide, because committing suicide means interfering with the work of gods and nature. They bid farewell to each other, and order their forces to march to their respective positions.

SCENE (*ii*)

Brutus asks Messala to ride fast and hand over some written order to his troops. Forces of Octavius are cold, perhaps, tired. So, Brutus' forces should make a sudden attack to overpower and defeat those forces.

SCENE (*iii*)

It is another part of the field. There is panic in the ranks of Cassius. Cassius tells Titinius that he himself had to kill his flag-bearer, because he was running away from the battle-field. Cassius has run away. He is on a hill, quite far away from Antony's forces. He sees certain troops in the distance, and sends his man, Titinius to find whether they are friends or foes. He also asks his slave, Pindarus to climb up the hill and see what happens to Titinius. This time fate also plays a dirty trick on Cassius. Pindarus sees some soldiers on horsebacks rushing towards Titinius. Some of them get down. Titinius also gets down. They surround Titinius and shout. These are victorious troops of Brutus. They, in fact greet Titinius with shouts of joy, and give a garland to be offered to Cassius. But poor Pindarus misunderstands the whole thing. He takes those soldiers for enemies, and thinks that Titinius has been taken prisoner. He gives this wrong report to Cassius. It breaks Cassius' heart. Cassius gives Pindarus his sword and orders him to thrust it into his heart. Pindarus does that and Cassius falls with these words "Caesar thou art revenged, even with the sword that killed thee" Titinius returns with Messala. Titinius finds Cassius' dead body. He also kills himself with that sword. Messala, who had gone to find out Pindarus, returns with Brutus. They lament the cruel mistake which led to the death of Titinius and Cassius, and then they go back to the battle-field.

SCENE (*iv*)

Antony's soldiers capture Lucilius. They think him to be Brutus. Lucilius also poses to be Brutus. Antony reaches there and tells the soldiers that they are mistaken. He orders them to keep Lucilius in safe custody, because he is a good man, and Antony wants to have good men as his friends.

SCENE (*v*)

This is the last scene of the play. Brutus finds that he has lost the battle. He requests his friends to stab him, but they refuse. At last he asks Strato to hold his sword. Then Brutus runs on it. Octavius and Antony arrive. They see what has happened. Antony pays a glowing tribute to Brutus. He calls him the noblest Roman of them all. He says that all other conspirators were jealous of Caesar. Brutus had joined them only for the common good of all the Romans. Octavius says that Brutus will be given an honourable burial which is due to a brave warrior. Then, the victorious generals go away to share the glories of their grand victory.

JULIUS CAESAR

TEXT

ACT I

Scene I—Rome, A Street

Enter : Flavius, Marullus and certain Commoners over the stage.

Flav. Hence ! home, you *idle creatures,* get you home :
Is this a holiday ? What ! know you not,
Being *mechanical,* you ought not walk
Upon a *labouring day* without the *sign*
Of your profession ? Speak, what *trade* art thou ?

First Com. Why, sir, a carpenter.

Mar. Where is thy leather *apron* and thy *rule* ?
What dost thou with thy best *apparel* on ?
You, sir, what trade are you ?

Sec. Com. Truly, sir, *in respect of a fine workman. I am but,* as you would say, *a cobbler.*

Mar. But *what trade art thou ?* Answer me *directly.*

Sec. Com. A trade, sir, that I hope I may *use with a safe conscience* : which is, indeed, sir, a *mender of bad soles.*

Mar. What trade, thou *knave* ? thou *naughty* knave, what trade ?

Sec. Com. Nay, I *beseech* you, sir, *be not out* with me : yet *if you be out,* sir, *I can mend you.*

Mar. What meanest thou by that ? Mend me thou *saucy* fellow !

Sec. Com. Why, sir, *cobble you.*

Flav. Thou art a cobbler, *art thou ?*

Sec. Com. Truly, sir, all that I live by is with the *awl* ; I *meddle* with no tradesman's *matters,* nor women's matters ; *but with awl* I am, indeed, sir, a *surgeon*, to old shoes ; when they are *in great danger*, I *re-*

Hence—go away; be off; leave this place. **Idle creatures**—do-nothings; idlers. **Mechanical**—ordinary craftsmen ; ordinary labourers. **Labouring day**—a working day (a day which is not a holiday). **Sign of your profession**—clothes and tools which working men should wear and use on their professional duty. **Trade**—Profession; line; occupation. **Apron**—a loose cloth or garment worn over the front part of the body to keep the clothes clean. **Rule**—foot rule, **Dost**—do. **Thou**—you. **What dost thou...?**—what are you doing...?. **Apparel**—clothes, dress. **In respect of**—in comparison with; as compared to. **Fine workman**—skilled worker. **In respect of a fine workman**—As compared to a skilled workman. **I am but**—I am only. **A cobbler**—a mender of shoes. [The word has two meanings—cobbler means 'a bungler'; or 'a mender of shoes'. **What trade art thou**—what is your job; what is your profession. **Directly**—plainly, without beating about the bush. **Use**—practice; follow. **With a safe conscience**—without feeling ashamed of it. **Mender of bad soles**—mender of the worn out soles or souls. **Knave**—poor fellow. **Naughty**—worthless; good-for-

PARAPHRASE

ACT I

Scene I—Rome, A Street

Enter : Flavius, Marullus and certain Commoners.

Flav. Go away, you idle fellows, go back to your homes. Is it a holiday ? You are manual labourers and you should know that on a working day you should move about wearing your working clothes and having your tools which are the signs of your respective professions. Tell me, you fellow, what is your profession ?

First Com. My profession, Sir ? I am a carpenter.

Mar. Where, then, is your leather apron and your foot-rule ? Why are you wandering about in your finest clothes ? And, you fellow ? What is your profession ?

Sec. Com. To speak the truth, Sir, as compared to a skilled worker I am only an unskilled mender of shoes.

Mar. What is your profession ? Give me a straight answer.

Sec. Com. I have a profession, Sir, which I can follow without feeling ashamed of it. I am really, Sir, a mender of worn out (*bad*) soles. [*There is a play on the word 'soles' and 'souls'. He suggests that he can reform bad souls like that of Marullus. Simple meaning is that he repairs bad or worn out soles of the shoes (जूतों के तले)*]

Mar. You foolish rogue, tell me plainly what your profession is.

Sec. Com. I request you, sir, not to be angry with me. If you are angry with me, I can mend you also. [*If your shoes are worn out I can mend them.*]

Mar. You impudent fool ! What do you mean when you say that you can mend me ?

Sec. Com. Well, Sir, I mean that I can repair your shoes.

Flav. So, you are a cobbler. Are you a cobbler ?

Sec. Com. Yes Sir, I earn my livelihood only with the awl. I do not interfere with any man's or woman's business ; my business is with awl [*a play on the word 'awl' (मोची का औजार, सुतारी, सुआ) and 'all' सब)*] I am, sir, a mender of old shoes. When the shoes are badly worn out I repair them

---

nothing. **Beseech**—request. **Be not out**—do not be angry [or do not show me torn portion of your heels or any part of your shoe. **If you be out**—if you are angry [or if your shoes are out at heels]. **I can mend you**—I can mend your shoes [or I can set you right]. **Saucy**—impudent; insolent. **Cobble you**—mend your shoes (or mend you), set you right. **Art thou**—are you? **Awl**—shoe maker's tool. **Meddle**—interfere. **Matters**—affairs. **But with awl**—I work with my awl [or I interfere with or work for all]. **Surgeon**—mender. **In great danger**—shoes in a totally hopeless condition. **Recover**—mend or restore to health.

cover them. As *proper men as* ever *trod* upon *neat*'s *leather* have gone upon my *handiwork.*

Flav. But *wherefore* are not in thy shop to–day ?
Why dost thou *lead* these men about the streets ?

Sec. Com. Truly, sir, to *wear out their shoes,* to get myself into more work. But, indeed, sir, we make holiday to see Caesar, and to *rejoice in his triumph.*

Mar. Wherefore rejoice ? *What conquest* brings he home ?
What *tributaries* follow him to Rome.
To grace in *captive bonds* his chariot-wheels ?
You *blocks,* you stones, you worse than *senseless things !*
O you *hard* hearts, you cruel men of Rome,
Knew you not Pompey ? Many a time and *oft.*
Have you climbed up to walls and *battlements,*
To towers and windows, yea, to chimney-tops,
Your infants in your arms, and there have sat
The livelong day, with *patient expectation,*
To see great Pompey *pass the streets of Rome* ;
And when you saw his chariot *but* appear,
Have you not made *an universal shout.*
That Tiber trembled underneath her banks.
To hear the *replication* of your sounds,
Made in her *concave shores* ?
And do you now put on your best *attire* ?
And do you now *cull out a holiday ?*
And do you now *strew* flowers in his way
That comes in triumph over *Pompey's blood* ?
Be gone !
Run to your houses, fall upon your knees,
Pray to the gods to *intermit* the *plague*
That needs must light on *this ingratitude,*

Proper men—fine men. **As**—who. **Trod**—Walked. **Neat's leather**—shoes made of ox's skin. **Handiwork**—work done by my hands.

Wherefore—why; what for. **Lead**—leading. **Wear out their shoes**—to make them wear out their shoes by walking. **Rejoice in his triumph**—to feel glad at Caesar's victory; to celebrate Caesar's victory (over sons of Pompey). **Triumph**—victory. **What conquest**—what new territory or country has Caesar conquered. **Tributaries**—the conquered Princes and rulers who will pay tribute to Caesar. **To grace**—to add glory to. **Captive bonds**—chains of slavery. [It was a custom in Rome that the defeated Princes were brought as slaves tied to the chariot of the Victorious Commander. Tied to the chariot, they were taken out in a victory procession through the streets of Rome.] **Blocks**—unfeeling fools. **Senseless things**—lifeless and unfeeling things like stones. **Hard**—cruel. **Knew you not Pompey**—did you not know Pompey [the noblest man of Rome who started a civil war against Caesar and was defeated by Caesar. Now Caesar has returned after defeating and killing Pompey's sons.

and make them strong. I have repaired the shoes of the finest men who walk in shoes made of calf-leather.

Flav. But why are you not in your workshop to-day ? Why are you walking about with these people in the streets ?

Sec. Com. Well, sir, to tell you the truth, I am doing so to make people wear out their shoes. If they wear out their shoes I shall get more work, and make more money. But really we are taking this day as a holiday to see Caesar enter Rome at the head of a victory procession. We want to take part in the celebration of Caesar's victory.

Mar. What reason do you have for rejoicing ? What new country has Caesar conquered ? What conquered kings and princes does he bring chained to his chariot to add glory to him and to pay him tribute. You stupid, senseless, hard-hearted Romans ! You are senseless and unfeeling like stones. Have you forgotten Pompey ? In the past, many times, when Pompey was to pass through the streets of Rome, you used to climb up the walls, and parapets (खाई के पास की दीवार), towers, windows and even chimney tops; with your children in your arms the whole day long you used to wait eagerly to catch a glimpse of Pompey the Great, passing through the streets of Rome. And as soon as you saw his chariot, you would shout so loud that your cheers would be echoed and re-echoed from the hollow banks of the river Tiber. The river Tiber used to tremble out of terror when she heard your shouts echoed from her hollow banks. Yet you have chosen this day as a day of rejoicing, and you have come out dressed in your finest clothes ; and you now scatter flowers in the path of the man who returns victorious after killing the sons of Pompey ! Go away. Run back to your houses, fall upon your knees and pray to gods to save you from that terrible punishment which must fall upon you for your ungratefulness (कृतघ्नता).

Oft—often. **Battlements**—fortified walls. **The livelong day**—the whole day long. **Patient expectation**—waiting patiently for his arrival. **Pass the streets of Rome**—pass through the streets of Rome in grand victory processions. **But**—only. **An universal shout**—shouting all together. **That**—so that. **Tiber**—a river flowing through Rome. **Trembled**—shook in fear. **To hear**—on hearing. **Replication**—echo. **Concave shores**—hollow banks. **Attire**—dress, clothes. **Cull out a holiday**—choose this day as a holiday ; a day of rejoicing. **Strew**—scatter. **That**—who. **Comes in triumph**—returns after defeating and killing. **Pompey's blood**—the sons of Pompey. **Intermit**—put off ; withhold, check. **Plague**—the terrible punishment, calamity. **That**—which. **Needs must**—must necessarily, **Light**—come down upon, fall upon. **This ingratitude**—the ungrateful Romans who have forgotten Pompey's services to Rome.

Flav. Go, go, *good countrymen*, and for this fault ;
Assemble all the poor men of your *sort* ;
Draw them to Tiber banks, and *weep your tears*
Into the channel, till the *lowest stream.*
Do kiss the most *exalted shores of all* [Exeunt all the Commoners]
See whether their *basest metal be not moved* :
They *vanish tongue-tied in their guiltiness.*
Go you down that way towards the Capitol ;
This way will I, *Disrobe* the *images,*
If you do find them *deck'd* with *ceremonies.*

Mar. May we do so ?
You know it is the feast of Lupercal.

Flav. It is no matter; let no images
Be hung with *Caesar's trophies, I'll about.*
And drive away the *vulgar* from the streets;
So do you too, where you *perceive* them *thick.*
(*These growing feathers pluck'd* from Caesar's wing
Will make him *fly an ordinary pitch,*
Who *else* would *soar above the view of men,*
And keep us all in *servile* fearfulness.) [Exeunt]

Scene II—A Public Place

Flourish. Enter : Caesar ; Antony, for *the course ;*
Calpurnia, Portia, Decius, Cicero, Brutus,
Cassius and Casca ; a great crowd following,
among them a *Soothsayer.* After them Marullus and Flavius.

Caes. Calpurnia

Casca. Peace, ho ! Caesar speaks

[Music ceases.]

Caes. Calpurnia !

Cal. Here, my lord.

Caes. Stand you *directly* in Antonius' way,
When he doth run his course. Antonius !

Good countrymen—Flavius is gentler and more polite to the common people. He is not abusive like Marullus. **Assemble**—gather. **Sort**—class, kind. **Weep your tears**—weep and shed your tears. **Into the channel**—into the river. **Lowest**—shallowest, the bottom. **Stream**—rivulet. **Do kiss**—touch. **Exalted shore of all**—the highest point of the banks. **See**—these words are addressed to Marullus. **Basest metal**—the most worthless and meanest man among them. **Be not moved**—has not been affected. **Vanish**—disappear ; move away. **Tongue-tied**—silent, without even moving the tongue. **In their guiltiness**—conscious of their guilt or fault. **Disrobe**—remove the decorations from. **Images**—statues. [These tribunes are displeased with Caesar's growing power]. **Decked**—decorated. **Ceremonies**—decorations, ribbons, scarves and etc. **Caesar's trophies**—tokens, emblems of signs of Caesar's victory. **I'll about**—I will go round the streets. **Vulgar**—the common people ; the mob. **Perceive**—

Flav. Go, go home, my good countrymen. Call all your fellow work-men to do penance for this wrong that you have done. Take them all to the banks of river Tiber, and there weep and shed tears of repentance till the lowest stream of the river may rise and touch the highest point on the banks.

[*All the Commoners go away*]

See, our words have affected them deeply. Even the meanest man among them has also been moved, because they have gone away without a word of objection. They have become conscious of their guilt. You go down that way towards the Capitol (*a hill on which stood a big temple*). I will go to this way. If you find statues of Caesar decorated with scarves (रंगीन रूमाल) and ribbons, remove all those decorations.

Mar. But may we do so on this holy festival day? You know to-day is the day of holy festival of Lupercal. Will our act of disrobing Caesar's statues not be taken as an unholy or sinful act.

Flav. It does not matter. Let no decorations and tokens of Caesar's victory remain hanging on his statues. I will go round the city and drive the common people home from the streets. You also should drive them home wherever you find them crowded. If we tear away these feathers (*honours*) from Caesar's wings, he will not be able to fly high above us all. Otherwise, he is ambitious, He will like to fly in heaven and reach beyond the sight of men ; he would like to be one of the gods. He will become a powerful dictator and make us, Romans, his slaves full of his fear.

Scene II—A Public Place

Flourish. Enter : Caesar, Antony, for the course ;

Calpurnia, Portia, Decius, Cicero, Brutus, Cassius and Casca ; great crowd following, among them a Soothsayer.

Caes. Calpurnia,

Casca. Keep quiet ! every one ! listen ! Caesar is going to speak.

Caes. Calpurnia ! [Music stops]

Cal. I am here, my lord

Caes. When Antony runs the race, you immediately stand in his path, Antonius.

---

see. **Thick**—crowded. **These growing feathers**—honours and trophies heaped on Caesar. **Plucked**—torn away; removed. **Fly an ordinary pitch**—fly not very high, will become a man of ordinary means and power. [Flavius means that these honours heaped on Caesar are making him the most powerful man in Rome.] **Else**—otherwise. **Soar**—fly high. **Above the view of men**—high in heaven, beyond the sight of men, become a superman. **Servile**—slavish. **Flourish**—loud sound of trumpets. **The course**—the race to be run on the occasion of Lupercalia. **Soothsayer**—fore-teller. **Peace, ho ! Caesar speaks**—these words spoken by Casca show that Caesar is very powerful and popular. All must be silent when Caesar speaks. **Here**—I am here. **Directly**—immediately ; right.

Ant. Caesar, my lord ?

Caes. Forget not in your *speed*, Antonius.
To touch Calpurnia ; for our *elders* say,
The barren, touched in this holy *chase*,
Shake off their *sterile curse,*

Ant. I shall remember :
When Caesar say, "do this", it is *perform'd.*

Caes. *Set on* ; and *leave no ceremony* out

[Flouris]

Sooth. Caesar !

Caes. Ha ! *Who calls ?*

Casca. *Bid every noise be still* ; peace yet again !

Caes. Who is it in the *press that* calls on me ?
I hear a *tongue, shriller* than all the music,
Cry, "Caesar !" Speak ; *Caesar is turn'd to hear.*

Sooth. *Beware* the *ides of March.*

Caes. What man is that ?

Bru. A soothsayer *bids you beware the ides of March.*

Caes. *Set* him before me ; let me see his face.

Cas. Fellow, come from the *throng* ; look upon Caesar.

Caes. *What say'st thou* to me now ? Speak once again.

Sooth. Beware the ides of March.

Caes. He is a *dreamer* ; let us leave him : *Pass.*

[*Sennet.* Exeunt all but Brutus and Cassius.

Cas. Will you go see *the order of the course* ?

Bru. Not I.

Cas. I pray you, do.

Bru. I am not *gamesome* I *do lack* some part.
Of that *quick spirit* that is in Antony.
Let me not *hinder*, Cassius, your desires ;
I'll leave you.

Speed—great speed while running the race. **Elders**—elderly people. **The barren**—childless women. **Chase**—race. **Shake off**—get rid of ; are cured of. **Sterile curse**—the curse of barrenness or childlessness. **Performed**—done. **Set on**—proceed. **Leave no ceremony**—do not forget to perform rites and rituals that must be performed on this occasion. **Who calls ?**—who is calling me ? **Bid**—let, ask. **Every noise be still**—let no one make any noise. **Press**—crowd. **That**—who. **Tongue**—voice of a man. **Shriller**—sharper ; louder. **Caesar is turned to hear**—Caesar is ready to listen [Caesar's tune is full of pride and haughtiness—instead of saying 'I' he uses his 'name'—as if he were a great king.] **Beware**—be careful about ; guard yourself against. **Ides of March**—15th of March. **Bids you**—asks

Ant. Yes, my lord.

Caes. Antony, when you run the race, do not forget to touch Calpurnia ; because our wise old people say that a barren woman is cured of her barrenness if she is touched by the runner who runs the race on the feast of Lupercal. [*A childless woman can bear children if and etc.*]

Ant. I shall not forget it. As soon as Caesar says "Do this", it is done at once.

Caes. Proceed then, and do not forget to perform all the ceremonies that should be performed on this occasion.

Sooth. Caesar !

Caes. Who calls me ?

Casca. Let there be no noise. Let there be silence again.

Caes. Who is it that calls from the crowd. I hear a voice which is louder than all the sounds of the trumpets. It called me by my name. Let him speak, Caesar is ready to listen.

Sooth. Remember the 15th of March.

Caes. Who is that man ?

Bru. He is a foreteller who warns you against the ides (15*th*) of March.

Caes. Bring him here. Let me see his face.

Cassius. Fellow, come from the crowd and stand before Caesar.

Caes. What do you want to say ? Speak once again.

Sooth. Remember the danger that awaits you on the 15th of March.

Caes. He is a day-dreamer. Let us pay no heed to what he says. Let us move on.

[*Flourish of trumpets. All go except Brutus and Cassius.*]

Cassius. Will you go to see how the race goes on ?

Brutus. No, I will not.

Cassius. I request you to do so.

Brutus. No, I am not fond of games and sports. My temperament is not as lively and gay as that of Antony. But I do not want to prevent you from attending the race. I will, therefore, take leave of you. (Cassius)

---

you ; tells you ; warns you. **Beware the ides of March**—to take care of the 15th of March. **Set**—present. **Throng**—crowd. **Say'st**—say. **What say'st thou**—what do you say ? **Dreamer**—a day-dreamer ; one who imagines things. **Pass**—proceed. **Sennet**—sound of trumpets to welcome a great man. **The order of the course**—how the race goes. **Gamesome**—fond of games and sports. **Do lack**—do not have. **Quick spirit**—lively nature, dynamism. **Hinder**—stand in the way of, block.

Cas. Brutus, I do *observe* you now *of late* :
I have not from your eyes that *gentleness*,
And *show of love*, as *I was wont to have*
You bear too stubborn and too strange a hand
Over your friend that loves you.

Bru. Cassius,
Be not deceived ; if I have *veil'd my look,*
I turn the trouble of my countenance
Merely upon myself. Vexed. I am
Of late, with *passions of some difference*
Conceptions only *proper to myself,*
Which give some soil, perhaps, to my *behaviours* ;
But let not therefore my good friends be grieved
(Among which number, Cassius, be you one),
Nor *construe* any further my *neglect,*
Than that poor Brutus, *with himself at war,*
Forgets the shows of love to other men.

Cas. Then, Brutus, I have much *mistook* your *passion* ;
By means whereof, this breast of mine hath *buried*
Thoughts of great value, *worthy cogitations.*
Tell me, good Brutus, can you see your face ?

Bru. No, Cassius : for the eye sees not itself,
But by *reflection*, by some other things.

Cas. *'Tis just* :
And it is very much *lamented*, Brutus,
That you have no such mirrors as will *turn*
Your hidden worthiness into your eye,
That you might see your *shadow*. I have heard,
Where many *of the best respect* in Rome
(*Except immortal Caesar*), Speaking of Brutus.
And groaning *underneath* this *age's yoke*
Have wish'd that noble *Brutus had his eyes.*

Observe—watch. **Of late**—for a few days now ; recently. **Gentleness**—(here) kindness. **Show of love**—expression of love ; demonstration of love. **I was wont to have**—I was accustomed to have ; I usually got. **You bear too...loves**—you deal with me harshly, though I am all love for you. **Bear**—(here) behave. **Stubborn**—hard ; harsh. **Strange**—unfriendly, that of an enemy [you deal with me like an enemy]. **Be not deceived**—do not be mistaken. **Veiled my look**—kept my face covered or hidden. **I turn...myself**—I turn my troubles only on myself ; I try to keep my troubles only to myself. [I do not want my friends troubled by my troubles]. **Vexed**—troubled ; worried. **Passions of some difference**—some conflicting emotions. **Conceptions**—thoughts. **Proper to myself**—that concern myself alone. **Which**—these thoughts. **Give some soil**—stain ; make bad. **Behaviours**—actions ; dealings with others. **Construe**—interpret. **Neglect**—coldness, indifference. **With himself at war**—torn between conflicting emotions. **Forgets ... men**—forgets to show love and courtesy to

Cassius. Brutus, I have been lately watching you very carefully. I find that now your looks are not so full of love and tenderness for me as they used to be once. You are treating me harshly. I am your friend, yet you deal with me as with an enemy and like a stranger. [*You do not give me that love and affection now as you used to give formerly. You have grown harsh to me.*]

Brutus. Do not misunderstand me, Cassius. If at times I keep my face hidden, it is because I want to keep my sadness to myself alone. I do not want to trouble my friends with my own troubles. [*My troubled looks are there not because of any ill will for my friends, but because of my purely personal troubles*]. For some time now I have been troubled by some conflicting emotions, But these thoughts concern only myself. These troubling thoughts, perhaps, make my behaviour look harsh. But my good friends should not feel worried about these personal troubles of mine, and I consider you, one of my good friends.

Nor should my friends attribute my indifference to any other cause except this that I have been disturbed by conflicting emotions, and so, some times I have forgotten to show love and courtesy to my friends.

Cas. Then, Brutus, I have really misunderstood your feelings. And because of this misunderstanding I have kept many important thoughts hidden in my mind. I should have communicated these thoughts to you much earlier. Tell me, dear Brutus, can you see your own face ?

Bru. No, Cassius, I cannot do that. Because eye cannot see itself. It can see itself only when it is reflected in a mirror or something else.

Cas. It is true ; and it is to be regretted that you have no one to show you your real self like a mirror. [*You have no one to show you your real worth and greatness.*] I have heard that many highly respected men of Rome, except god-like Caesar, have been discussing Brutus. And they have all been feeling sorry for the injustice and oppression of these present times ; they have all wished that Brutus could see his worth as clearly as others see it.

---

his friends. **Mistook**—misunderstood. **Passion**—feelings. **By means whereof**—because of which ; as a result of which [of this misunderstanding]. **This breast of mine**—my heart. **Buried**—hidden, not shared. **Worthy**—valuable ; of great importance. **Cogitations**—ideas. **Reflection**—when it is reflected in a mirror. **'Tis just**—it is right ; you are right ; it is true. **Lamented**—is a matter of regret. **Turn**—reflect ; reveal show. **Shadow**—reflection. **Of the best respect**—of the highest reputation, most respected. **Except immortal Caesar**—except god-like Caesar [there is satire or irony in the word 'immortal']. **Underneath**—under. **Age's yoke**—the injustice and tyranny of the present times. **Brutus had his eyes**—Brutus was not blind to his own worth and capability; Brutus could see his worth clearly.

Bru. Into what *dangers* would you lead me, Cassius,
That you would have me *seek* into myself
For *that which is not in me* ?
Cas. *Therefore*, good Brutus, be prepared to hear :
And, since you know you cannot see yourself
So well as by *reflection, I, your glass*,
Will *modestly discover* to yourself
That of yourself which you yet know not of.
And be not *jealous on* me, gentle Brutus:
Were I a *common laugher*, or did use
To *stale* with ordinary oaths my love
To every *new protester* : if you know
That I do *fawn on* men, and *hug* them hard,
And *after scandal* them ; or if you know
That I *profess myself*, in *banqueting*.
To all the *rout*, then *hold* me dangerous.
[Flourish and shout]
Bru. What means this shouting ? I do fear the people.
Choose Caesar for their king.
Cas. Ay, do you fear it ?
Then must I think *you would not have it so* ?
Bru. I would not, Cassius; yet I love him well.
But wherefore do you *hold* me here so long ?
What is it that you would *impart* to me ?
If it be *aught* toward the *general good*,
Set honour in one eye and death *i'* the' other.
And I will look *on both indifferently* ;
For, *let the gods so speed me* as I love
The name of honour more than I fear death.
Cas. I know *that virtue* to be in you, Brutus,
As well as I do know your *outward favour*.
Well, honour is the subject of my story.
I cannot tell what you and other men
Think of this life; but for my single self,
I had as lief not be, as live to be
In awe of such a thing as I myself.

Dangers—dangerous missions. **Seek**—discover ; see. **That which ... me**—that worth which, I know, I don't have. **Therefore**—as far as that is concerned. **Reflection**—image in the mirror. **I, your glass**—I serve as a glass where you can see your true image. **Modestly**—truly, without any exaggeration. **Discover**—reveal ; disclose. **That of yourself**—that side of your personality. **Jealous on**—suspicious of. **Common laugher**—an ordinary person not to be taken seriously ; a laughing stock, a mere clown or joker. **Stale**—to cheapen ; to make cheap. **New protester**—every new comer who professes love for me. **Fawn on**—meanly flatter. **Hug**—embrace. **After**—afterwards ; at their back. **Scandal**—defame. **Profess**

Bru. Into what dangerous plot are you trying to drag me, Cassius ? Why do you want me to see in me those virtues which I do not really possess.

Cas. So far as that is concerned, you must be prepared to listen to me. As you know that you cannot see your real self unless it is reflected by some mirror, I will serve as a mirror for you and without any exaggeration I will reveal to you those qualities which you possess, but of which you are not aware. Don't have any suspicions about me, gentle Brutus. If I am a common clown (*joker*) or if I am in the habit of making my love cheap by swearing love for every new comer who professes love for me or even if you know that I flatter people on their faces and then talk ill of them at their back ; if you know that I profess love to a whole crowd of merry makers gathered at a feast, then you may consider me dangerous.

[Flourish and shout]

Bru. What does this shouting mean. I am afraid that people are choosing Caesar to be their king.

Cas. Are you really afraid of it ? Then, I think, you do not want this to happen.

Brutus. No, Cassius, I would not want this, though I love Caesar very much. But why have you detained me here for so long ? What do you want to communicate to me ? If it is a matter concerning the welfare of the people, then for this public good I will look on death and honour quite impartially [*For people's welfare even death would be as dear to him as honour*]. Let gods so help me. Because I love honour more than I fear death [*My love of honour is greater than my love of life or fear of death*].

Cas. I know, Brutus, that you have this love of honour. I know it as well as I know your outward appearance. Well, honour is the subject of my talk. I do not know what you and other people think about this life. But as far as I am concerned I would rather die than live in fear of Caesar who is just a man like me.

---

myself—pretend to be ; pose to be. **Banqueting**—feasting. **Rout**—vulgar merry makers ; crowd of foolish people. **Hold**—consider. **You would not have it so**—you would not allow it to happen ; you would not allow Caesar crowned as a king. **Hold**—detain. **Impart**—communicate ; tell. **Aught**—anything. **General good**—good of the people. **On both**—on death and honour. **Indifferently**—impartially. **Let the gods so speed me**—let gods so help or favour me. **Speed me**—help me ; favour me. **That virtue**—love of honour. **Outward favour**—looks, outward appearance. **I had as lief not be**—I would as willingly die ; would as willingly not live. **In awe**—in fear. **Thing as I myself**—Caesar who is just a man like me.

I was born free as Caesar ; so were you :
We *both have fed as well* ; and we can both
Endure the winter's cold as well as he :
For once, upon a *raw* and *gusty* day,
The *troubled* Tiber *chafing with her shores,*
Caesar said to me, "Darest thou, Cassius, now
Leap in with me into this *angry flood,*
And swim to *yonder point* ? *Upon the word,*
Accoutred as I was, I *plunged in*
And *bade* him follow ; so indeed, he did.
The *torrent* roar'd : and we did *buffet* it.
With *lusty sinews,* throwing *it* aside,
And *stemming* it with *hearts of controversy :*
But *ere* we could arrive the point proposed,
Caesar cried, "Help me, Cassius or I sink !"
I, as *Aeneas* our great ancestor,
Did from the flames of Troy upon his shoulder.
The old Anchises bear, so from the waves of Tiber
Did I the tired Caesar : and this man
Is now become a god ; and Cassius is
A wretched creature, and must *bend his body,*
If Caesar carelessly *but nod* on him.
He had a *fever* when he was in Spain,
And when the *fit* was on him, I *did mark*
How he *did shake* : 'tis true, *this god* did shake :
His coward lips did from their colour fly ;
And, that same eye whose *bend doth awe* the world
Did lose his *lustre* : I did hear him *groan* :
Ay, and that tongue of his, that bade the Romans
Mark him and write his speeches in their books,
Alas, it cried, "Give me some drink, Titinius,"
As a sick girl. Ye gods ! it doth *amaze me,*
A man of such a *feeble temper* should
So *get the start of* the majestic world
And *bear the palm* alone.

[Flourish and shout]

Both have fed as well—both of us were brought up as well as Caesar. **Endure**—face. **Raw**—very cold ; biting cold. **Gusty**—stormy. **Troubled**—angry and flooded ; in flood. **Chafing with her shores**—striking or beating angrily against her banks [because they were restraining her—the river Tiber. **Angry flood**—noisy water of the river in flood. **Yonder point**—that distant point. **Upon the word**—as soon as he spoke these words. **Accoutred**—dressed. **Plunged in**—jumped into the river. **Bade**—asked. **Torrent**—flooded river. **Buffet**—strike; beat [with arms and legs as they swam]. **Lusty**—strong. **Sinews**—muscles. **It**—the

I was born as free as Caesar ; so were you, Brutus, we both have been brought up as properly as Caesar. We both can endure the biting cold of winter as well as Caesar. I remember once on a cold stormy day the river Tiber was in flood. The flooded Tiber was angrily striking against her banks. At that time Caesar said to me, "Do you have courage, Cassius, to jump into this flooded river and swim to that point there." Though I was fully dressed, yet as soon as Caesar spoke, I at once jumped into the river, clothes and all, and asked Caesar to follow me, which he did. The flooded river roared angrily. We beat the strong currents with our strong muscles. We fought against the currents with great courage and spirit of competition ; but before we could reach the goal, Caesar lost courage and cried, "Help me, Cassius, or I sink." Then I rushed to his help. I bore tired Caesar on my shoulder and saved him from drowning in the flooded river. I saved Caesar just as Aeneas, our great ancestor had borne (*carried*) his old father Anchises on his shoulder from the flames of the burning city of Troy. But, now this very Caesar is worshipped as a god, while Cassius (*who once saved Caesar*) is regarded as a petty-creature who must bow down to Caesar, if Caesar only nods at him.

When Caesar was in Spain, he had an attack of fever. I saw, how Caesar trembled. Yes, it is true, this Caesar who has become a god now, did tremble. His lips lost their healthy red colour and turned pale. His eyes whose mere glance now fills terror in the hearts of the people, lost their brightness ! I heard him crying in pain ; his voice, which now proudly orders Romans to listen to him and write down his speeches in books, cried in pain, "Give me something to drink, Titinius." He cried pitiably like a sick girl. I am really very much surprised that such a weak man should surpass all in this grand world and should carry away the prize of victory.

[Shouts and blowing of trumpets]

---

water. **Stemming**—opposing; resisting. **Hearts of controversy**—with great courage and spirit of competition. **Ere**—before. **Aeneas**—the great ancestor of Romans. He brought his old father Anchises out of the burning city of Troy. **Bend his body**—bow low. **But**—only. **Nod**—shake head ; bend one's head. **Fit of fever**—attack of fever. **Did mark**—noticed, saw. **Did shake**—trembled. **This god**—this Caesar who is now worshipped as a god. **His coward lips ... fly**—Caesar lost his healthy red colour and became white and lifeless. **Bend**—slight movement ; look, glance. **Doth**—does. **Awe**—terrify ; fill with terror. **Lustre**—brightness, shine. **Groan**—crying in pain. **Mark him**—listen to him attentively and with respect and fear. **Doth amaze me**—shocks me; stupefies me. **Feeble**—weak. **Temper**—temperament; constitution. **Get the start of**—should surpass, dominate. **Bear the palm**—carry the prize.

Bru. Another general shout !
I do believe that these *applauses are*
For some new honours that are *heap'd on* Caesar,

Cas. Why, man, he doth *bestride* the narrow world
Like a *Colossus* : and we petty men
Walk under his huge legs, and peep about
To find ourselves *dishonourable graves.*
Men at some time are masters of their fates :
The fault, dear, Brutus, is not in our *stars,*
But in ourselves, that we are *underlings.*
Brutus, and Caesar : what should be in that, "Caesar" ?
Why should that name be *sounded* more than yours ?
Write them together, yours is *as fair* a name ;
Sound them, it, doth become the mouth as well ;
Weigh them, it is as heavy ; *conjure with 'em,*
"Brutus" will *start* a spirit as soon as "Caesar".
Now, in the names of all the gods at once,
Upon what *meat* doth this our Caesar feed,
That he is grown so great ? *Age,* thou art *shamed* !
Rome, thou hast lost the *breed* of *noble bloods* !
When went there by an age since the *great flood,*
But it was *famed with* more than with one man ?
When could they say, till now, that talk'd of Rome,
That her wide walls *encompass'd* but one man ?
Now is it Rome indeed, and *room enough,*
When there is in it but one only man ?
O, you and I have heard our *fathers* say,
There was a Brutus once that would have *brook'd*
The *eternal devil* to *keep his state* in Rome.
As easily as a king.

Applauses—cheers ; shouts of joy. **Heaped on**—showered on. **Bestride**—stands with legs wide apart. **Colossus**—something very big and important ; a huge statue [at the harbour of Rhodes. It was such a huge statue that big ships could move under its legs.] **Dishonourable graves**—poor graves in which they will lie buried like slaves, and not honourable, free men. **Stars**—stars under which we were born. **Underlings**—inferior creatures ; subordinates. **Sounded**—spoken. **As fair**—as good. **Sound**—speak out ; pronounce. **Them**—names of Caesar and Brutus. **It**—the name of Brutus. **Doth become the mouth as well**—is as sweet sounding as that of Caesar. **Conjure with them**—if you use both the names as incantation or special magic words to call up spirits [angels or souls of dead men]. **Start**—call up: move. **Meat**—food. **Age**—our times; the age of Brutus, Cassius and Caesar. **Shamed**—you (age) are put to shame. **Breed**—race. **Noble bloods**—men of spirit and courage. **When went there by an age**—there never was any such age. **Great flood**—the great flood caused by Zeus, the highest Roman god, to destroy mankind. **Famed with**—was made famous by;

Brutus. This is another shout from the crowd. I think these loud cheers are raised for some fresh honours showered on Caesar. *[I believe they (people) are showering fresh honours upon Caesar.]*

Cas. Why, my friend, Caesar is now a mighty man. He stands like a huge statue over our narrow world. We petty people walk under his legs [*just as ships used to pass under the legs of the huge statue (Colossus) of Apollo at the harbour of Rhodes*]. We just look about timidly to find graves for ourselves in which we may lie buried like poor slaves. There are times when man is the maker and master of his own fate. Dear Brutus, we should not blame our stars under which we were born. We should blame ourselves that we submit to slavery and subordination. Compare the two names, Brutus and Caesar. What is there in the name of Caesar that it is spoken more often than yours. Write these two names side by side ; your name looks as charming as Caesar's. If you pronounce them, your name is as sweet sounding as that of Caesar ; if you weigh them, yours is as weighty as Caesar's. If you use these names as incantations (मंत्र) or magical words to call up spirits, your name will as easily call up a spirit (*ghost*) as his name. In the name of all the gods. I ask what special food this Caesar eats that he has become so powerful. O Age, you must feel ashamed of such things, O Rome, you have lost the power to produce noble men of spirit. Never since the great flood of destruction has there been any age in which Rome was not famous for more than one great men. When till now, people talking about Rome could say that the wide walls of Rome contained only one man. Can we call it Rome, now when there is room enough in it only for one great man. (*Now in Rome there is no room for any other great man than Caesar*). O, you and I have heard our forefathers say that once there was a Brutus, an ancestor of yours, who would tolerate rather the everlasting Satan than a king ruling over Rome. [*For him a king ruling over Rome was as bad as the Satan ruling over her*].

---

was known for. **Encompassed**—contained. **Room enough**—space enough. **Fathers**—forefathers. **Brook'd**—tolerated. **Eternal devil**—everlasting Satan [Satan is the mightiest enemy of goodness]. **Keep his state**—rule over.

Bru. That you do love me, I am *nothing jealous* ;
What you would work me to, I have some *aim* :
How I have thought of this and of these times,
I shall *recount* hereafter ; *for this present*,
I would not, (*so* with love I might *entreat* you)
Be any further *moved.* What you have said,
I will consider ; what you have to say,
I will with patience hear, and find a time
Both *meet* to hear, and answer, such *high* things.
Till then, my noble friend, *chew upon this* :
Brutus *had rather* be a *villager*,
Than to repute himself a son of Rome
Under these hard conditions as this time
Is *like* to *lay upon us.*

Cas. I am glad that my weak words
Have struck but thus much *show of fire* from Brutus.

Bru. The games are done, and Caesar is returning.

Cas. As they pass by, *pluck* Casca by the sleeve ;
And he will, (*after his sour fashion*), tell you
What *hath proceeded worthy note* to-day.

Enter Caesar *and his Train.*

Bru. I will do so—But, look you, Cassius,
The *angry spot* doth glow on Caesar's *brow.*
And all the rest look like a *chidden train* ;
Calpurnia's cheek is pale ; and Cicero
Looks with such *ferret and such fiery eyes*
As we have seen him in the Capitol,
Being cross'd in conference by some senators

Cas. Casca will tell us what the matter is.

Caes. Antonius !

Ant. Caesar ?

Caes. Let me have men about me that are fat ;
Sleek headed men, and *such as sleep o' nights.*
Yond Cassius has a *lean and hungry* look :
He thinks too much ; such men are dangerous.

Nothing jealous—not at all doubtful ; have no doubt about it. **Aim**—guess; only a vague idea. **Recount**—tell; explain. **For this present**—for the time being. **So**—if. **Entreat**—request. **Moved**—urged; persuaded. **Meet**—proper. **High**—important. **Chew upon this**—think over it again and again; ponder over it. **Had rather**—would rather be ; would like to be. **Villager**—a rustic. **Than to repute himself**—than to be called ; than to be known as. **A son of Rome**—a free citizen of Rome. **Like**—may. **Lay upon us**—impose on us; thrust upon us. **Show of fire**—show of warmth; feeling of sympathy for the cause of freedom and

Brutus. I am not at all doubtful that you love me dearly. I can also guess what you want me to do. I shall tell you some other time what I have thought about this matter and this age of ours. For the time being, I will request you as a friend not to persuade me any further. I will think over all that you have said. I will find some proper time patiently to hear what more you have to say ; and to answer important questions you may raise. Till then, my noble friend, keep it in mind and ponder (*think*) over it that Brutus would rather be called a rustic than a citizen of Rome in the humiliating conditions which this present age is likely to thrust upon us.

Cassius. I am glad that my weak words have produced such warmth and feelings in your heart.

Bru. The games are over, and Caesar is coming back.

Cas. As the people pass by, catch Casca by the sleeve and hold him, and he (*Casca*), in his usual sarcastic manner, will tell you what worth-hearing has happened today.

Re-enter Caesar and his followers

Brutus. I will do so. But see, Cassius, Caesar's face is red with anger. The people following him look like servants badly rebuked by the master whom they follow. Calpurnia's cheeks are pale and Cicero's eyes are red with anger. They look like the red eyes of a ferret. His eyes are as red with anger as we have seen them in the Capitol whenever he has been opposed by some senator during a debate.

Cas. Casca will tell us what has happened.

Caes. Antony.

Antony. Well, Caesar,

Caes. I want to have around me men who are healthy and who enjoy sleep at night. That Cassius there, looks thin and hungry. He thinks too much ; such men are dangerous.

---

honour. **Pluck**—draw aside and hold. **After his sour fashion**—in his usual sarcastic manner. **Hath**—has. **Proceeded**—happened. **Worthy note**—worth noting; worth remembering. **And his train**—and his followers. **Angry spot**—expression of anger. **Brow**—forehead, here it means, face. **Chidden train**—servants rebuked by the master. **Ferret and such fiery eyes**—red with anger like the eyes of a ferret. [Cicero, the great orator is angry, because he disliked what had happened during the celebrations]. **Being crossed**—when he was opposed; when he was contradicted. **In conference**—during some debate or discussion. **Sleek-headed**—with well-combed hair [because people careful about their dress and appearance are not like dangerous conspirators with lean looks and dishevelled hair]. **Such as sleep o' nights**—who enjoy sound sleep at night. **Yond Cassius**—that Cassius standing there. **Lean and hungry**—looks like a thin and hungry man.

Ant. Fear him not, Caesar, he's not dangerous ;
He is a noble Roman and *well given.*

Caes. *Would* he were fatter ! But I fear him not ;
Yet *if my name were liable to fear.*
I do not know the man I should avoid.
So soon as that *spare* Cassius. He reads much ;
He is a great observer, and he *looks*
Quite through the deeds of men ; he loves no plays.
As thou dost, Antony; he hears no music ;
Seldom he smiles, and smiles in such a *sort,*
As if he *mock'd* himself, and *scorn'd* his spirit
That could be moved to smile at anything
Such men as he *be* never *at heart's ease*
Whiles they behold *a greater* than themselves;
And therefore are they very dangerous.
I rather tell thee what is to be fear'd
Than what I fear ; for always I am Caesar.
Come on my right hand, *for this ear is deaf.*
And tell me truly what thou *think'st* of them.

[Sennet, Exeunt Caesar and all his Train but Casca.

Casca. You pull'd me by the cloak ; *would you* speak with me ?

Bru. Ay, Casca ; tell us what *hath chanc'd* to-day,
That Caesar looks so *sad.*

Casca. Why, you were with him, were you not ?

Bru. I should not then ask Casca what had chanc'd.

Casca. Why, there was a crown offered him; and, being offered him, he *put it by* with the back of his hand, thus ; and then the people *fell a-shouting.*

Bru. What was the second noise for ?

Casca. Why for that too.

Cas. They shouted thrice ; what was the last cry for ?

Casca. Why, for that too.

Bru. Was the crown offered him thrice ?

Casca. *Ay, marry, was't* and he put it by thrice, every time *gentler* than other ; and at every putting-by, *mine honest neighbours* shouted.

Well given—well disposed, having good intentions. **Would**—I wish. **If my name ... fear**—If I, Caesar could ever be filled with fear [these words show how proud and haughty Caesar is]. **Liable to**—subject to. **Spare**—(here) lean and thin. **Looks quite through the deeds of men**—clearly understands the motives of people's actions. **Seldom**—very rarely, hardly. **Sort**—way ; manner. **Mocked**—laughed at ; ridiculed. **Scorned**—looked down upon ; despised ; hated. **Be**—are. **At heart's ease**—contented ; satisfied. **A greater**—some one greater in authority or superior to them. **For this ear is deaf**—another weakness of Caesar. Caesar suffers from physical weakness too. His left ear is deaf. **Think'st**—thinks. **Would**

Antony. You need not be afraid of him. He is not a dangerous man. He is a noble Roman, and is well disposed. [*He has no evil nature or evil intention*]

Caes. I wish he were fatter than he is. But I am not afraid of him. Still if I could ever fear anything. I do not know any other man than that lean looking Cassius whom I should like to keep away. He reads a lot. He is a keen observer of man, manners and motives. He sees through the acts of men and discovers their real motives. He does not like to see plays staged in the theatres as you do. He enjoys no music. He smiles very rarely, and even when he smiles, he smiles in such a way as if he were laughing at himself and hating his spirit which was weak enough to smile at anything. Such men as he are never contented so long as they see any man greater or more powerful than they are. So, such men are very dangerous. Mind you, I tell you what should be feared. I am not talking about what I fear. [*because Caesar cannot fear anything*] Come to my right, for I am deaf in the left ear, and tell me what you think of Cassius.

[The blowing of trumpets, and Caesar and all his followers except Casca go]

Casca. You pulled me by the cloak. Do you want to talk to me ?

Brutus. Yes, Casca ; tell us what happened to-day that has made Caesar so sad and serious.

Casca. Why, you were with him ; were you not ?

Brutus. If I were there, I would not ask you, Casca, to tell me what happened there.

Casca. Well, people offered him a crown. But he pushed that crown aside with the back of his hand in this way [*here Casca moves his hand to show how Caesar did it*] and, then the people began shouting.

Brutus. What was the cause of the second shouting ?

Casca. Well, it was just for the same reason.

Cassius. They shouted three times. Why did they shout the third time ?

Casca. Well, the third time too they shouted for the same reason.

Brutus. Was the crown offered to him three times ?

Casca. Yes, by Mary, it was offered to him thrice and Caesar pushed it aside three times. Every time he did it more politely than before : and every time he pushed it aside and every time those honest (*or foolish*) fellows near me shouted.

---

you—do you want to. **Hath**—has. **Chanc'd**—happened. **Sad**—serious; sullen ; gloomy. **Put it by**—rejected it, put it away, pushed it aside. **Fell a-shouting**—began shouting. **Ay marry**—by Virgin Mary (the mother of Jesus Christ); it is a kind of oath. **Wasn't**—it was not. **Gentler**—more politely. **Mine honest neighbours**—the people [here honest is ironical].

Cas. Who offered him the crown ?

Casca. Why, Antony.

Bru. Tell us the manner of it, gentle Casca.

Casca. I can as well be hang as tell the manner of it : It was mere *foolery*: I did not *mark it.* I saw Mark Antony offer him a crown ; – yet, 'twas not a crown *neither,* 'twas one of these *coronets ;* – and, as I told you, he put it by once ; but for all that, to my thinking, he would *fain* have had it. Then he offered it to him again ; then he put it by again ; but to my thinking, he was very *loath to lay his fingers off it.* And then he offered it the third time ; he put it the third time by ; and *still* as he refused it, the *rabblement hooted,* and clapped their *chopped* hands and threw up their *sweaty* night-caps, and uttered such a deal of *stinking* breath because Caesar refused the crown, that it had almost *choked* Caesar ; for he *swounded,* and fell down at it. And for mine own part, I *durst not* laugh, for fear of opening my lips and receiving the bad air.

Cas. But, *soft,* I pray you ; what, did Caesar swound ?

Casca. He fell down in the market-place, and *foamed at mouth* and was speechless.

Bru. 'Tis very like : he hath the *falling-sickness.*

Cas. No, Caesar *hath it* not; but you, and I,
And honest Casca, *we have the falling-sickness.*

Casca. I know not what you mean by that ; but I am sure. Caesar fell down. If the *tag rag people* did not clap him, and hiss him, according as he pleased and displeased them, *as they use to do* the *players* in the theatre, I am no *true* man.

Bru. What said he when he *came unto himself* ?

Casca. Marry, before he fell down, when he perceived the *common herd* was glad he refused the crown, *he plucked me ope his doublet* and offered them his throat to cut. *An* I had been *a man of any occupation,* if I would not have taken him *at a word,* I would I might go to hell among the rogues. And so he fell.

Tell ... of it—tell us the manner in which it was done. **Foolery**—all nonsense ; a foolish show. **Mark it**—notice it. **Neither**—now we should say either [Shakespeare uses double negative to emphasize the negative]. **Coronets**—laurel crowns [laurel is an ever-green shrub ; its leaves were used by Greeks as an emblem of victory. Caesar was offered a crown made of laurel leaves.] **Fain**—gladly. **Loath**—unwilling. **To lay his fingers off it**—take his fingers off that crown. **Still**—always. **Rabblement**—the crowd, the masses. **Hooted**—shouted, cried. **Chopped**—rough hands; hands with cracks because of hard manual labour. **Sweaty**—soaked in sweat and therefore foul smelling. **Stinking**—bad smelling. **Choked**—suffocated. **Swounded**—fainted. **Durst**—dared [These words show Casca's contempt for the crowd]. **Soft**—(here) wait. **Foamed at mouth**—emitted foam from the mouth. **'Tis**—it is. **Very like**—very likely. **Falling sickness**—epilepsy. **Hath**—has. **It**—this falling sickness epilepsy). **We ... sickness**—It is we who suffer from sickness of falling under Caesar's

Cas. Who offered the crown to him?

Casca. Well, it was Antony who did that.

Brutus. Tell us in detail how it all happened, my dear Casca.

Casca. I would rather be hanged than be able to describe how it all happened. It was such a foolish show that I just did not see it. I saw Mark Antony offered him a crown, but it was not a crown (*made of gold or silver*), it was a laurel crown (*made of laurel leaves*) and as I have already told you, Caesar put it aside once. But in my opinion he would have gladly accepted that crown. [*His rejection of it was only a pose to please the people*]. It was offered to him again, and he pushed it aside once again, but I think he was quite unwilling to take his hand off the crown [*Casca means, that in the heart of his hearts Caesar loved the crown and wanted to be the king of Rome*]. And Antony offered the crown for the third time, and for the third time he declined (*refused*) it ; and each time he refused it, the crowd shouted and clapped their cracked and rough hands. They threw up their dirty caps soaked in sweat (*perspiration* पसीना). And they so much filled the atmosphere with their foul smelling breath that Caesar was suffocated with that. He fell down and fainted. As for myself, I dared not open my mouth to laugh, lest I should breathe the air poisoned by the bad breath of the crowd.

Cas. But wait a moment, I request you to tell me if Caesar really fainted.

Casca. Yes, he fell down in the market place, and foam (झाग) came out of his mouth. He was unable to speak.

Bru. It is just possible, for Caesar suffers from epilepsy (मिरगी).

Cas. No, Caesar does not suffer from this disease. I think it is we who suffer from this sickness of falling before Caesar.

Casca. I do not understand what you mean by saying that ; but I am sure that Caesar did fall. I tell you the truth that the beggarly people clapped, hissed and cheered as Caesar's actions pleased and displeased them. They did so just as they cheer or hoot out actors in the theatres. Take me to be a liar if they did not do all that I have described.

Brutus. What did Caesar do when he recovered his consciousness.

Casca. Well, before he fainted, he saw that the people were pleased at his refusal of his crown and I saw that he pulled open his doublet or

---

domination; we have fallen to be slaves of Caesar. **Tag-rag people**—riff raff; the crowd of low, foolish people. **As they use to do**—as they do. **Players**—actors. **True**—honest. **Came unto himself**—came to senses ; recovered his senses. **Common herd**—the crowd of common people [Casca has great contempt for the common people; he considers them no better than sheep and cows.] **Herd**—mob; crowd. **He plucked me ope his doublet**—I saw that he pulled open his coat. **An**—if. **Man of any occupation**—a mechanic or a craftsman such as a carpenter or a cobbler and etc., a working man. **At a word**—at his word.

When he came to himself again, he said, if he had done or said anything *amiss,* he desired *their worships* to think it was his *infirmity.* Three or four *wenches.* Where I stood, cried, "*Alas, good soul* !" and forgave him *with all their hearts ;* but there's *no heed to be taken of them* ; if Caesar had *stabbed* their mothers, they *would have done no less.*

Bru. And after that, he came *thus sad away* ?

Casca. Ay.

Cas. Did Cicero say anything ?

Casca. Ay, he spoke *Greek.*

Cas. To what *effect ?*

Casca. Nay, an I tell you that, *I'll ne'er look you i' the face again* ; but those that understood him smiled at one another, and shook their heads ; but for mine own part *it was Greek to me.* I could tell you more news too ; Marullus and Flavius, for pulling scarfs off Caesar's images, are *put to silence.* Fare you well. There was more foolery yet, if I could remember it.

Cas. Will you *sup* with me to-night, Casca ?

Casca. No, I am *promised forth.*

Cas. Will you dine with me to-morrow ?

Casca. Ay, if I be alive, *and your mind hold,* and your dinner worth the eating.

Cas. Good: I will expect you.

Casca. Do so. Farewell, both. [Exit]

Bru. What a *blunt* fellow is this grown to be !
He was *quick mettle* when he went to school.

Cas. So is he now in *execution.*
Of any bold or noble *enterprise,*
However he *puts on* this *tardy form.*
This *rudeness is a sauce to his good wit*
Which gives men *stomach to digest* his words.
With *better appetite.*

Amiss—wrong. **Their worships**—the crowd ; those foolish people who were noble men for Caesar [There is an irony in these words]. **Infirmity**—weakness. **Wenches**—poor young women. **Alas ! good soul**—how sad ! the good fellow suffers from such a weakness. **With all their hearts**—fully and readily. **Heed**—notice. **No heed to be taken of them**—there is no need of taking any notice of them. **Stabbed**—murdered ; stabbed to death. **Would have done no less**—would have done the same thing, and forgiven Caesar. **Thus sad**—sad in this way. **Ay**—yes. **Greek**—for Romans Greek was a language of truly learned people. **Effect**—purpose. **Nay**—no. **An**—if. **I will ... again**—then I will tell a lie (for I do not know Greek) and so I will be ashamed of facing you again. **It was Greek to me**—I could not understand it ; it was something unintelligible to me. **Put to silence**—dismissed ; deprived of their office. **Sup**—take supper (last meal of the day). **Promised forth**—engaged ; already engaged. **And your mind hold**—if your mind does not change. **Blunt**—dull ; not sharp ; stupid. **Quick mettle**—of sharp intelligence. **So**—so intelligent and sharp. **Execution**—

coat and permitted the crowd to cut his throat if they wished to do that. If I had been a mechanic and man of action I would have taken him at his word and would have cut his throat. If I had not done that I wish I might have gone to the company of sinners in hell. And after that Caesar fell down. As soon as he came to his senses (होश में आना) he begged them to forgive him, because it was the result of his weakness (*his falling sickness*) Three or four young women standing near me cried "Poor fellow", and they forgave him fully and sincerely. But we need not take any notice of what they said and did, because they would have forgiven Caesar even if he had murdered their own mothers.

Brutus. And after that, he came away so sad and serious.

Casca. Yes.

Cas. Did Cicero say something.

Casca. Yes, he spoke something in Greek.

Cas. To what purpose ?

Casca. No, I cannot tell you that. For if I tell you that I will be telling lies and so I will be ashamed of facing you in future. I just did not understand him, but those who did, smiled at one another and shook their heads. But for me, it was something which I could not understand. I can give you one more news. Marullus and Flavius have been removed from their office (*post*) because they were removing scarves and decorations from Caesar's statues. Good bye to you. Quite a few other foolish things were said and done, but I don't remember them.

Cas. Will you take your supper with me to-night, *Casca* ?

Casca. No, thank you ; I have already an engagement this night.

Cas. Well, then, would you come to dine with me tomorrow ?

Casca. Yes, I may, if I am alive tomorrow, if your mind does not change, and if your dinner is worth eating (*tasty, delicious*).

Cas. Very well ; I will be expecting you

Casca. Yes, do ; good bye to both of you. [Casca goes]

Brutus. How dull and stupid has this fellow become ? He had sharp intelligence when he was a school going boy.

Cas. He (*Casca*) is still sharp in carrying out noble plans which require boldness. He only pretends to be dull. His roughness of manners is like a tasty sauce to his intelligence ; it gives taste and flavours to the dish of his intelligent comments and make his listeners.

---

carrying out ; performance. **Enterprise**—job; task, plan. **Puts on**—covers himself with ; wears. **Tardy form**—show of dullness. **Rudeness**—roughness. **Is a sauce to his good wit**—makes his intelligence palatable and acceptable (just as sauce makes food tasty (palatable). **Stomach**—hunger for ; desire for. **Digest**—enjoy; receive. **Better appetite**—with greater hunger and enjoyment (relish) with more taste.

Bru. And so it is. For this time I will leave you :
Tomorrow, if you please to speak with me,
I will come home to you ; or if you will,
Come home to me, and I will wait for you.

Cas. I will do so ; till then *think of the world.* [Exit Brutus]
Well, Brutus, thou art noble ; yet, I see,
Thy honourable *metal* may be *wrought*
From that it is disposed: therefore, it is *meet*
That noble minds *keep* ever with their *likes* :
For who so firm that cannot be *seduced* ?
Caesar doth *bear me hard* ; but he loves Brutus :
If I were Brutus now, and he were Cassius,
He should not *humour* me. I will this night,
In several *hands,* in at his windows throw,
As if they came from several citizens,
Writings, all *tending to* the *great opinion.*
That Rome holds of his name ; wherein *obscurely*
Caesar's ambition shall be *glanced at* :
And after this, let Caesar seat him sure ;
For we will *shake him* or *worse days endure.* [Exit]

Scene III—The Same, A Street

[Thunder and lightning. Enter, from opposite sides,
Casca, with his sword drawn, and Cicero.]

Cic. *Good even,* Casca : *brought you Caesar home* ?
Why are you breathless ? and why *stare you so* ?

Casca. Are you not moved, when all the *sway of earth.*
Shakes like a thing *unfirm* ? O Cicero !
I have seen tempests. When the *scolding winds*
Have *rived* the *knotty oaks*, and I have seen
The *ambitious* ocean *swell,* and *rage* and foam,
To be exalted with the threatening clouds :
But never till to-night, never till now,
Did I go through a *tempest* dropping fire.

Think of the world—think of the world around you ; state of affairs in Rome. **Metal**—disposition, spirit ; nature. **Wrought**—changed; influenced. **From that it is disposed**—from its nature (inclination). **Meet**—proper. **Keep**—associate ; live in the company of. **Likes**—people like them; people of their nature and temperament. **For**—because. **Who**—which man. **Firm**—strong; of strong character. **Seduc'd**—misled; led astray. **Bear me hard**—has ill-will or grudge against me. **Humour**—influence; affect. **Hands**—hand writings. **As if they came**—as if they were written. **Tending to**—pointing to. **Great opinion**—high esteem of Brutus. **Obscurely**—darkly. **Glanced at**—hinted at. **Seat him sure**—sit safely on his throne of power. **Shake him**—throw him down from his high position. **Or worse days endure**—and if we fail to over-throw him we will have to suffer bad times under his tyranny.

listen to him and enjoy his talks with greater hunger and zest. [Casca's roughness makes his intelligent and witty remarks more enjoyable].

Bru. You are quite right . Now I must leave you. If you wish to speak about this matter any further, I will, then, either come to your place tomorrow, or if you care to come to my place, I will wait for you.

Cas. I will do so. Till then, ponder (*think*) over the present state of affairs in Rome.

[Brutus goes]

Well, Brutus, you have a noble character, no doubt. But I find that your noble nature can also be easily influenced and changed from its natural nobleness. It is, therefore, proper that men of noble character should keep company with men who are noble like them. For no man is so strong-minded as cannot be misled [Even the most noble minded man can be misled.] Caesar bears me ill-will, but he loves Brutus. If I were Brutus and Brutus were Cassius, he would not be able to influence me as I am influencing him (Brutus) now. To-night I will throw letters written in different hand-writings into the windows of his house. The subject of all these letters will be the high esteem in which Brutus is held by the citizens of Rome. In these letters Caesar's ambition will not be directly mentioned, but only indirectly (*darkly*) hinted at. And after this, Caesar may sit safe and secure on the seat of his power, (without knowing what is being conspired against him), we will either throw him from his position of power or we shall have to suffer greater tyranny if we fail to throw him.

[Cas goes]

Scene III—The Same, A street

[Thunder and lightning. Enter from opposite sides.
Casca with his sword drawn, and Cicero.]

Cic. Good evening, Casca. Did you accompany Caesar home ?
Why are you breathless ? Why do you look so scared ?

Casca. Are you not frightened ? The whole earth is shaking like something unstable. O Cicero, I have seen terrible storms in which the roaring winds have split strong oak trees. I have seen the waves of the tempest-tossed ocean rising high to touch the clouds but never before have I seen such a storm as this which is raining fire.

Good even—good evening. **Brought you Caesar home**—did you accompany Caesar home ? **...re you so**—why do you look scared (stare). **Sway of earth**—the whole realm of the earth; the whole regular movement of the earth. **Unfirm**—unstable; unsteady. **Scolding winds**—roaring winds, stormy winds. **Rived**—split. **Knotty**—hard. **Oaks**—a very huge tree with very hard wood [oak wood was used in building ships in olden times]. **Ambitious**—having the ambition to rise to the skies. **Swell**—rise high. **Rage**—become violent with anger; be violently angry. **To be exalted with**—to rise as high as. **Tempest-tossed**—stormy high tides.

Either there is a *civil strife* in heaven,
Or else the world, too *saucy* with the gods,
Incenses them to send destruction.

Cic. Why, saw you anything *more wonderful* ?

Casca. A common slave— you know him well by sight—
Held up his left hand, which did flame, and burn
Like twenty torches join'd, and yet his hand,
Not sensible of fire remain'd *unscorched,*
Besides,—I ha' not since *put up my sword*—
Against the Capitol I met a lion,
Who *glazed upon* me, and went *surly* by,
Without *annoying me.* And there were *drawn*
Upon a heap a hundred *ghastly* women,
Transformed with their fear, who swore they saw
Men, all in fire, walk up and down the streets,
And yesterday the *bird of night* did sit,
Even at noon-day upon the market-place,
Hooting and shrieking. When these *prodigies*
Do so *conjointly meet,* let not men say,
"*These are their reasons,*—they are natural ;"
For, I believe, they are *portentous* things
Unto the *climate* that *they point upon,*

Cic. Indeed, it is a *strange-disposed times* :
But men may *construe* things *after their fashion,*
Clean from the purpose of the things themselves.
Comes Caesar to the Capitol tomorrow ?

Casca. He doth ; for he *did bid* Antonius
Send word to you, he would be there tomorrow.

Cic. Good night then, Casca ; this *disturbed sky*
Is not to walk in.

Casca. Farewell, Cicero. [Exit Cicero.]

Civil strife—civil war. **Saucy**—insolent; impudent; disrespectful. **Incenses**—provokes; makes angry. **More wonderful**—more awe inspiring than the things you have already described ; more frightening. **Not sensible of**—not feeling. **Unscorched**—unburnt. **Put up my sword**—put my sword in its sheath. **Against**—in front of. **Glazed upon**—looked angrily. **Surly**—angrily. **Annoying me**—injuring me. **Drawn upon a heap**—huddled into a crowd. **Ghastly**—ghost-like. **Transformed with their fear**—changed beyond recognition by their fear. **Bird of night**—an owl (a bird of ill-omen). **Prodigies**—terrible omens. **Conjointly meet**—coincide ; meeting or happening at the same time. **These are their reasons**—that these happenings (omens) have natural causes. **Portentous things**—Ominous. **Unto**—to. **Climate**—country. **They point upon**—in which they appear. **Strange disposed times**—times full of strange happenings. **Construe**—interpret. **After their fashion**—in their own

Either there is a civil war among the gods in heaven, or the men of this world have been sinful, and disrespectful. So gods, in their anger, are sending death and destruction to punish mankind.

Cicero. Why, have you seen anything more awe-inspiring (*fearful*) than the storm ?

Casca. I saw an ordinary slave, well-known to you. He lifted up his hand which was burning and flaming like twenty torches put together, and yet his hand did not feel the heat, and remained unburnt. I met a lion in front of the Capitol and I have kept my sword drawn since then. The lion glared (*looked angrily*) at me, but, then passed by angrily without injuring me. And there were a hundred ghost-like women crowded together and changed beyond recognition, because of their fear. Those women swore that they had seen men covered up in flames, walking up and down the streets. Only yesterday, an owl sat hooting (उल्लू का बोलना) in the forum (market place) in broad day light. When so many evil omens occur together in this way, let people not say that they have simple and natural causes. Because I believe these are ominous things and a supernatural warning to the country in which they appear.

Cicero. These are strange times, indeed, when strange things happen. But people may explain them in their own way. And their explanation may be entirely different from the real meaning of such happenings. Is Caesar coming to the Capitol tomorrow ?

Casca. Yes, he is coming, because he told Antony to inform you that he would be in the Senate House tomorrow.

Cicero. Good night, Casca. The sky is so disturbed that we should not remain out of doors.

Casca. Good-bye, Cicero. [Exit Cicero]

---

way. **Clean**—different. **Clean... themselves**—in a way entirely different from the real meaning of these strange happenings. [We see that Casca is timid and superstitious] **He doth**—he does; he will. **Did bid**—asked. **Send Word**—to inform. **Disturbed sky...in**—the sky is so disturbed that it is not good to walk under it.

Enter : Cassius.

Cas. Who's there ?

Casca. A Roman.

Cas. *Casca, by your voice.*

Casca. Your *ear* is good, Cassius, *what night* is this !

Cas. A very pleasing night to honest men,

Casca. Who ever knew the heavens *menace* so ?

Cas. Those that have known the earth so *full of faults.*
For my part, I have walk'd about the streets
Submitting me unto the *perilous* night,
And, thus *unbraced,* Casca, as you see,
Have *bared my bosom* to the *thunder-stone,*
And when the *cross* blue lightning seem'd to *open*
The breast of heaven, I did present myself.
Even in the aim and very flash of it.

Casca. But wherefore did you so much *tempt* the heavens ?
It is the *part of* men to fear and tremble,
When the most mighty gods by *tokens* send
Such dreadful *heralds* to *astonish us*.

Cas. You are *dull.* Casca: and those *sparks of life.*
That should be in a Roman, you do *want,*
Or *else* you use not. You look pale, and *gaze,*
And *put on fear,* and *cast yourself in wonder,*
To see the strange *impatience* of the heavens,
But if you would consider the true cause
Why all these fires, why all-these *gliding* ghosts,
Why birds and beasts *from quality and kind;*
Why *old men fool* and children *calculate.*
Why all these things change, from their *ordinance,*
Their natures and *performed faculties,*
To *monstrous quality,* why, you shall find
That heaven hath *infused* them with these spirits

Casca...voice—by your voice I can recognise you to be casca. **Ear**—sense of hearing. **What night**—what sort of horrible night ! **Menace**—threaten. **Full of faults**—Full of evils. **Submitting me**—exposing myself to. **Perilous**—dangerous. **Unbraced**—With my doublet unbuttoned. **Bared my bosom**—exposed my breast; offered my naked breast. **Thunderstone**—thunderbolt. **Cross**—forked; zig-zag. **Open the...heaven**—tear open, rend the heart of heaven. **Even in the aim and very flash of it**—just at the point at which the flash of lightning was aimed. **Tempt**—provoke; take liberties with. **part**—duty. **Tokens**—signs, omens. **Heralds**—messengers [of their wrath (anger)]. **Astonish**—stun; to give a

Enter : Cassius

Cas. Who is there ?

Casca. A Roman.

Cas. By your voice I guess you are Casca.

Casca. Your sense of hearing is very sharp, Cassius. What a strange night it is!

Cas. It is a very pleasant night for all those who are honest.

Casca. Who have ever seen the sky so threatening ?

Cas. Those people who know how full of evil this earth is have seen heavens threatening so. As far myself I have been moving up and down the streets and have not tried to save myself from the dangers of this night. I have moved with my doublet unbuttoned like this and have exposed my naked breast to the thunderbolt. When the terrible flash of lightning seemed to be tearing open the breast of the sky, I stood directly in the path of its flashes.

Casca. But why did you take such liberties with the forces of nature ? It is the duty of men to fear and tremble when most mighty gods send such omens and messengers to shock and stun them.

Cas. You are stupid, Casca. You either lack that courage and understanding which a true Roman should have, or if you have it you do not use it. You look pale and frightened. Seeing the disturbance of heavens you have thrown yourself into a state of abject fear. But try to think what the real cause of all this is. Why there is this rain of fire from the sky ? Why are these ghosts moving swiftly about ? Why do birds and beasts behave in a way contrary to their nature and character ? Why do old men, who should be wise, behave like fools and why do children and fools act prudently and wisely ? Why do all these things change from their natural behaviour and behave in an unnatural way ? If you think over it, you will find that heaven has filled them with these qualities to serve as means of

---

terrible shock or blow. **Dull**—stupid [here: Cassius calls Casca stupid only to excite him. Otherwise he knows that Casca is not stupid. He told so to Brutus]. **Sparks of life**—courage and heroic spirit. **Want**—lack. **Else**—Otherwise. **Gaze**—stare. **Put on fear**—show signs of fear. **Cast yourself...wonder**—throw yourself into a state of wonder. **Impatience**—disturbance. **Gliding**—moving about smoothly and continuously. **From quality and kind**—change their nature and character; behave in an unnatural way. **Old men fool**—old men behave like fools. **Calculate**—prophesy or act prudently. **Ordinance**—normal practice; natural behaviour. **Preformed faculties**—qualities which God had given them originally. **Monstrous quality**—abnormal or unnatural. **Infused**—filled.

To make *them instruments of fear and warning*
Unto some monstrous state.
Now could I, Casca, name to thee a man
Most like this dreadful night.
That thunders, *lightens,* opens graves; and roars
As doth the lion in the Capitol.
A man no mightier than thyself, or me,
In personal action, yet *prodigious* grown
And fearful, as these strange *eruptions* are

Casca. 'Tis Caesar that you mean: is it not, Cassius ?

Cas. Let it be who it is: for Romans now
Have *thews* and limbs like to their ancestors ;
But *woe* the *while* ! our fathers' *minds are dead,*
And we are govern'd with our mother's spirits ;
Our *yoke* and *sufferance* show us womanish.

Casca. Indeed, they say the senators tomorrow
Mean to *establish* Caesar as a king :
And he shall wear his crown by sea and land,
In every place, *save* here in Italy.

Cas. I know where I will *wear* this dagger then ;
Cassius from bondage will deliver Cassius ;
Therein, ye gods, you make the weak most strong ;
Therein, ye gods, you tyrants do defeat :
Nor stony tower, nor walls of *beaten brass,*
Nor airless *dungeon,* nor strong *links of iron,*
Can be *retentive* to the strength of spirit ;
But life being *weary of these worldly bars,*
Never lacks power to *dismiss* itself
If I know this, know all the world besides,
That part of *tyranny* that I do bear
I can *shake off at pleasure.* [Thunder still.]

Casca. So can I :
So every *bondman* in his own hand bears,
The power to *cancel his captivity.*

Them—abnormal or unnatural happenings. **Instruments of fear and warning**—means of threat and terrible warning. **Unto**—of. **Some monstrous state**—abnormal state of affairs ; terrible conditions. **Lightens**—shows out bursts of passion like sudden flashes of lightning. **Personal action**—action as an individual. **Prodigious**—supernaturally threatening. **Eruptions**—outbreaks of nature; disturbance of nature. **Thews**—muscles. **Woe the while**—alas! for these times! **Minds are dead**—the minds and heroic spirit of our ancestors are dead in us. **Yoke**—slavery. **Sufferance**—the patience with which we endure our slavery. **Establish**—make. **Save**—except. **Wear**—Put; sheath; thrust. **Therein**—in that; in giving man power to kill himself; in the use of the dagger to kill one's ownself. **Beaten brass**—hammered and solid brass. **Dungeon**—underground prison cell. **Links of iron**—chains. **Be retentive**—

fear and terrible warning of some coming danger or disaster. And I can tell you, even now, the name of a man who is very much like this fearful night. He thunders, shows sudden outbursts of anger and passion; he causes the dead bodies to come out of the graves and walk upon the earth; he roars like a lion in the Capitol. As an individual this man is no more powerful than you or I, but he has become supernaturally threatening like these outbreaks of nature's anger on this night.

Casca. I think Cassius, you mean Caesar. Don't you ?

Cas. Never mind whom I mean. Romans still have the strong muscles and limbs like those of their forefathers. But the heroic spirit of their forefathers is now dead in them. Alas for these times! Now the Romans' are governed by the weak spirit of their mothers, Our slavery and the patience with which we endure it show that we have become womanish.

Casca. Indeed, they say that the senators intend to make Caesar the king of Roman empire. He will wear his crown all over the empire except in Italy.

Cas. If that happens, I shall, then stab myself with this dagger. In this way I will free myself from the chains of slavery. Gods have made a weak man strong by giving him power to free himself from slavery by killing himself. Cruel rulers are thus defeated. (*They can not enslave a man who has courage to free himself by killing himself*) Neither the stone-built prison-towers, nor the walls of solid hammered brass, nor the dark underground prison cells or iron chains can keep a brave man imprisoned. If a man is sick of slavery he can free himself by killing himself. I know this, and let the rest of the world also know that I have within me the power to free myself, at will, from the tyranny under which I suffer.

Casca. I can also free myself like this. In this way every slave has the power to put an end to his slavery.

---

restrain or imprison. **Weary of**—tired of; sick of. **Worldly bars**—obstacles ; checks on the freedom of spirit. **Dismiss**—free itself by committing suicide. **Tyranny**—oppression; cruelty and injustice. **Shake off at pleasure**—throw off at will. **Bond man**—prisoner; slave. **Cancel**—to put an end to; finish, destroy. **Captivity**—slavery.

Cas. And why should Caesar be a tyrant, then ?
Poor man ! I know, he would not be a *wolf.*
But that he sees the Romans *are but sheep* :
He *were* no lion, were not Romans *hinds.*
Those that with haste will make a mighty fire.
Begin it with weak straws. What *trash* is Rome ;
What rubbish, and what *offal* when it *serves.*
For the *base matter* to *illuminate*
So *vile* a thing as Caesar! But O grief,
Where hast thou led me? I, perhaps, speak this
Before a *willing bondman ;* then I know
My answer must be made; but I am arm'd
And dangers are to me *indifferent.*

Casca. You speak to Casca, and to such a man
That is no *fleering tell tale,* Hold, my hand :
Be factious for *redress* of all these *griefs.*
And I will set this foot of mine as far
As who goes farthest.

Cas. There's a *bargain made*
Now know you. Casca, I have *moved* already
Some certain of the noblest minded Romans
To *undergo* with me an enterprise
Of *honourable dangerous consequence*;
And I do know *by this* they stay for me,
In *Pompey's porch* : for now, this fearful night,
There is no *stir* or walking in the streets ;
And the *complexion* of the *element,*
In favour's like the work we have in hand,
Most bloody, fiery, and most terrible.

Casca. Stand close awhile, for here comes one in haste.

Cas. 'Tis Cinna ; I do know him by *his gait* :
He is a friend.

Enters Cinna

Cinna where haste you so ?

Cinna. To find out you. Who's that ? Metellus Cimber ?

Wolf—a tyrant. **Are but sheep**—are only submissive like sheep ; cowards. **Were**—would be. **Hind**—deer, a timid animal ['deer' has another meaning 'menial servants']. **Trash**—rubbish ; useless. **Offal**—waste matter such as dry twigs fallen from a tree, shavings from a piece of wood. **Serves for**—serves as. **Base matter**—worthless material fit only to be burnt. **Illuminate**—to make bright, to brighten, to glorify. **Vile**—worthless. **Willing bond man**—one who is a willing slave; one who accepts slavery willingly. **my ... must be made**—then, I know I shall have to answer for my words. **Indifferent**—of no importance; [I am indifferent to all dangers]. **Fleering**—sneering; contemptuous. **Tell-tale**—a tale-bearer;

Cas. But why, then, does Caesar rule over us like a tyrant ? Poor man! I know that Caesar would not be a wolf (*cruel ruler*) if he did not find Romans to be like submissive sheep ; he would not be a lion if Romans were not timid like deer (हिरण). Those who want to make a big fire very quickly begin with straw and other waste material which catches fire quickly. We Romans are like straw, refuse and waste material serving as fuel to feed the flames of glory of a worthless man like Caesar. But my grief has made me a fool. I fear, I may be speaking all this to a man who is happy to be a slave. In that case, I know, I will have to answer for my words. But I am well-armed and prepared to meet any dangers. I just don't care for any dangers.

Casca. You speak to Casca. I am not a man who betrays his friends with a mocking smile. I am no tale-bearer who discloses the secrets confided to him. Hold my hand, organise a party to remedy the ills and evils prevailing in Rome, and I assure you that in achieving this aim I will go with you as far as any one else may. [*I will do as much as any one else can*].

Cas. Well ! now it is a pact between you and me. Let me tell you, Casca, that I have already persuaded some of the noblest Romans to join me in an adventure which is both dangerous and honourable. And I know, by this time, they must be waiting for me in the Portico of Pompey's theatre. Because on this fearful night the streets are deserted and lonely, and the outward appearance of the sky is as bloody, fiery and fearful as the work which we are going to do.

Casca. Hide, and keep still for a short while, because some one is coming in a hurry.

Cas. O, it is only Cinna, I can recognise by the manner of his walking.

He is a friend.

Enters Cinna

Cinna, where are you going in such a hurry ?

Cinna. In search of you. Is that Metellus Cimber ?

---

informer. **Be factious**—form a faction (party, group). **Redress**—remedy, cure. **Griefs**—grievances ; troubles. **Bargain made**—an agreement entered into. **Moved**—stirred up; excited; roused. **Undergo**—undertake. **Honourable...consequence**—honourable but also dangerous results. **By this**—by this time. **Pompey's porch**—the portico of the theatre built by Pompey. [**Portico**—the roof resting on pillars at the entrance of a building]. **Stir**—movement of people. **Complexion of the element**—condition of the sky. **In favour's like**—in appearance is like. **Stand close**—stand hidden. **Awhile**—for a short time. **Gait**—manner of walking.

Cas. No, it is Casca ; one *incorporate*
To our attempts. Am I not *stay'd for* Cinna ?

Cinna. *I am glad on't.* What a fearful night is this!
There's two or three of us have seen strange sights.

Cas. Am I not stay'd for ? Tell me.

Cin. Yes, you are.
O Cassius, if you could
But win the noble Brutus to our party—

Cas. *Be you content :* Good Cinna, take this paper,
And look you lay it in the *praetor's chair.*
Where Brutus may but find it ; and throw this
In at his window; set this up with wax
Upon *old Brutus' statue* : all this done,
Repair to Pompey's porch where you shall find us.
Is Decius Brutus, and Trebonius, there ?

Cin. All *but* Metellus Cimber : and he's gone
To seek you at your house. Well I will *hie*
And so *bestow* these papers as you bade me,

Cas. That done, repair to Pompey's theatre. [Exit Cinna]
Come, Casca, you and I will yet, *ere day.*
See Brutus at his house : three parts of him
Is ours already ; and the man entire
Upon the next *encounter yields him ours.*

Casca. O, he sits high in all the people's hearts ;
And that which would appear offence in us,
His *countenance,* like richest *alchemy,*
Will change to *virtue* and to *worthiness.*

Cas. Him and his worth, and our great need of him
You have right well *conceited.* Let us go,
For it is after *midnight* ; and ere day,
We will awake him, and *be sure of him.* [Exeunt]

Incorporate—joined ; united with us and our cause. **Stay'd for**—awaited ; are they not waiting for me ? **I am glad on't**—I am glad to hear that Casca has joined the conspiracy. **But**—Only. **Be you content**—be easy; don't worry. **Praetor's**—magistrate's (Brutus was a Magistrate). **Chair**—the seat on which the magistrate sits to settle disputes. **Where Brutus may but**—where only Brutus may. **Old Brutus**—Lucius Junius Brutus. **Repair**—go. **But**—except. **Hie**—make haste. **Bestow**—place. **Ere day**—before day-break. **Encounter**—meeting. **Yields him ours**—surrenders himself to us. **Countenance**—favour; approval. **Alchemy**—the art of turning base metal into gold. **Virtue**—goodness. **Worthiness**—honour. **Conceited**—thought; judged. **After mid-night**—past mid-night. **Be sure of him**—make ourselves sure of his support.

Cas. No, he is Casca, who has joined us in what we plan to do. Are they not waiting for me, Cinna ?

Cinna. I am glad to hear that Casca has joined our group. What a fearful night this is! Two or three of us have seen strange things happening.

Cas. Tell me, are they not waiting for me ?

Cinna. Yes, they are waiting for you. I wish, Cassius, that you could, somehow, win noble Brutus to our side.

Cas. Don't you worry about that? Good Cinna, take this paper and see that you put it in the chair in which Brutus sits as a magistrate and in which he alone can find it; throw this paper through the window into his room, and paste this paper on the statue of old Brutus, the noble ancestor of Marcus Brutus. When you have done all this, reach the porch of Pompey's theatre, where you shall find us. Are Decius Brutus and Trebonius present there?

Cinna: Everyone except Metellus Cimber is there, and he has gone to look for you at your house. Well, I will make haste and place these papers just as you have asked me to place them.

Cas. Having done that, reach Pompey's theatre.

(Cinna goes)

Come Casca, we will call on Brutus before day-break. More than half of him is already with us, and on our next meeting, with a little presentation, he will be wholly ours.

Casca. O, he is held in highest esteem by the people ; what may appear wrong if done by us alone will become worthy and honourable if it is supported by Brutus. Brutus' approval will change even our evil deeds into good and honourable acts, just as alchemy changes baser metal into gold.

Cas. You have rightly judged the worth of Brutus and his great importance for us. But, let us go now; it is already past mid-night. We will meet before day-break and make ourselves sure of his support.

(They go)

ACT II

Scene I—Rome, Brutus's Orchard

Enter Brutus.

Bru. *What* Lucius, ho !
I cannot, by the *progress* of the stars,
Give guess how near to day. Lucius, I say !
I would it were my fault to sleep so soundly.
When, Lucius, when ? awake, I say ! What, Lucius !

Enter Lucius.

Luc. Call'd you, my lord ?

Bru. Get me *a taper* in my *study*, Lucius :
When it is lighted, come and call me here.

Luc. I will, my lord. [Exit.

Bru. *It* must be *by his death* : and, for my part,
I know no personal cause to *spurn* at him,
But *for the general.* He *would be* crowned :
How that might change his nature, there's the question.
It is *a bright day* that *brings forth the adder,*
And *that craves wary walking*. Crown him ?—that ;
And then, I grant, we put a *sting* in him.
That at his will he may do *danger* with
The *abuse* of greatness is, when it *disjoins*
Remorse from power; and to speak truth of Caesar,
I have not known when his *affections swayed*
More than his *reason. But 'tis a common proof,*
That *lowliness is young ambition's ladder.*
Whereto the climber-upward turns his face ;
But when he once attains the *upmost round.*
He then unto the ladder, turns his back,
Looks in the clouds, scorning the base degrees
By which he *did ascend.* So Caesar may ;
Then lest he may, *prevent.* And, since the *quarrel*

What—a call to attract attention. **I can't**—I cannot tell. **Progress**—position and movement. **Give guess**—guess; make a guess. **How near to day**—how near the day-break is. **I would**—I wish. **When**—an exclamation of impatience; when will you get up? **Taper**—candle. **Study**—room used for work or study. **It**—freedom of Rome. **By his death**—death of Caesar. **Spurn at him**—strike him down ; kick him away. **For the general**—for the good of all people ; for public welfare. **Would be**—would like to be. **Bright day**—warm and sunny day. **Brings forth**—brings out (of its hole or hatches out of its egg.) **Adder**—a poisonous snake. **A bright day ... adder**—brightness of Caesar's glory as a king will change him into a poisonous snake. **Craves**—demands. **Wary**—careful ; cautious. **That craves**

ACT II

Scene I—Rome, Brutus's Orchard

Enter: Brutus in his garden.

Bru. Get up, Lucius ! I want you. From the positions and movement of the stars, I cannot guess how near it is to day-break. Lucius, I say, where are you ? I wish I also could sleep so soundly as this Lucius does. What is this ? Lucius ! Don't you hear me ? Wake up, Lucius. Come here.

Enter : Lucius

Luc. Did you call me, my lord ?

Bru. Light a candle in my study, Lucius, and tell me when you have lighted it.

Luc. I will do so, my lord. (Lucius goes out)

Bru. It is clear that Rome can be free only if Caesar dies. So far as I am concerned, I have no reason why I should strike him down. It is only for the general good of Rome that I can do that. Caesar would like to be crowned a king. But the real question is how this change will influence him and his nature. A snake comes out of its hole only when the day is warm and sunny, and then, we have to walk carefully. Shall we crown him king ? But if we do that, I am sure that we then, give him a sting to do more harm if he wants to do that. Power is misused when it is used without mercy. And, to speak the truth about Caesar, I have never seen Caesar being ruled by his passions instead of his reason [*he has always been reasonable and just*]. But, it is a matter of common experience that, in the beginning, an ambitious man uses humility only as a ladder to climb up ; but as soon as he reaches the highest rung, he turns his back on the lower steps by which he had risen up. Then he begins to look higher up to the clouds and aspires to reach them. It may be so with Caesar also. So we should try to check it before it happens. And this is the cause of my complaint against Caesar.

---

wary walking—Caesar is like a deadly poisonous snake. We should be careful of his growing power. **Sting**—fangs, power to harm us. **Do danger with**—work any mischief with that power ; do any harm to us. **Abuse**—misuse. **Disjoins**—separates. **Remorse**—pity ; kindness. **Disjoins remorse**—when a powerful man like Caesar loses pity and kindness. **Affections**—feelings. **Swayed**—ruled ; governed ; influenced. **Reason**—sense of right judgement. **But ... proof**—matter of general experience. **Lowliness**—humility. **Lowliness ... ladder**—pose of humility, it means that an ambitious man uses humility as a ladder to rise to power. **Upmost round**—highest position ; the highest rung. **Looks in the clouds**—looks higher up ; aspires to reach as high as the clouds. **Scorning**—hating. **Base degrees**—lower rungs (or steps). **He did ascend**—he climbed up. **Prevent**—anticipate; prevent the happening of such a thing. **Quarrel**—cause of complaint.

Will *bear no colour for the thing he is.*
Fashion it thus : that *what he is, augmented,*
Would run to *these and these extremities* ;
And therefore think him as a serpent's egg,
Which, *hatched,* would *as his kind,* grow mischievous
And *kill him in the shell.*

Re-enter Lucius.

Luc. The taper burneth in your *closet,* sir.
Searching the window for a *flint,* I found.

[Gives him a letter.]

This paper, thus sealed up ; and, I am sure
It did not lie there when I went to bed.

Bru. Get you to bed again ; it is not day.
Is not to-morrow, boy, the *ides of March* ?

Luc. I know not, sir

Bru. Look in the calendar, and bring me word.

Luc. I will sir, [Exit.]

Bru. The *exhalations whizzing* in the air.
Give so much light that I may *read by them.*

[Opens the letter, and reads]

"'Brutus, thou sleep'st awake, and *see thyself.*
Shall Rome, etc.—Speak, strike, *redress* !"
"Brutus thou *sleep'st* : awake !"—
Such *instigations* have been often dropped
Where I have took them up.
"Shall Rome, etc." Thus must I *piece it out* ;
Shall Rome stand *under one man's awe* ? What, Rome ?
My *ancestors* did from the streets of Rome.
The Tarquin drive, when he was call'd a king.
"Speak strike, redress !"—Am I *entreated*
To speak and *strike* ? O Rome, I make the promise,
If the redress will follow, *thou receivest*
Thy full petition at the hand of Brutus !

Bear no colour—have no excuse ; no justification. **For the thing he is**—for the kind of person Caesar is at present. **Fashion it thus**—put the matter in this way. **He**—Caesar. **What he is**—what is his power at present. **Augmented**—made higher or more powerful; increased and added. **These and these**—such and such; from one extreme to the other. **Extremities**—excesses (of tyranny). **Hatched**—made to let out the young one. **As his kind**—according to its nature. **Kill him in the shell**—kill him before it comes out of the egg [We should kill Caesar before he becomes all powerful and dangerous]. **Closet**—study. **Flint**—a piece of stone used to strike a spark to make fire. **Ides of March**—middle or 15th of March. **Exhalations**—shooting stars. **Whizzing**—rushing fast making a hissing sound **Read**

But I will have no excuse, since Caesar at present has given us no cause of complaint. We should, therefore, put it this way that if his powers increase he will act in such and such cruel and extreme ways. We should consider him a serpent's egg, which, if hatched, will naturally produce a dangerous snake. We should, therefore kill it in the egg. [*We should kill Caesar before he becomes all powerful and a danger to the freedom of Rome*]

Re-enter Lucius

Luc. I have lit the candle in your study, Sir. But as I was looking about the window for a flint, I found this sealed letter. And I am sure that this letter was not there when I went to bed.

[Giving him the letter]

Bru. You go to sleep again, it is not yet morning. Is tomorrow not the ides (15th) of March?

Luc. I do not know, Sir.

Bru. Go and look at the calendar. and, then, tell me.

Luc. I will, Sir.

Bru. The shooting *stars* (*meteors*) flashing across the sky give me so much light that I can read the letter in it.

(Opens the letter and reads)

"Brutus, you are asleep: Wake up and know yourself and your real worth. Shall Rome etc. Raise your voice (*for freedom of Rome,*) take up arms against tyranny, and set the wrongs right. Brutus, you are asleep ; wake up !" Such letters prompting me to rise up and act have often been dropped at places from where I have picked them up; "Shall Rome etc." In this way I must fill in the blanks in the letter and understand what it means—"Shall Rome suffer under the tyranny of one man" ? What, Rome! When Tarquin proclaimed himself king of Rome, my ancestors drove him out of the streets of Rome. "Speak, strike, and remedy the wrongs." Do they (*Romans*) ask me to raise a voice against tyranny, and act to put an end to it ? O, Rome, I promise that I will give you all that you ask for. If my speaking and striking can set right the wrongs, I will surely do that.

---

by them—read in the light of the stars. **Sleep'st**—sleep. **See thyself**—know your worth ; see what you really are. **Redress**—set things right; give justice to the people. **Instigations**—exciting letters; provocative letters. **Piece it out**—fill up the blanks. **Under one man's awe**—under fear of one man (Caesar). **Ancestors**—Lucius Junius Brutus who drove Tarquin out of Rome when he became a cruel king. **Entreated**—requested ; asked. **To speak**—to speak for the cause of the people or general good. **Strike**—act ; take up arms. **Thou ... Brutus**—O, Rome, you will get from Brutus all that you ask for.

Re-enter : Lucius

Luc. Sir, March is *wasted fifteen days.* [Knocking within]

Bru. 'Tis good. Go to the gate; somebody knocks.
[Exit Lucius]
Since Cassius first *did whet* me against Caesar,
I have not slept.
Between the *acting* of a *dreadful thing*
And the *first motion,* all the *interim* is
Like a *phantasma* or a *hideous* dream:
The *genius* and the mortal *instruments*
Are then in council and *the state of man*
Like to a little kingdom, *suffers* then,
The nature of an insurrection.

Re-enter ; Lucius

Luc. Sir, 'tis your *brother* Cassius at the door,
Who doth desire to see you ?

Bru. Is he alone ?

Luc. No, sir, there are *moe* with him.

Bru. Do you know them ?

Luc. No, sir : their hats are *pluck'd about* their ears.
And half their faces *buried* in their *cloaks*,
That by no means I may *discover* them
By any mark of *favour.*

Bru. Let 'em enter. [Exit Lucius.]
They are *the faction.* O conspiracy,
Sham'st thou to show thy dangerous *brow* by night,
When evils are most free ? O, then by day
Where wilt thou find a *cavern* dark enough
To *mask thy monstrous visage* ? Seek none, conspiracy ;
Hide it in smiles and *affability* ;
For if thou *path, thy native semblance on,*
Not *Erebus* itself *were dim enough*
To hide thee *from prevention.*

Wasted ... days—fifteen days of March are gone [he means that it is fifteenth of March—a part of fifteenth day is also gone, and it is morning]. **Did whet**—sharpened my hate ; instigate ; rouse. **Acting**—execution; translating a thought or feeling into action. **A dreadful thing**—a terrible deed. **First motion**—the first impulse (feeling) to do it. **Interim**—interval ; the time in between. **Phantasma**—nightmare; dreadful dream. **Hideous**—dreadful ; terrible. **Genius**—the immortal spirit of man. **Mortal instruments**—bodily powers of man. **Are ... council**—are in conflict ; are debating. **The state of man**—the self of man which is like an organized orderly state (kingdom). **Suffers**—experiences. **The ... insurrection**—a kind of rebellion or mutiny. **Brother**—brother-in-law (Cassius). **Moe**—more. **Plucked about**—pulled over. **Buried**—hidden. **Cloaks**—overcoats without sleeves. **That**—so that. **Discover**—

Re-enter ; Lucius

Luc. Sir, fifteen days of March are gone.

[Knocking within.]

Bru. That is all right. Go to the gate, somebody is knocking.

[Lucius goes.]

I have not been able to sleep ever since Cassius instigated (*excited*) me against Caesar. The period between the first thought (*or impulse*) of a dreadful deed and its actual doing is like a horrible dream. The spirit of man and his bodily powers are, then, in a debate (*soul is torn between decision and indecision*) and man's self becomes like a state in a condition of rebellion or civil war.

Re-enter Lucius

Luc. Sir, it is your brother-in-law, Cassius, who is at the gate. He wants to meet you.

Bru. Is he alone ?

Luc. No, Sir, there are more persons with him.

Bru. Do you know them ?

Luc. No, Sir, their hats are pulled over their ears and half their faces are so hidden under their cloaks that I can in no way recognize them by their features.

Bru. Let them enter. [Lucius goes.]

They are the party of conspirators. O conspiracy, do you feel so ashamed of showing your dreadful face even in the darkness of night when evil things move about most freely. If such is the case in the night, where then, will you find a cave dark enough to hide your dreadful face during the day ? You, O Conspiracy, need not seek any place to hide your face. Cover your face with sweet smiles and show of politeness. Because, if you move about in your real appearance, not even the darkness of hell would be able to hide you from being recognised and checked.

---

recognize. **Favour**—features ; appearance. **The faction**—the party or a group (of conspirators). **Brow**—face. **When...free**—when evil things move about freely in darkness. **Cavern**—cave. **Mask**—cover, hide. **Thy**—your. **Monstrous**—dreadful. **Visage**—face ; figure. **Affability**—gentleness, politeness. **Path**—walk about. **Thy ... on**—in your true colours, real appearance. **Thy native semblance**—your original shape or appearance. **Erebus**—the dark region under the earth through which the souls of the dead reach the under-world. **Were**—would be. **Dim enough**—dark enough. **From prevention**—can prevent you from being discovered or recognised ; from being discovered and checked.

Enter the conspirators, Cassius, Casca, Decius, Cinna, Metellus Cimber and Trebonius.

Cas. I think we are *too bold upon your rest :*
Good morrow, Brutus; do we trouble you ?

Bru. I have been *up this hour* ; awake all night.
Know I these men that come along with you ?

Cas. Yes, every one of them ; and no man here
But honours you; and every one doth wish
You had but that opinion of yourself
Which every noble Roman *bears* of you.
This is Trebonius.

Bru. He is welcome hither.

Cas. This, Decius Brutus.

Bru. He is welcome too.

Cas. This, Casca ; this, Cinna ; and this Metellus Cimber.

Bru. They are all welcome.
What *watchful cares* do *interpose* themselves
Betwixt your *eyes and night* ?

Cas. *Shall I entreat a word* ?

[Brutus and Cassius whisper apart.]

Dec. Here lies the east : doth not the day break here ?

Casca. No.

Cin. O, pardon, sir, it doth ; and yon grey lines
That *fret the clouds,* are *messengers* of day.

Casca. You shall confess that you are both deceived.
Here, as I point my sword, sun arises ;
Which is a great way *growing on* the south
Weighing the youthful season of the year.
Some two months hence, up higher towards the north
He first presents his fire : and the *high east*
Stands, as the Capitol, directly here.

Bru. Give me your hand *all over,* one by one.

Cas. And let us *swear our resolution.*

Bold—overconfident or rude. **Too ... rest**—taking too much liberty in intruding upon your time of rest. **Up**—awake. **This hour**—for one hour. **Bears**—keeps. **Watchful cares**—cares that keep you awake and alert. **Interpose**—come between. **Betwixt**—between. **Eyes and night**—what worries have kept your eyes open at night when they ought to have closed in sleep. **Shall ... word**—Shall I be permitted to speak a word to you ? **Fret the clouds**—adorn or decorate the clouds. **Messengers**—announcers. harbingers. **Growing on**—approaching ; encroaching on. **Weighing**—considering ; keeping in mind. **Youthful ... year**—

Enter the conspirators, Cassius, Decius, Cinna, Metellus Cimber and Trebonius.

Cas. I fear we are disturbing your night's rest. Good morning, Brutus. Are we really disturbing you ?

Bru. I have been wide awake the whole night and have been out of my bed for over an hour. Do I know all these men who have come with you ?

Cas. Yes, you know all of them and there is no man here who does not respect you; everyone of them wishes that you should think of yourself as highly as every noble Roman thinks of you. This is Trebonius.

Bru. He is welcome here.

Cas. This is Decius Brutus.

Bru. He too is welcome.

Cas. This is Casca, this Cinna and this is Metellus Cimber.

Bru. They are welcome. What anxieties do keep you awake, and stand between your eyes and your night's rest (*prevent you from sleeping*) ?

Cas. May I have a word with you ?

| Brutus and Cassius talk in whispers.

Dec. On this side is the east. Does not the sun rise here ?

Casca. No.

Cin. Excuse me, Sir, it does rise there ; and those grey lines of brightness which decorate the clouds show that the day-dawn is near.

Casca. You will have to admit that both of you are mistaken. The sun rises in the direction in which I am pointing my sword. It rises farther to the south (*of east*) because it is the beginning of the year. In about two months' time the sun will rise in the due east, a little farther north than it does now. The due east is in this direction in which stands the Capitol.

Bru. Let me shake hand with you one by one.

Cas. And let each one of us take an oath that we will be firm in our determination to act (against Caesar).

---

the early part of the year. **He**—the sun. **First ... fire**—the sun rises. **High east**—due east. **All over**—all of you. **Swear ... resolution**—take an oath to be firm in our determination (against Caesar).

Bru. No, not an oath. If not the *face of men.*
The *sufferance* of our souls, the *time's abuse*—
If these be motives weak, *break off betimes,*
And every man *hence* to his *idle bed* ;
So let *high-sighted tyranny range on.*
Till each man drop *by lottery.* But *if these,*
As I am sure they do, *bear fire enough*
To *kindle cowards* and to *steel with valour*
The *melting spirits* of women, then, countrymen,
What need we any *spur* but our own cause
To prick us to redress ? What other bond
Than *secret Romans,* that have spoke the word
And will not *palter* ? and what other oath
Than honesty to *honesty engaged,*
That this shall be, or we will *fall for it* ?
Swear priests, and cowards, and man *cautelous,*
Old feeble carrins, and such suffering souls
That welcome wrongs ; unto bad causes swear
Such creatures as men doubt ; but do not *stain*
The *even virtue* of our enterprise,
Nor the *insuppressive mettle* of our spirit
To think that our cause or our performance
Did need an oath: when every drop of blood
That every Roman bears, and nobly bears,
Is guilty of a *several bastardy,*
If he do break the smallest particle
Of any promise that hath passed from him.

Cas. But what of Cicero ? Shall we *sound him* ?
I think he will *stand very strong with us.*

Casca. Let us not leave him out.

Cinna. No, by no means.

Face of men—the discontented and sad faces of Romans suffering under the tyranny of an ambitious man (Caesar). **Sufferance**—suffering; distress. **Time's abuse**—tyranny of the present days; evil and injustice prevalent at the time. **Break off betimes**—disperse at once. **Hence**—go from here. **Idle bed**—to his bed to lie in it as an idle man ; lie in bed doing nothing. **High sighted tyranny**—tyranny which can see from great heights. **Range on**—go on unrestrained ; widespread. **By lottery**—by chance (just when the eyes of the tyrant happen to see him). **These**—the motives mentioned by Brutus. **Bear... enough**—have sufficient power. **Kindle cowards**—excite or rouse even cowards to action. **Steel with valour**—make strong with courage. **Melting spirit**—soft and weak nature. **Spur**—goading; excitement; encouragement. **To prick**—to goad; to excite; to incite. **Secret Roman**—honourable Romans pledged to keep a secret. **Palter**—deceive or betray; be insincere. **Than...engaged**—the oaths of honour exchanged. **Fall for it**—die for it. **Cautelous**—deceitful; crafty.

Bru. No, there is no need of taking any oath. If the sad faces of our fellow citizens, the pain and suffering of our souls and the evils of the present time are not reasons strong enough to keep us united, let us, then, disperse at once, and let each one of us return home to lie in his bed and idle away his time; let this injustice and tyranny reign supreme till each man dies as the eyes of this tyranny happen to fall on him. But, I am sure these reasons are strong enough to make even the cowards brave and strong and to fill even the soft and weak spirits of women with courage. Then, my countrymen, we do not require anything except our cause that incites and encourages us to act for freedom from Caesar's tyranny. What other bond do we require except the fact that we are honourable Romans who would never betray the cause or disclose their secrets ? This oath is enough that we are honourable Romans who have given an honest word that we will either achieve our goal or die for it. Only priests, cowards, deceitful men and weak old people who are no better than dead bodies, and those down-troddens who have no courage to oppose injustice, need swear or take oaths. Only distrustful people swear when their cause is unjust. But we should not spoil the steadfast goodness of our cause and the indomitable force of our spirit by thinking that our cause or its execution needs any oath taking. Every drop of blood of a noble Roman is impure if he breaks even a part of a promise made by him.

Cas. What about Cicero ? Shall we try to know his mind ? I think he shall support us very strongly.

Casca. Let us not leave him out of our party.

Cinna. No, by no means.

Old...carrins—weak old people who are no better than dead bodies. **Stain**—spoil. **Even virtue**—steadfast goodness. **Insuppressive mettle**—indomitable; unconquerable nature. **Several bastardy**—great impurity of blood ; many of us not born of our parents. **Sound him**—try to know what he thinks. **Stand...us**—he will support us very strongly.

Met. O, let us have *him* for his *silver hairs*
Will *purchase* us a *good opinion*
And buy men's voices to *commend* our deeds ;
It shall be said, his *judgement ruled our hands* ;
Our youths and wildness shall *no whit* appear,
But all be *buried* in his *gravity.*

Bru. O, name him not ; let us not *break with him,*
For he will never follow anything.
That other men begin.

Cas. Then leave him out.

Casca. Indeed, he is not fit.

Dec. Shall no man else be *touched but* only Caesar ?

Cas. Decius, well *urged.* I think it is not *meet,*
Mark Antony, so well beloved of Caesar,
Should outlive Caesar ; we shall find *of him,*
A *shrewd contriver,* and you know, his *means*,
If he *improve* them, may well *stretch so far*
As to *annoy us all* ; which to prevent,
Let Antony and Caesar fall together.

Bru. Our *course* will seem too bloody, Caius Cassius,
To cut the head off and then *hack* the limbs,
Like *wrath* in death and *envy* afterwards
For Antony is but a limb of Caesar ;
Let us be *sacrificers*, but not *butchers Caius*,
We all stand up against *the spirit of Caesar,*
And in the spirit of men there is no blood ;
O, that we then could *come by* Caesar's spirit,
And not *dismember* Caesar ! But, alas,
Caesar must bleed for it. And, gentle friends,
Let's kill him boldly, but not *wrathfully* ;
Let's carve him as a dish fit for the gods,
Not *hew* him as a *carcass* fit for *hounds* ;
And let our hearts, as *subtle* masters do,
Stir up their servants, to an *act of rage,*
And *after* seem to *chide* 'em. This shall make.

Him—Cicero. **Silver hairs**—white hair which show him a respectable wise old man. **Purchase us**—get for us ; buy us. **Good opinion**—reputation. **Commend**—praise; approval. **Judgement**—wisdom. **Ruled**—guided; directed. **Our hands**—our actions. **No whit**—not in the least. **Buried**—hidden under. **Gravity**—seriousness, solemnity. **Break with him**—disclose our secret to him. **Touched**—harmed; killed. **But**—except. **Urged**—said; suggested. **Meet**—proper. **Of him**—in him. **Shrewd contriver**—mischievous plotter; clever schemer. **Means**—resources ; sources of power. **Improve**—turns to advantage. **Stretch so far**—will go so far ; extend himself so much or become so powerful. **Annoy**—harm. **Course**—

Met. O, let us have him in our party, because his white hair will win for us the good opinion of the people ; his old age will make people support our cause. They will, then, say that our actions and hands were guided by Cicero's mature wisdom. Our youth and inexperience will not in the least be noticed, because it will be covered by his maturity and seriousness. [*Cicero's seriousness will hide our rashness and inexperience of youth.*]

Bru. Do not mention his name. Let us not disclose our secrets to him. Because he will never take part in anything started by any man other than himself.

Cas. Then, let us leave him out.

Casca. He is, in fact, not a suitable man,

Dec. Shall no other man, except Caesar, be killed ?

Cas. Well said, Decius. I think, Mark Antony, whom Caesar loves so much, should not live after Caesar's death. For he will prove to be a mischievous plotter ; and you know if he turns his resources to advantage, he can greatly harm all of us. So in order to prevent him from harming us, Antony should also be killed along with Caesar.

Bru. If we do that; our course of action will appear to be bloodthirsty, Cais Cassius. It will be cutting the head of a man first and then cutting him limb by limb. You know, Antony is only a limb of Caesar. It will look as if we killed Caesar in a fit of malicious anger and after that killed Antony out of jealousy. Let us behave like persons who are offering sacrifice on a holy altar and not like butchers who kill senselessly. We are against the ambitious spirit of Caesar. But the spirit of man is not made of flesh and blood. We wish, we could find the spirit of Caesar and kill it without killing his body, but alas ! Caesar's blood must be shed; without that his spirit cannot be killed. And, my good friends, let us kill him boldly but not angrily. Let us kill him as if we were making an offering of his body to gods. We should not kill him senselessly just to throw his body to dogs. Our hearts should first incite our bodily powers and passions to do an act of violence, and, then, should pretend to rebuke them, just as cunning masters first instigate their servants to an act of violence and, then, rebuke them to make a show of anger. If we act in this way, then, it will be thought that our act of murdering Caesar is just an act of sacrifice.

---

action. **Hack**—cut into pieces. **Wrath**—anger. **Envy**—jealousy. **Sacrificers**—Let us behave like those who will sacrifice Caesar at the holy altar of freedom. **Butchers**—slaughterers. **Spirit of Caesar**—Caesarism; the tyrannical tendency of Caesar ; Caesar's authoritarianism. **Come by**—get; find. **Dismember**—to cut limb by limb. **Wrathfully**—angrily; with anger and ill-will. **Carve him**—cut ceremoniously. **A dish**—as an offering for gods. **Hew**—cut to pieces. **Carcass**—dead body. **Hounds**—hunting dogs. **Subtle**—clever; cunning. **Stir up**—incite. **Their servants**—bodily organs, hands, passions and etc. **Act of rage**—violent act. **After**—afterwards (when the deed is done). **Chide**—rebuke.

Our purpose *necessary* and not *envious* ;
Which so appearing to the common eyes,
We shall be called *purgers*, not murderers,
And for Mark Antony, think not of him ;
For he can do no more than Caesar' arm.
When Caesar's head is off.

Cas. Yet I fear him :
For in the *ingrafted love* he bears to Caesar—

Bru. Alas, good Cassius, do not think of him ;
If he loves Caesar, all that he can do
Is to himself,—*take thought* and die for Caesar ;
And that *were much he should* ; for he is *given.*
To sports, to *wildness,* and much company.

Treb. There is *no fear in him* ; let him not die ;
For he will live, and laugh at this hereafter.

[Clock strikes.]

Bru. Peace ! count the clock,

Cas. The clock hath *stricken* three.

Treb. 'Tis time to part,

Cas. But it is doubtful yet.
Whether Caesar will come forth to-day, or no ;
For he is superstitious grown *of late,*
Quite from the *main opinion* he held once
Of *fantasy* of dreams, and *ceremonies* ;
It may be, these *apparent prodigies.*
The unaccustomed terror of this night,
And the persuasion of his *augurers,*
May hold him from the Capitol to-day.

Dec. Never, fear that ; if he be so *resolved,*
I can *o'ersway him* ; for he loves to hear
That *unicorns* may be *betrayed* with trees,
And bears with glasses' elephants with *holes,*
Lions with *toils* and men with flatterers.
But when I tell him he hates flatterers
He says he does, being then most flattered.
Let me work ;
For *I can give his humour the true bent.*
And I will bring him to the Capitol.

Necessary—an act done out of necessity or compulsion. **Envious**—done out of malice or ill-will. **Purgers**—healers, purifiers (who heal through sacrifice) ; those who have purged Rome of such a tyrant like Caesar. **Ingrafted**—deeply rooted. **Take thought**—become

Caesar was done to death out of necessity and out of ill will. And if the common people look at it this way, they will call us the purifiers of Rome and not the murderers of Caesar. And as for Mark Antony, you just don't think about him, because after Caesar's murder, he will be as helpless and harmless as dead Caesar's arm.

Cas. Yet I am afraid of him because of his deep rooted love for Caesar.

Bru. Alas, good Cassius, do not think about him. If he loves Caesar so much, he can harm only himself with that love. He may grow sad and kill himself. But, this also will be too much for him, because he very much fond of games, merry-making and company of boon or close companions.

Treb. There is no need being afraid of him ; don't kill him. Because, if he lives, he will only laugh at his murder of Caesar.

[Clock strikes]

Bru. Silence ; count the strokes of the clock.

Cas. The clock has struck three.

Treb. It is time that we were gone.

Cas. But it is not yet certain whether Caesar will come out today or not. Because recently he has become superstitious. His belief in omens, dreams and strange fancies is different from what it used to be. It is very probable that these unusual horrors of this night and the advice of his soothsayers may prevent him from coming to the Capitol to-day.

Dec. Do not be afraid of that probability. Even if Caesar is determined not to come, I can over-rule his decision, for he is fond of hearing that it is easy to trap unicorns with the help of trees, and bears with the help of mirrors which can blind them, to trap elephants by digging ditches, and to catch lions with the help of nets. It is easy to deceive men by flattering them. But when I tell Caesar that he hates flatterers, he will say that he does hate them ; and that is the best way to flatter him. You leave it to me to work upon his mind, and I am sure that I shall be able to turn his disposition (*temperament*) in the right direction, and will be able to bring him to the Capitol.

---

sad. **Were...should**—even that would be too much for him to do. **Wildness**—riotous living. **No fear in him**—there is nothing to be feared in him. **Stricken**—struck. **Of late**—recently. **Quite from**—contrary to. **Main opinion**—general opinion. **Fantasy**—strange imaginings; fancy. **Ceremonies**—portents; omens. **Apparent**—that are appearing clearly. **Prodigies**—omens; warnings. **Unaccustomed**—unusual. **Augurers**—foretellers; soothsayers. **May hold him from**—may prevent him from going to the Capitol ; keep him back. **Resolved**—determined. **Oversway**—influence him, persuade him. **Unicorn**—a horse-like animal with one horn. **Betrayed**—deceived; caught; trapped. **Holes**—pits; ditches. **Toils**—nets; snares. **Let me work**—let me do this job of influencing Caesar. **I...bent**—I can turn bis disposition (temperament) in the right direction ; I can bend him to move according to our plan.

Cas. Nay, we will all of us be *there* to fetch him,
Bru. By the eighth hour : is that the *uttermost* ?
Cin. Be that the uttermost, and fail not then,
Met. Caius Ligarius doth *bear Caesar hard,*
Who rated him for speaking well of Pompey :
I wonder, none of you have thought of him,
Bru. Now good Metellus, go along *by him* ;
He loves me well, and I have given him reasons ;
Send him but *hither,* and I'll *fashion him.*
Cas. The morning comes *upon's* : *we'll* leave you, Brutus.
And, friends, disperse yourselves ; but all remember
What you have said, and show yourselves true Romans.
Bru. Good gentlemen, *look fresh and merrily.*
Let not your looks put on our purposes,
But *bear it* as our Roman actors do,
With *untired spirits* and *formal constancy.*
And so, good morrow to you every one.

[Exeunt *all but* Brutus]

Boy ! Lucius ! Fast asleep ? It is no matter ;
Enjoy the heavy *honey-dew of slumber* ;
Thou *hast* no *figures nor no fantasies*,
Which *busy care* draws in brains of men ;
Therefore, thou sleep'st so sound.

Enter : Portia

Por. Brutus, my lord !
Bru. Portia, what mean you ? Wherefore rise you now ?
It is not for your health thus to *commit*
Your weak *condition* to the *raw-cold* morning.
Por. Nor for yours neither. You've *ungently,* Brutus,
Stole from my bed : and yesternight, at supper,
You suddenly arose, and walked about,
Musing and sighing, *with your arms across,*
And when I ask'd you what the matter was,
You *stared upon me* with *ungentle* looks ;
I *urged* you further ; then you *scratch'd your head.*

There—at Caesar's house. **Uttermost**—latest hour. **Bears...hard**—bears ill will to Caesar ; doesn't like Caesar. **Who**—Caesar. **Rated**—rebuked, scolded. **By him**—to his house. **Hither**—here (at Brutus' place). **Fashion him**—mould him for our purpose ; win him to our side. **Upon's**—upon us. **We'll**—we will. **Look...merrily**—appear to be gay. **Let...purposes**—let not our appearance show our real plans. **Purposes**—plans, designs, intentions. **Bear it**—carry it, do it. **Untired spirits**—without any sign of strain or tiredness. **Formal constancy**—dignified composure ; honourable self-control. **Honey...slumber**—sound, sweet and refreshing

Cas. No, we will all be at Caesar's house to bring him to the Capitol.

Bru. By eight o'clock in the morning. That should be the latest hour.

Cin. Yes, let that be the latest hour, and let us not fail to reach there by that time.

Met. Caius Ligarius bears ill-will to Caesar who, once, scolded him for speaking in praise of Pompey. I am surprised that none of you has even mentioned his name.

Bru. Now, good Metellus, you go to his house; he loves me very much, and I have convinced him that he should join us. You just send him here, and I will persuade him to be with us.

Cas. The morning is near. We will leave you, Brutus. Now, my friends, let us go. But remember what you have promised, and be true Romans.

Bru. Good gentlemen, look to be fresh and cheerful. Let not our looks betray our plans (*let our appearances not show what we want to do*). But carry yourselves with that self-possession and dignity with which Roman actors play their parts on the stage. So good morning to you all.

[They all, except Brutus go.]

Boy ! Lucius ! Are you fast asleep ? Well, it does not matter. Enjoy the sweet, sound and refreshing sleep that has over-powered you. You have no disturbing thoughts or fancies which disturb the people who have worries and anxieties. That is the reason why you sleep soundly.

Enter : Portia

Por. Brutus, my Lord !

Bru. What do you mean, Portia ? Why have you got up so early ? It is not good for your health to expose your weak constitution (कमजोर शरीर) to the cold morning wind in this way.

Portia. But this exposure (खुला वातावरण) is not good for your health also. It was very unkind of you that you left my bed stealthily. Last night too, at supper, you got up all of a sudden and walked about with your arms folded. You sighed and it looked as if you were lost in deep thought. And when I asked you what the matter was, you only looked angrily at me. I pressed you again to tell me all about it, but you scratched your head in perplexity.

---

sleep. **Hast**—has. **Figures...fantasies**—no disturbing dreams or figments of imagination. **Busy care**—rush and worries. **It is...health**—It is not good for your health. **Commit**—expose. **Condition**—(poor) state of the body; health. **Raw-cold**—bitter and biting. **Ungently**—unkindly, cruelly. **Stole**—left stealthily. **Musing**—lost in thought, thinking. **With...across**—with your arms folded. (the pose of a man lost in deep thoughts). **Stared...me**—looked at me. **Ungentle**—unkind. **Urged**—pressed. **Scratched... head**—showed that you were perplexed and in confusion.

And *too impatiently* stamp'd with your foot
Yet I insisted, yet you answer'd not,
But, with an angry *wafture* of your hand,
Gave sign for me to leave you : So I did.
Fearing to *strengthen* that impatience
Which seem'd too much *enkindled,* and *withal*
Hoping it was but an *effect of humour,*
Which sometimes *hath his hour with* every man
It will not let you eat, nor talk, nor sleep;
And could it work so much upon your *shape*
As it hath much *prevailed on* your *condition*
I *should not know you, Brutus.* Dear my Lord.
Make me acquainted with your cause of grief.

Bru. I am not well in health, and that is all.

Por. Brutus is wise, and were he not in health
He would *embrace the means to come by it.*

Bru. Why, so I do–Good Portia, go to bed.

Por. Is Brutus sick, and is it *physical.*
To walk *unbraced,* and suck up the *humours*
Of the *dank* morning? What, is Brutus sick ?
And will he steal out of his *wholesome* bed
To *dare* the *vile contagion* of the night,
And *tempt* the *rheumy* and *unpurged* air
To add unto his sickness ? No, my Brutus:
You have some *sick offence with your mind,*
Which by the right and virtue of *my place,*
I ought to know of : and upon my knees,
I *charm you,* by my once *commended* beauty,
By all your vows of love, and that great vow
Which did *incorporate* and make us one,
That you *unfold* to me, your self, your *half,*
Why you are *heavy,* and what men to-night
Have *had resort* to you : for here have been
Some six or seven, who did hide their faces
Even from darkness.

Too impatiently—highly agitated and restless. **I insisted**—I pressed for the answer. **Wafture**—gesture, movement, waving. **Strengthen**—increase. **Enkindled**—roused, excited. **Withal**—moreover. **Effect of humour**—a sign of one's passing mood. **Hath his hour with**—has its hold over ; dominates. **shape**—appearance; looks. **Prevailed on**—affected. **Condition**—state of mind. **I...Brutus**—I should not know you for Brutus (you do not look like Brutus). **Embrace**—adopt. **Embrace the means**—take measures (to get healthy again). **Come by**—get. **Physical**—healthy ; good for health. **Unbraced**—unbuttoned. **Humours**—dampness. **Dank**—damp. **Wholesome**—warm and comfortable. **Dare**—take the risk of. **Vile contagion**—foul infection of the damp night. **Tempt**—risk. **Rheumy**—Causing cough or cold. **Unpurged**—

And then you stamped the floor with your foot. When I pressed you further you made no answer, but with angry gesture (*motion*) of your hand you gave me a hint that I should leave you ; so I left you because I did not want to increase your impatience which was already very much roused. I just hoped that it was merely a passing mood which gets hold of every man at some time. But this bad mood does not let you eat or talk or sleep ; if it affected your physical appearance as much as it has affected your mind, I should, then, not be able to recognize you. Brutus, my lord, tell me the cause of your sadness.

Bru. I am not in good health, and that is the only reason.

Portia. You are a wise man. If you were not in good health, you would take necessary steps to regain your health.

Bru. That is exactly what I am doing, my good Portia, you go to bed.

Portia. Is Brutus unwell ? And is it a cure that you move about with your cloak unbuttoned and inhale the damp air of the morning ? Can you be unwell ? If you are/were unwell, why would you leave your warm and comfortable bed. If you were ill why would you expose yourself to the infectious vapours and invite the unpurified air to worsen your illness ? No, my Brutus, there is some mental trouble which causes this illness, and as your dear wife, I have every right to know what troubles your mind. Brutus, I bend down on my knees. I pray you in the name of my beauty which once you admired so much. I pray you in the name of your vows of love for me, and in the name of that vow of marriage which united us and made us one. I pray you to disclose to me, to your wife, your better half, what it is that troubles your mind ? Who were those men who came to you tonight ; because some six or seven persons have been here, and even in the darkness of the night, they kept their faces covered.

---

unpurified by the heat of the sun. **Sick offence**—harmful sickness. **With your mind**—the sickness is not physical but mental ; it has affected your mind. **My place**—my place as your wife. **Charm you**—request you ; entreat you. **Commended**—admired. **Incorporate us**—made us one; joined us together. **Unfold**—disclose. **Half**—your better half (wife). **Heavy**—sorrowful ; depressed. **Had resort**—had come.

Bru. Kneel not, gentle Portia.

Por. I should not need, if you were gentle Brutus.
Within the bond of marriage, tell me, Brutus,
Is it excepted I should know no secrets
That *appertain* to you ? Am I yourself
But, as it were *in sort or limitation* :
To keep with you at meals, comfort your bed,
And talk to you sometimes ? Dwell I but in the *suburbs*
Of your good pleasure ? If it be no more,
Portia is Brutus' *harlot*, not his wife.

Bru. You are my true and honourable wife ;
As dear to me as the *ruddy drops*
That *visit* my sad heart.

Por. If this were true, then should I know this secret.
I grant, I am a woman : but *withal*
A woman that Lord Brutus *took to wife* ;
I grant, I am a woman ; but withal
A woman well-reputed'—Cato's daughter.
Think you I am no stronger than my sex,
Being so fathered, and so husbanded ?
Tell me your *counsels,* I will not disclose 'em.
I have made *strong proof* of my *constancy,*
Giving myself a *voluntary wound*
Here in the thigh : can I bear that with patience.
And not my husband's secrets ?

Bru. O ye gods,
Render me worthy of this noble wife ?

[Knocking within.]

Hark, hark ! one knocks : Portia, go in awhile ;
And by-and-by thy bosom shall *partake*
The secrets of my heart ;
All my *engagements* I will *construe* to thee,
All the *charactery of my sad brow ;*
Leave me with haste. [Exit Portia]

Within...marriage—in the contract of marriage. **Is it excepted**—is this reservation made that ; are there some issues excluded from the sacred contract of marriage ? **Appertain**—belong. **In sort or limitation**—in a limited degree; only for some specified period. **Suburbs**—Outskirts ; doesn't live in his heart [harlots or prostitutes used to live in the suburbs of London or other big towns. Portia here means that Brutus should take her as his wife and not as a prostitute]. **Harlot**—a hired mistress. **Ruddy drops**—red drops of blood. **Visit**—circulate in. **Withal**—at the same times. **Took to wife**—married. **Being...husbanded**—having such a noble father and such a noble husband. **Counsels**—thoughts, what is there in your mind. **Strong proof**—a difficult test or trial. **Constancy**—firmness. **Voluntary wound**—a

Bru. Do not bow down before me, gentle Portia.

Por. If you were kind Brutus, it would not be necessary for me to kneel before you. Is there any such reservation made in our marriage contract that I should not know any secrets belonging to you ? Do I belong to you only in a limited sense ? Am I to be with you only at meal times? Am I only to sleep with you in your bed, and talk to you sometimes ? Do I live only in the outskirts (बाह्य भाग) of your heart and not in the centre of it ? If it is so, I am your hired mistress, not your dear wife.

Bru. You are my true and honourable wife. You are as dear to me as the red drops of blood which circulate through my heart.

Portia. If this were true, then I should know this secret of yours I admit that I am a woman, but at the same time I am a woman whom lord Brutus married and took as his wife. I grant that I am a woman, but at the same time I am a woman with a high reputation, I am the daughter of no less a man than Cato. Do you think that being the daughter of Cato and the wife of Brutus, I am no stronger than an ordinary woman ? Tell me all about your thoughts and plans. I will not disclose them. I have tested my power of endurance very severely by giving my thigh a deep wound of my own accord. If I can bear that pain with patience, shall I not be able to keep the secrets of my husband ?

Bru. O Gods, make me worthy of this noble wife.

[Knocking inside

Listen! Someone is knocking. Go inside for a short while, Portia, and soon I will explain to you all my plans and all that is written on my sad face [*I will tell you all that worries me and all that I plan to do*) ; leave me quickly. [Portia goes

---

wound which I gave of my own accord. **Hark**—listen. **By and by**—soon ; in a short-while. **Bosom**—heart. **Partake**—share. **My engagements**—all that I have promised to do. **Construe**—explain. **Charactery...brows**—what is written on sad face or forehead.

Enter Lucius and Ligarius

Bru. Lucius, who's that knocks ?
Luc. Here is a sick man *that would spake* with you.
Bru. Caius Ligarius that Metellus *spake* of.
Boy, stand aside—Caius, Ligarius ! *how* ?
Lig. *Vouchsafe* good morrow from a *feeble* tongue.
Bru. O, *what a time* have you *chose* out, brave Caius.
To wear a kerchief ! *Would you were not sick* !
Lig. I am not sick, if Brutus have in hand.
Any *exploit* worthy the name of honour.
Bru. Such an exploit have I in hand, Ligarius,
Had you a *healthful* ear to hear of it.
Lig. By all the gods that Romans bow before,
I here *discard* my sickness ! Soul of Rome !
Brave son, *derived from honourable loins* !
Thou, like an *exorcist*, hast *conjured up*
My *mortified* spirit. Now bid me run,
And I will *strive with* things impossible ;
Yea, get the better of them. *What's to do ?*
Bru. A piece of work that will make sick men *whole.*
Lig. But are not some whole that we must make sick ?
Bru. That must we also. What it is, my Caius,
I shall unfold to thee, as we are going
To whom it must be done.
Lig. *Set on your foot,*
And with a heart *new fired* I follow you
To do I know not what : but it *sufficeth* [Thunder
That Brutus leads me on.
Bru. Follow me, then. [Exeunt]

Scene II—A Room in Caesar's Palace

Thunder and lightning. Enter Caesar, in his night-gown

Caes. Nor heaven nor earth have *at peace* to-night :
Thrice hath Calpurnia in her sleep cried out,
"Help, oh ! They murder Caesar !" Who's within ?

That would—who would like to ; who wants to. **Spake**—spoke. **How**—how is that ; how are you ? **Vouchsafe**—be good enough to accept. **Feeble**—weak. **What a time**—you have chosen a wrong time. **Chose**—chosen. **To...kerchief**—to be ill ; to tie the head with a handkerchief because of sickness. **Would...sick**— I wish you were not sick now. **Exploit**—enterprise ; some important work or mission. **Had you**—if you had. **Healthful**—healthy ; bold. **Discard**—give up; banish. **Derived...loins**—born of noble ancestors. **Exorcist**—one who drives away evil spirits; magician. **Conjured up**—raised up with the help of magic. **Mortified**—dead ; lifeless.

Enter Lucius and Ligarius

Bru. Lucius who is that knocks ?

Luc. Here is a sickman who wants to talk to you.

Bru. It is Cais Ligarus about whom Metellus spoke to me. Boy, you stand aside Cais Ligarius, how now ? *(or how are you ?).*

Lig. Be kind enough to accept good morning from a weak and sickman.

Bru. O, what a wrong time you have chosen to fall ill, and tie a handkerchief round your head ! I wish that you were not ill.

Lig. I am not ill if Brutus has some work of honour for me.

Bru. Well, Ligarius, I really have such an-enterprise for you, if only you were Healthy enough to listen to what I have to tell you.

Lig. By all the gods of Rome I throw away my sickness right now. Great Roman ! you brave descendant of noble ancestors ! Like a magician you have revived my dead spirit. Now tell me to run, and I will struggle against greatest difficulties and dangers. What is there to be done ?

Bru. It is something which will make-sick men healthy.

Lig. But are there not some healthy men whom our action will make sick ?

Bru. Yes there are. I will, however, tell you all about it as we go to him against whom we have to act.

Lig. Start at once, and I will follow you with a heart full of new energy and enthusiasm. I do not know what I am going to do, but it is enough for me that Brutus is leading me.

Bru. Follow me then.

Scene II—A room in Caesar's Palace

Thunder and Lightning. Enter Caesar in his night gown.

Caes. Both, the heaven and the earth have been quite disturbed tonight.

Three times Calpurnia cried out in her dream "Help, Oh ; they murder Caesar." Who is there inside ?

Strive with—Struggle against. **Yea**—yes. **What's...do**—what is to be done. **Whole**—healthy. **To whom**—to the house of the person to whom. **Set...foot**—move; proceed. **New fired**—full of fresh energy and enthusiasm. **Sufficieth**—is sufficient. **At peace**—calm.

Enter a Servant

Serv. My lord ?
Caes. Go *bid* the priests do *present* sacrifice,
And bring me their *opinion of success.*
Serv. I will, my lord. [Exit

Enter Calpurnia

Cal. What mean you, Caesar ? think you to walk forth ?
You shall not *stir out* of your house to-day.
Caes. Caesar *shall forth ;* the things that threaten'd me.
Ne'er look'd but on my back ; when they shall see
The face of Caesar, they *are vanished.*
Cal. Caesar, I never *stood on ceremonies,*
Yet now they *fright* me. *There is one within.*
Besides the things that we have heard and seen,
Recounts most horrid sights seen by the *watch.*
A lioness hath *whelped* in streets ;
And graves have *yawn'd* and *yielded up their dead* !
Fierce fiery warriors fought upon the clouds,
In ranks and squadrons and *right form of war,*
Which *drizzled* blood upon the Capitol ;
The noise of battle *hurtled* in the air,
Horses did neigh-and dying men did groan,
And ghosts did *shriek* and *squeal* about the streets.
O Caesar ! these things are *beyond all use.*
And I do fear them.
Caes. What can be avoided
Whose end is purposed by the mighty gods ?
Yet Caesar shall go forth ; for these *predictions*
Are to the world in general as to Caesar.
Cal. When beggars die there are no *comets* seen :
The heavens themselves *blaze forth* the death of princes.
Caes. Cowards *die many times* before their deaths ;
The *valiant* never taste of death *but* once.
Of all the wonders that I yet have heard,
It seems to me most strange that men should fear ;
Seeing that death, a *necessary end,*
Will come when it will come.

Bid—ask. **Present**—immediate; at once. **Opinion of success**—bring the news if the sacrifices gave the desired success. **Success**—result of the sacrifice. **Stir out**—move out. **Shall forth**—go out. **Are vanished**—they (dangers) disappear at once. **Stood on ceremonies**—attached importance to omens and rituals. **Fright**—frighten. **There...within**—there is a servant in our palace. **Recounts**—narrates; describes. **Watch**—city guards; night watchmen. **Whelped**—brought forth her young ones. **Yawned**—opened wide. **Yielded...dead**—let out

Enter a servant

Serv. Yes my lord ?

Caes. Go to the priests and ask them to offer a sacrifice at once, and bring me the result, good or bad. *(Let me know whether I will fare well or not).*

Serv. I will do so, my lord. [*goes*

Enter Calpurnia

Cal. What do you mean, Caesar ? Do you think of going out ? You shall not move out of your house today.

Caes. Caesar shall certainly go out. I have never yet seen things that can threaten me. They are always at my back. As soon as I turn my face to them (*threatening things; dangers*) they disappear at once.

Cal. Caesar, I have never attached any importance to omens, but now they frighten me. There is a servant within who has been relating some dreadful scenes seen by the night-watchman, in addition to those that we have ourselves seen and heard. A lioness has brought forth her young ones in the street. Graves have opened wide and dead bodies buried in them have moved out. Divisions of soldiers with flaming bodies fought upon the clouds in a regular order of war ; blood rained upon the Capitol. The noise of the battle clattered and clashed in the air. Horses were heard neighing, and dying soldiers were heard groaning and crying out of pain. Ghosts were heard screaming and raising shrill cries. O Caesar, these are all abnormal things and I am afraid of them.

Caes. It is impossible to avoid what has been decided and designed by mighty gods. Yet Caesar will go out, because these omens are meant as much for the world in general as for me.

Cal. When beggars (*poor ordinary people*) die, their death is not foretold by the appearance of shooting stars in the sky ; but when kings are about to die, the sky itself proclaims (*declares*) their death.

Caes. Cowards are always afraid of death. So they die many times before their actual death (*they die every time the fear of death gets hold of them*). But brave men suffer death only once. I have known many strange things, but of all these, the most wonderful thing is as to why men should be afraid of death, when they know that it is inevitable, and it must come at its right time.

---

dead bodies buried in them. **In ranks and squadrons**—in a battle array. **Right form of war**—regular order of war. **Drizzled**—rained; dropped. **Hurtled**—clattered; clashed; rang loudly. **Shriek**—cry. **Squeal**—utter shrill cries. **Beyond all use**—quite unusual; quite abnormal **Whose end...gods**—whose death or ruin has already been decided by gods ; what is designed or decided by the powerful gods. **Purposed**—designed ; destined ; determined. **Predictions**—omens. **Comets**—shooting stars. **The heavens**—sky and other heavenly bodies. **Blaze forth**—proclaim. **Die many times**—die as many times as the fear of death, gets hold of their imagination. **Valiant**—brave. **But**—only. **Necessary end**—inevitable; unavoidable.

Re-enter Servant

What say the *augurers ?*

Serv. They *would not have you* to *stir forth* to-day,
Plucking the *entrails* of an *offering* forth,
They could not find a heart within the beast.

Caes. The gods do this *in shame of cowardice :*
Caesar should be a *beast* without a heart
If he should stay at home to-day for fear,
No, Caesar shall not ; danger knows full well
That Caesar is more dangerous than he.
We are two lions *litter'd* in one day,
And I the elder and more terrible;
And Caesar shall go forth.

Cal. Alas, my lord,
Your wisdom is *consumed in* confidence.
Do not go forth to-day : call it my fear
That keeps you in the house, and not your own.
We'll send Mark Antony to the Senate-House,
And he shall say you are not well to-day;
Let me, upon my knee, *prevail* in this.

Caes. Mark Antony shall say I am not well ;
And *for thy humour,* I will stay at home.

Enter : Decius

Here's Decius Brutus, he shall tell them so.

Dec. Caesar *all hail* ! Good morrow, worthy Caesar :
I come to fetch you to Senate-House.

Caes. And you are come in *very happy time,*
To *bear my greeting* to the senators,
And tell them that I will not come today ;
Cannot, is false ; and that I dare not, falser:
I will not come today—tell them so Decius.

Cal. Say he is sick.

Caes. Shall Caesar send a lie ?
Have I in conquest *stretch'd mine arm so far,*
To be *afeared* to tell *greybeards* the truth ?
Decius, go tell them Caesar will not come.

Augurers—foretellers. **Would not...you**— would not allow you. **Stir forth**—go out. **Entrails**—intestines. **Offering**—the animal sacrificed by the priests. **In shame of cowardice**—to put cowards to shame. **Beast**—wild animal and not a man. **Littered**—born; brought forth. **Consumed**—destroyed ; ruined (by overconfidence). **Prevail**—have my own way. **For thy humour**—to satisfy your wish. **All hail**—wish you all health and happiness.

Re-enter Servant

What is the opinion of the foretellers ?

Servant. They advise you not to go out of your house today. When they removed the intestines (आंतें) of an animal offered as a sacrifice, they discovered that the animal had no heart.

Caes. The gods have done so in order to put cowards to shame. If, because of fear, I stay at home to-day, it will mean that I am no better than a beast without a heart. No, Caesar shall not stay at home. Danger knows that Caesar is more dangerous than danger itself. Danger and I are like two lions born on the same day, and I am the elder of the two and far more dreadful. Therefore Caesar shall go out.

Cal. I am sorry, my lord, that your overconfidence has destroyed your wisdom. Do not go out to-day. Say that is my fear, and not yours that keeps you at home. We will send Mark Antony to the Senate and he will tell them that you are not well. I request you, on my knees, to let me have my own way in this matter.

Caes. All right, then, let Mark Antony say that I am not well. I will stay at home just to satisfy your whim.

Enter : Decius

Here is Decius Brutus. He shall tell so.

Dec. Good morning Caesar ! May you be all healthy and happy ! I have come to take you to the Capitol.

Caes. You have come at the right moment, to convey my greetings to the senators and tell them that I will not come to-day. It will be untrue to say that I cannot come, and it will be a greater lie to say that I am afraid of coming. Just tell them, Decius, that I will not come.

Cal. Tell them he is not well.

Caes. Shall Caesar send a lie ? Have I extended my power to distant lands and won great victories only to be afraid of speaking the truth to a few old men (*senators*) ? No Decius, simply tell them that Caesar will not come.

Very happy time—at the right time. **Bear my greeting**—convey my greetings. **Stretched my arm so far**—have extended my power to distant lands ; extended the might of my arms. **Afeared**—afraid. **Greybeards**—old men ; old senators.

Dec. Most mighty Caesar, let me know some cause,
Lest I be laugh'd at when I tell them so.
Caes. The cause is in my will ; I will not come ;
That is enough to satisfy the Senate.
But *for your private satisfaction,*
Because I love you, I will let you know :
Calpurnia here, my wife, *stays me* at home :
She dreamt to-night she saw my statue,
Which, like a fountain with an hundred *spouts,*
Did run pure blood ; and many *lusty* Romans
Came smiling, and did bathe their hands in it,
And these does she *apply for* warnings and *portents.*
And evils *imminent* ; and on her knee
Hath begg'd that I will stay at home to-day.
Dec. This dream is all *amiss interpreted* :
It was a *vision* fair and fortunate.
Your statue *spouting* blood in many pipes
In which so many smiling Romans bathed,
Signifies that from you great Rome shall *suck*
Reviving blood, and that great men shall *press*
For *tinctures, stains, relics* and *cognizance* :
This by Calpurnia's dream is signified.
Caes. And this way have you well *expounded* it.
Dec. I have when you have heard what I can say :
And know it now : the Senate have *concluded*
To give this day a crown to mighty Caesar.
If you shall send them word you will not come,
Their minds may change. Besides, it were a *mock*
Apt to be *rendered* for some one to say,
Break up the Senate till another time,
When Caesar's wife shall meet with better dreams."
If Caesar hide himself, shall they not whisper,
"Lo, Caesar is afraid" ?
Pardon me, Caesar ; for my dear, *dear love*
To your proceeding bids me tell you this,
And reason to my love is liable.

Private—personal. **For...satisfaction**—for your personal satisfaction; to satisfy your personal curiosity. **Stays me**—keeps me, detains me. **Spouts**—openings, jets. **Lusty**—strong. **Apply for**—take for, regard as. **Portents**—omens. **Imminent**—just about to happen. **Amiss interpreted**—mis-interpreted, wrongly interpreted. **Vision**—dream. **Spouting**—throwing out. **Signifies**—shows. **Suck**—draw, get. **Reviving blood**—fresh blood giving new life ; Caesar's blood giving new life to Romans. **Press**—crowd round you. **Tinctures**—red colour of your blood. **Stains**—stains of your blood on their handkerchief (to be kept as mementoes). **Relics**—memorials. **Cognizance**—badges of honour [He means that Romans will dip their

Dec. Most powerful Caesar, give me some reason for your not coming to the Senate House, so that the senators may not laugh at me when I give them your message.

Caes. The only reason is that I have decided not to go ; so I will not go. My decision should be enough to satisfy the senators. But to satisfy your personal curiosity, I will tell you the reason simply because I love you. It is Calpurnia, my wife, who makes me stay at home. She had a dream last night. In her dream she saw my statue which like a fountain with many spouts (*openings*) sent forth pure blood ; and many strong Roman citizens with smiling faces crowded round it and bathed their hands in that blood. She regards this dream as an omen, a warning, pointing to some evil that is about to fall on me. And on her knees, she has requested me to stay at home to-day.

Dec. This dream has been wholly misinterpreted. It was a dream foretelling some good fortune. Your statue sending forth blood through many openings and the smiling Romans bathing their hands in it shows something good. It shows that from you Rome will receive new blood and new life. [*You will make Romans stronger and more prosperous*]. And great Romans will crowd round you to get relics and memorials. They will dip their handkerchiefs in your blood and keep them as holy relics obtained from some saint or martyr. This is the meaning of Calpurnia's dream.

Caes. This way you have certainly given a better explanation of this dream.

Dec. Yes, you will fully agree to my explanation when you have heard what I have yet to tell you. Let me tell you that the Senate has resolved to give mighty Caesar a crown. If now you send them the message that you will not come, they may change their decision. Moreover, some one may laugh at it and make a joke of it. He may taunt saying, "Let the Senate disperse until Caesar's wife has a happier dream. If you do not go to the Senate, they may say that even Caesar is afraid. Excuse me, Caesar my deep love for you and my great interest in your welfare makes me speak like this. My judgement tells me that I should not speak like this, but my love for you over-rules my judgement.

---

handkerchiefs in Caesar's blood, as in the blood of a saint or Martyr, and keep them as memorials and badges of honour.] **Expounded**—explained. **Concluded**—decided. **Mock**—joke. **Apt**—likely. **Rendered**—made in reply. **Break up**—disperse. **Break up...better dreams**—disperse the Senate until Caesar's wife has a better dream. **Dear love**—deep love. **To your proceeding**—for your advancement, your welfare. **And reason...liable**—my reason (judgement) is subordinate to my love. [My reason might prevent me from speaking to you in this way. But my love for you has over-ruled my judgement.

Caes. How foolish do your fears seem now, Calpurnia !
I am ashamed I *did yield to them.*
Give me my *robe, for* I will go.

[Enter Publius, Brutus, Ligarius, Metellus, Casca, Trebonius, and Cinna]

And look where Publius is come to *fetch* me.
Pub. Good morrow, Caesar.
Caes. Welcome Publius,
What, Brutus, *are you stirr'd* so early too ?—
Good morrow Casca,—Caius Ligarius,
Caesar was ne'er so much your enemy.
As that same *ague* which hath *made you lean,*
What is't o'clock ?
Bru. Caesar, *'tis strucken* eight.
Caes. I thank you for your pains and courtesy.

Enter Antony

See ! Antony, that *revels long o' nights,*
Is *notwithstanding up*. Good morrow, Antony.
Ant. *So* to most noble Caesar.
Caes. Bid them *prepare within ;*
I am to blame to be thus waited for,
Now, Cinna ; now, Metellus, what, Trebonius !
I have an hour's talk *in store for you* ;
Remember that you *call on me to-day* ;
Be near me, *that* I may *remember you.*
Treb. Caesar, I will ; [*Aside*] and so near will I be,
That your best friends shall wish I had been *further.*
Caes. Good friends, go in, and taste some wine with me ;
And we, like friends, will *straightaway* go together.
Bru. [*Aside*] That *every like is not the same,* O Caesar,
The heart of Brutus *yearns* to think upon !

[Exeunt.

Did yield to them—surrendered to your fears; was influenced by your fears. **Robe**—cloak, dress. **For**—because. **Fetch**—take. **Are you stirr'd**—are you out of your bed. **Ague**—a fit of fever. **Made you lean**—made you weak, lean and thin. **'Tis strucken**—it has struck. **Revels long o' nights**—makes merry late during the nights. **Notwithstanding**—inspite of that, yet. **Up**—awake and ready. **So**—the same (good morning). **Prepare**—get ready (wine and etc. to welcome the guests). **Within**—in the house. **In store for you**—waiting and ready for you ; reserved only for you. **Call on me to-day**—come to me. **That**—so that. **Remember you**—remember to talk to you. **Aside**—to himself (a thing not be heard by any one else). **Further**—farther, far away from. **Straightaway**—at once. **Every...same**—every one who looks to be a friend is not a real friend ; everyone is not what he looks like. **Yearns**—grieves, feels sad.

Caes. Now, Calpurnia, you see, how foolish your fears are ! I feel ashamed that I was influenced by them. Bring my dress, and I will go.

[Enter : Brutus, [*Caius*] Ligarius, Metellus, Casca, Trebonius, Cinna, and Publius]

And see, there is Publius, who has come to take me to the Senate House.

Pub. Good morning Caesar !

Caes. Welcome, Publius. And, Brutus, are you also out of your bed so early to-day ? Good morning, Casca, Caius Ligarius, you think me to be your enemy, but your fever has proved a deadlier enemy than I. It has made you so weak, lean and thin. What is the time ?

Bru. It is just eight o'clock.

Caes. I thank you for the trouble you have taken and the courtesy you have shown in coming (*to take me to the Senate House*).

Enter : Antony

See, even Antony who makes merry late in the nights is up so early this morning. Good morning Antony !

Ant. I wish you the same, most noble Caesar.

Caes. Tell the persons in the house to keep wine ready. I am to be blamed for keeping the Senate waiting for me. Now, Cinna, Metellus and Trebonius, is that you ? I have to talk to you for an hour. Keep in mind to be near me, so that I may remember to talk to you.

Treb. Caesar, I will do so (*to himself*). I will be so near you that those who love you will wish that I were far away from you.

Caes. Now, my good friends, come in and taste some wine with me. After that like good friends, we will go together to the Senate House.

Bru. (*to himself*) O Caesar, it makes me sad to think that all those who look like friends are not real friends. (*It gives me pain to think that things or people are not what they appear to be.*)

[They go.

Scene III—A Street near the Capital

Enter Artemidorus, reading a paper

Art. "Caesar, *beware of* Brutus ; take heed of Cassius ; come not near Casca ! *have an eye to* Cinna ; trust not Trebonius ; *mark well* Metellus Cimber : Decius Brutus loves thee not ; *thou hast wronged Caius Ligarius. There is but one mind in all* these men, and it is *bent* against Caesar. If thou *beest not* immortal, *look about* you ; *security gives way to* conspiracy. The mighty gods defend thee !"

Thy *lover,* Artemidorus

Here will I stand till Caesar pass along ;
And as *suitor* will give him *this.*
My heart *laments* that *virtue* cannot live
Out of the teeth of emulation,
If thou read this, O Caesar, may'st live ;
If not, the Fates with traitors do *contrive.* [Exit

Scene IV—Rome : Another part of the same street. Before the house of Brutus

Enter—Portia and Lucius

Por. I *prithee,* boy run to the Senate-House.
Stay not to answer me, but *get thee gone.*
Why dost thou stay ?

Luc. To know *my errand,* madam.

Por. I would have had thee there, and here again,
Ere I can tell thee what thou should'st do there.
O *constancy, be strong upon my side ;*
Set a huge mountain 'tween my heart and tongue !
I have a man's mind, but a woman's might,
How hard it is for women *to keep counsel* !—
Art thou here yet ?

Luc. Madam, what should I do ?
Run to the Capitol, and nothing else ?
And so return to you, and nothing else ?

Beware of—take care of. **Have an eye to**—keep an eye on, be watchful. **Mark well**—observe ; be watchful. **Thou...Ligarius**—you have harmed and hurt Ligarius. **One mind**—one aim, one purpose. **There is but one mind in all**—all these men (conspirators) have only one aim in their minds. **Bent**—directed, aimed. **Beest not**—are not. **Look about**—be careful. **Security**—freedom from care or suspicion. **Gives way to**—leaves the way open to, leads to. **Lover**—devoted friend. **Suitor**—petitioner, one who makes an appeal. **This**—this paper. **Laments**—feels sad to think that. **Virtue**—here it means virtuous or good persons like Caesar. **Out... emulation**—out of reach of envy and rivalry. [many people become jealous of such persons). **Emulation**—rivalry. **Contrive**—conspire. **Prithee**—pray you. **Get**

Scene III—A street near the Capitol

Enter Artemidorus reading a paper

Art. "Caesar, be on your guard from Brutus ; be careful about Cassius ; let not Casca come very close to you (*keep him at a distance*). Do not trust Trebonius ; keep a watchful eye on Metellus Cimber ; Decius Brutus hates you, and you have harmed and hurt Caius Ligarius (*So, he is hostile to you*). All these people have just one aim. Their aim is to harm you. If you are not immortal, you should be very watchful. Freedom from suspicion leaves the way open to conspiracy. (*If a man suspects nothing and trusts everyone, his enemies get a chance of plotting against him*). May gods protect you,

Your devoted friend ! Artemidorus."

I will stand just here till Caesar passes along. And then, as an ordinary petitioner, I will hand over this piece of paper to Caesar, as if it were a petition. I am grieved to think that virtuous people always fall victims to the jealousy of others. O Caesar, if you read this paper, you may avoid being killed by the conspirators ; but if you do not, then it means that fate is also in league with the conspirators. [*Fate is also favouring the conspirators*].

Scene IV—Another part of the same street, Before the house of Brutus

Enter Portia and Lucius

Por. I request you, boy, to run to the Senate House. Do not stay to answer me. Just be off. Why are you standing ?

Luc. To learn what I have to do, madam.

Por. I wish you were there and back again before I had time to tell you what you were to do. O, firmness, stand by me ; let me not lose my self-control. Put a huge mountain between my heart and my tongue [*so that my tongue may not speak out what my heart knows*] I have the mind of a man, but my self-control is as weak as that of a woman. It is really very difficult for a woman to keep a secret. Are you still here ?

Luc. Madam, what do you want me to do ? Do you want that I should just run down to the Senate House and do nothing else ? And then do you want that I should come back to you without doing anything else. [*Do you want that I should just run to the Senate House and return to you without doing anything else.*]

---

thee gone—be off, go straight away. **My errand**—my job, what I have to do. **Ere**—before. **Constancy**—self-control, firmness of mind. **Be...side**—give me strength and support, stand by me. **Set...tongue**—let a huge mountain stand as a wall between my heart and my tongue. [So that what is there in my heart (my husbands secret) may not come to the tip of my tongue]. **To keep counsel**—to keep a secret.

Por. Yes, bring me *word,* boy, if thy lord look well,
For *he went sickly forth* : and *take good note*
What Caesar doth, what *suitors press to him.*
Hark, boy ! what noise is that ?

Luc. I hear none, madam.

Por. Prithee, listen well ;
I heard a *bustling rumour,* like a *fray,*
And the wind brings it from the Capitol.

Luc. *Sooth,* madam, I hear nothing.

Enter the Soothsayer

Por. Come *hither,* fellow ; which way hast thou been ?

Sooth. At mine own house, good lady.

Por. What is't o'clock ?

Sooth. About the ninth hour, lady,

Por. Is Caesar yet gone to the Capitol ?

Sooth. Madam, not yet : I go to *take my stand,*
To see him pass on the Capitol.

Por. Thou hast some *suit* to Caesar, hast thou not ?

Sooth. That I have, lady : if it will please Caesar
To be so good to Caesar as to hear me :
I shall *beseech him* to *befriend himself.*

Por. Why, know'st thou any harm's *intended towards him* ?

Sooth. None that I know will be, much that I fear may *chance.*
Good morrow to you. Here the street is narrow :
The *throng* that follows Caesar *at his heels* ;
Of senators, of *praetors* common *suitors,*
Will crowd a *feeble* man almost to death :
I'll get me to a place more *void,* and there
Speak to great Caesar as he comes along. [Exit

Por. I must go in, *Ay me,* how weak a thing
The heart of woman is ! O Brutus,

Word—information ; message. **He...forth**—he was ill when he left the house. **Take good note**—watch carefully. **Suitors**—petitioners. **Press to him**—crowd round him ; approach him. **Hark**—listen. **Bustling rumour**—noise of crowds rushing about. **Fray**—fighting ; riot. **Sooth**—truly ; in truth. **Hither**—here. **Take...stand**—take my position. **Suit**—petition. **Beseech him**—request. **Befriend himself**—to take care of his own self ; to look after his own safety. **Intended...him**—aimed at him. **Chance**—happen. **Throng**—crowd. **At his heels**—close behind him. **Praetors**—magistrates. **Suitors**—petitioners. **Feeble**—weak. **Void**—more empty ; less crowded. **Ay me**—alas ! me.

Por. Yes, you run and bring me information if your master looks well, because he was ill when he left the house. Also notice carefully what Caesar does and what petitioners crowd round him. Listen, boy, what is that noise ?

Luc. I hear no noise, madam.

Por. I pray you listen carefully. It is the loud noise of rushing fighting, and rioting. It is the wind that brings the noise from Capitol.

Luc. In truth, madam, I hear nothing.

[Enter the Soothsayer]

Por. Come here, man, which way are you coming from ?

Sooth. From my own house madam.

Por. What time is it ?

Sooth. It is about nine o'clock.

Por. Has Caesar already gone to the Senate House ?

Sooth. Madam, not yet. I am going to take a position where I may be able to see him when he passes on his way to the Capitol ?

Por. Do you have any request to make to Caesar ?

Sooth. Yes, Madam, I do have a request to make to Caesar, if he is good enough to care for his own welfare and listens to me. I shall ask him to be careful about his own safety.

Por. Why, do you know of any dangerous plots against him ?

Sooth. I do not know for certain of any plot (*or danger*). But I think much harm, of which I am afraid, may happen to him. Good morning to you ! Here the street is narrow. The crowd of senators, magistrates and common petitioners that follow Caesar will crush a weak man like me to death. I must move to a less crowded place, and wait there to speak to great Caesar as he passes along.

[He goes

Por. I must go in, Alas ! the heart of a woman is really a very weak thing.

The heavens *speed thee* in thine *enterprise* !—
(*Aside*) Sure, the boy heard me. Brutus hath a *suit,*
That Caesar will not grant. (*Aside*) O, *I grow faint.*
Run, Lucius, and *commend me* to my lord :
Say, I am *merry :* come to me again,
And bring me word what he doth say to thee.

[*Exeunt severally.*

ACT III

Scene I—Rome, Before The Capitol

[A crowd of people in the street leading to the Capitol, among them Artemidorus and the Soothsayer. *Flourish,* Enter Caesar, Brutus, Cassius, Casca, Decius Metellus (Cimber), Trebonius, Cinna, Antony, Lepidus, Popilius and others]

Caes. (To the Soothsayer) The *ides of March* are come.
Sooth. *Ay*, Caesar; but not gone.
Art. *Hail, Caesar* ! Read this *schedule.*
Dec. Trebonius doth desire you to o'*er-read,*
At your best leisure, this his humble suit.
Art. O Caesar ! read mine first; for mine's a suit
That *touches* Caesar nearer ; read it, great Caesar.
Caes. *What touches us ourself shall be* last *served.*
Art. Delay not, Caesar; read it *instantly.*
Caes. *What,* is the fellow mad ?
Pub. *Sirrah, give place.*
Caes. What, *urge* you your petitions in the street ?
Come to the Capitol.

[Caesar goes up to the Senate-House, the rest following. All the Senators rise.]

Pop. I wish your *enterprise* to-day may *thrive.*
Cas. What enterprise, Popilius ?
Pop. Fare you well.

[Advances to Caesar.

Bru. What said Popilius Lena ?

Speed thee—God may help you to reach there soon ; may God give you success. **Enterprise**—work ; undertaking. **Suit**—appeal ; request to make. **I grow faint**—my heart grows weak within. **Commend me**—convey my greetings. **Merry**—in good spirits ; cheerful. **Exeunt severally**—they go one by one, and each on his or her own way. **Flourish**—a blowing of trumpets to announce the entry of an important person or procession. **Ides of March**—the fifteenth day of March. **Ay**—yes. **Hail Caesar**—greetings to you, Caesar. **Schedule**—document ; paper. **O'er read**—to-read ; to go through. **At...leisure**—when it is most convenient to you. **Touches**—concerns ; is in the interest of. **Touches us**—what affects

Brutus, may the gods grant you success in your work. (*to himself*). That boy has surely heard what I said. Brutus has a petition that Caesar will not grant. O, my heart is growing weak. Lucius, run and convey my greetings to my lord (*Brutus*). Tell him that I run and convey my greetings to my lord (*Brutus*). Tell him that I am in good spirits. Then, come back and tell me what he says to you.

[They go, each his or her own way

ACT III

Scene I—Rome, Before The Capitol

[A crowd of people; among them Artemidorus and the Soothsayer, Blowing of Trumpets. Enters Caesar, Brutus, Cassius, Casca, Decius, Metellus Cimber, Trebonius, Cinna, Antony, Lepidus, Publius, and Popilius]

Caes. (*To the Soothsayer*). The fifteenth of March (*Ides of March*) has come.

Sooth. Yes, Caesar, but it is not yet gone. (*The day is not yet over*)

Art. Greetings to you, Caesar ! Read this paper.

Dec. Trebonius requests you to read his petition when it is most convenient to you.

Art. O, Caesar read my petition first. Because it concerns you most; read it great Caesar.

Caes. What concerns our own interest will be dealt with last of all.

Art. Do not delay it, Caesar. Read it at once.

Caes. What, is this fellow mad ? [*that he wants me to read his petition right in the street*]

Pub. Fellow, get out of the way.

Caes. What is this ? Are you so foolish as to put forward your petition in the street ? Come to the Senate-House.

[Caesar and others enter the Senate-House]

Pop. I wish you every success in your work today.

Cas. What work, Popilius ?

Pop. May you fare well. (*he moves towards Caesar*)

Bru. What did Popilius Lena say to you ?

---

me ; concerns me [Caesar uses 'us' instead of 'me', he is proud, he behaves as if he were already a king.] **What touches us...last served**—what is related to me will be taken up only at the end. **Served**—attended to ; deals with. **Instantly**—immediately. **Sirrah**—fellow. **Give place**—get out of the way. **Urge**—press ; put forward. **Enterprise**—business. **Thrive**—may be successful.

Cas. He wish'd to-day our enterprise might thrive.
I fear our *purpose is discovered.*
Bru. Look, how he *makes to* Caesar: *mark* him.
Cas. Casca *be sudden,* for we fear *prevention,*
Brutus, what shall be done ? If this be known,
Cassius or Caesar never shall *turn back,*
For I will slay myself.
Bru. Cassius, be *constant* :
Popilius Lena speaks not of our purpose :
For look, he smiles, and *Caesar doth not change.*
Cas. Trebonius knows *his time* ; for look you, Brutus.
He draws Mark Antony *out of the way.*
[Exeunt Antony, Trebonius. Caesar and the Senators take their seats
Dec. Where is Metellus Cimber ? Let him go,
And *presently* prefer his suit to Caesar.
Bru. *He is address'd* : press near, and *second him.*
Cin. Casca, you are the first that *rears* your hand.
Caes. Are we all ready ? what is now *amiss.*
That Caesar and his Senate must *redress ?*
Met. Most high, most mighty, and most *puissant* Caesar
Metellus Cimber *throws before thy seat*
An humble heart :— (Kneeling
Caes. I must prevent thee, Cimber.
The *couchings,* and these *lowly courtesies,*
Might *fire the blood* of ordinary men,
And turn *pre-ordinance and first decree.*
Into the law of children. Be not *fond,*
To think that Caesar bears such *rebel blood*
That will be *thawed* from the *true quality*
With that which melteth fools ; I mean sweet words,
Low-crooked court'sies, and *base spaniel fawning.*
Thy brother *by decree* is *banished* :
If thou dost bend and pray and *fawn* for him.
I *spurn* thee like a *cur* out of my way.

Purpose—plan ; plot. **Is discovered**—has been detected ; has been found out. **Makes to**—moves towards ; advances towards. **Mark**—observe carefully. **Be sudden**—act promptly ; attack suddenly ; work speedily. **Prevention**—being forestalled ; being prevented from carrying out our plan. **Turn back**—return home. **Constant**—firm ; resolute. **Caesar...change**—expression on Caesar's face has not changed. **His time**—time when he is to act. **Out of the way**—aside. **Presently**—at once ; prepared. **He is addressed**—his name has been called. **Second him**—be next to him ; support him. **Rears**—raises. **Amiss**—wrong. **Redress**—set right ; remedy. **Puissant**—powerful. **Throws...seat**—offers at your feet. **Couchings**—this humble bowing and kneeling down. **Lowly courtesies**—those slave like

Cas. He expressed his wish that our plan might be successful to-day. I am afraid our plan has been found out (*Our secret is out*).

Bru. See, how he advances towards Caesar. Watch him carefully.

Cas. Be speedy (*quick*), Casca. For I fear we may be prevented from carrying out our plan. Brutus, what shall we do if our plot is disclosed and we fail, either Caesar or Cassius will not return home alive from the Capitol. For, I will kill myself.

Bru. Be firm. Popilius Lena is not speaking about our plan, because you can see, he is smiling, and the expression on Caesar's face has also not changed.

Cas. Trebonius knows when he is to act. See, Brutus, he has already taken Mark Antony away (*out of our way*).

[Antony and Trebonius go]

Dec. Where is Metellus Cimber ? Let him come forward and present his petition to Caesar.

Bru. He is ready. Move forward and join him to support him.

Cin. Casca, you are to be the first to raise your hand and attack Caesar.

Caes. Are we all ready ? What wrongs are there that Caesar and his Senate have to set right.

Met. O, most high and powerful Caesar, Metellus Cimber throws his humble self at your feet most humbly and respectfully.

[He kneels

Caes. I must prevent you from doing so, Cimber. This bowing down and slavish kneeling might touch and inflame the pride of an ordinary man. An ordinary man might, in a thoughtless and childish manner, change things already decided and ordained. Do not be so foolish as to think that Caesar has an unreliable temper. My temper cannot be melted and moved from its firmness by flattery. It (*flattery*) can move fools—this bowing, kneeling, this mean, dog-like fawning cannot move me. Your brother has been exiled under official orders. If for your brother, you bow down, flatter and behave like a poor fawning dog, I will kick you just as I kick a dog.

---

stoopings and kneeling down. **Fire the blood**—excite the pride ; inflame the pride. **Pre-ordinance...decree**—what has been already decided and ordered. **Into...children**—in a childish and thoughtless way. **Fond**—foolish. **Rebel blood**—unreliable temper ; fickle minded. **Thawed**—melted ; changed. **True quality**—stable quality ; noble nature. **Base...fawning**—mean creeping and crawling round the feet, like a dog. **Spaniel**—like a dog. **By decree**—by an official order. **Banished**—exiled. **Fawn**—flatter and behave like a poor dog. **Spurn**—kick. **Cur**—dog.

Know, Caesar *doth not wrong,* nor *without cause*
Will he be satisfied.

Met. Is there no voice more worthy than my own,
To *sound* more sweetly in great Caesar's ear
For the *repealing* of my banish'd brother ?

Bru. I kiss thy hand, but not in flattery, Caesar ;
Desiring thee that Publius Cimber may
Have an immediate *freedom of repeal.*

Caes. What, Brutus !

Cas. Pardon, Caesar ; Caesar, pardon :
As low as to thy foot doth Cassius fall,
To beg *enfranchisement* for Publius Cimber.

Caes. I could be well moved. If I were as you :
If I could pray to *move,* prayers would move me ;
But I am *constant* as the *northern star,*
Of whose true-fixed and *resting* quality
There is *no fellow* in the *firmament.*
The skies are painted with *unnumbered sparks.*
They are all fire, and every one doth shine
But there's but one in all doth *hold his place :*
So, in the world; 'tis *furnish'd well* with men.
And men are flesh and blood, and *apprehensive.*
Yet in the number, I do know but one
That *unassailable* holds on his rank,
Unshaked of motion : and that I am he,
Let me a little show it, even in this,
That I was constant Cimber should be banish'd,
And constant do remain to keep him so.

Cin. O Caesar,–

Caes. *Hence* ! *Wilt thou lift up Olympus* ?

Dec. Great Caesar,–

Caes. Doth not Brutus *bootless* kneel ?

Doth not wrong—does not do any injustice. **Without cause**—without convincing reason. **Sound**—to speak. **Repealing**—recalling from exile. **Freedom of repeal**—permission to return from banishment (exile). **Enfranchisement**—freedom ; grant the right of citizenship. **Move**—influence ; win favour. **Constant**—firm. **Northern star**—pole star. **Resting**—stable. **Fellow**—equal (no other star). **Firmament**—sky. **Unnumbered**—endless. **Sparks**—stars. **Hold his place**—remains firm. **Furnished well**—full of. **Apprehensive**—rational ; with the power of reasoning. **Unassailable**—firm. **Unshaked...motion**—unmoved ; unshaken by any movement. **Hence**—go away. **Olympus**—a mountain in Thessaly. **Wilt...olympus**—will you try to lift Mount Olympus [Caesar means that it is impossible to move him as it is impossible to lift mount Olympus.] **Bootless**—uselessly ; to no purpose.

You should know that Caesar never does any injustice, and so he will not be moved to change his decision without some convincing reason. [*In banishing your brother, I did nothing but justice, and now I cannot change that decision unless there is some convincing reason for it.*]

Met. Is there no other man more influential than I who could plead my brother's case in a sweeter and more persuasive voice ?

Bru. I kiss your hand, Caesar, but not to flatter you. I wish you to grant freedom to Publius Cimber to return from exile immediately.

Caes. What ! Brutus, you too, join such a prayer ?

Cas. Forgive me, Caesar, forgive me, I throw myself at your feet to beg freedom for Publius Cimber.

Caes. I could be easily moved if I were a weak man like you. If it were in my nature to pray to move others, the prayer of others, then, could move me. But I am fixed and firm like the Pole-star, which always remains unmoved in its position. No other star in the sky is the equal of the Pole-star in respect of its firmness. The sky is full of numberless stars; they all shine bright; but only one star of all these always keeps its position. It is just the same with this world of men. This world is full of men of flesh and blood. They have the power of reasoning, yet among these countless people, I know only one man who is firm and whom no attack can shake from his position. And that man is me, Caesar! Let me show you a bit of my determination and firmness even in this case of Cimber. I was determined that Cimber should be exiled, and I am still firm to keep him in exile.

Cin. O Caesar, —

Caes. Go away, will you be able to move mount Olympus ?

[*In trying to move me, you are trying to do what is impossible like moving the mount olympus*]

Dec. Most noble Caesar !

Caes. Did you not see that even Brutus fell on his knees in vain (*Even noble Brutus has failed to move me*).

Casca. Speak, hands for me.

[Casca stabs Caesar in the neck. Caesar catches hold of his arms. He is then stabbed by the other conspirators, and last by Marcus Brutus.]

Caes. *Et tu, Brute !*–Then fall, Caesar! [Dies
Cin. Liberty ! Freedom! Tyranny is dead !–
Run hence, proclaim, cry it about the streets.
Cas. Some to the common *pulpits*, and cry out,
"Liberty, freedom, and enfranchisement!"
Bru. People and senators, be not *affrighted ;*
Fly not ; stand still : – *ambition's debt* is paid.
Casca. Go to the pulpit, Brutus.
Dec. And Cassius too.
Bru. Where's Publius ?
Cin. Here, quite *confounded* with this *mutiny.*
Met. Stand fast together, lest some friend of Caesar's
Should *chance* –
Bru. Talk not of standing. Publius, *good cheer.*
There is no harm intended to your *person*
Nor to *no Roman else* : so tell them, Publius.
Cas. And leave us, Publius ; lest that the people.
Rushing on us, should do *your age* some *mischief.*
Bru. Do so : and let no man *abide* this deed.
But *we the doers.*

Re-enter Trebonius

Cas. Where is Antony ?
Treb. Fled to his house *amazed.*
Men, wives, and children stare, cry out and run
As it were *doomsday.*
Bru. Fates, we will know your pleasures :
That we shall die, we know : 'tis but *the time,*
And *drawing days out,* that men *stand upon.*
Casca. Why, he that cuts off twenty years of life
Puts off so many years of fearing death.

Speak...me—let my hands speak for me [let my hands do what others' speech failed to do—that is, move Caesar]. **Et tu, Brute**—you, too, Brutus—[these words show that seeing even Brutus stabbing him, Caesar was so shocked that words choked in his throat—but when he is reconciled to his fate, he speaks the rest of the sentence clearly]. **Pulpits**—raised platforms ; stages. **Affrighted**—frightened. **Fly**—run away. **Ambition's debt**—what ambitious Caesar deserved ; what was due to Caesar's ambition. **Confounded**—confused ; panicked. **Mutiny**—uproar ; sudden noise and confusion. **Chance**—happen to be here to do some mischief. **Good cheer**—be cheerful ; do not get panicky. **Person**—you and your body. **No...else**—or to any other Roman. **Your age**—your weak' old body. **Mischief**—harm. **Abide**—suffer for; pay the penalty for. **We the doers**—we who have murdered Caesar. **Amazed**—utterly confounded ; bewildered. **As it**—as if it were. **Doomsday**—the day of last judgement.

Casca. Let my hands speak for me! [*my hands will express what I want*] [They stab Caesar]

Caes. What, you too, Brutus ; then let Caesar die. [*If even so near and dear one as Brutus stabs Caesar, it is better for him* (Caesar) *to die*].

Cin. Liberty ! Freedom! the tyrant (*Caesar*) is dead! Run round and declare it in all the streets of Rome.

Cas. Let some of us go to the public stages and shout that we have attained liberty, freedom and equality for all.

Bru. Fellow citizens and senators, do not be frightened. Do not run away. Stand where you are. Ambitious Caesar has been paid what he deserved. Ambitious Caesar deserved death, and we have killed him.

Casca. Brutus, you go up the public stage, and speak to the people.

Dec. Let Cassius also do the same.

Bru. Where is Publius ?

Cin. He is here, quite panicky because of this noise and uprising.

Met. Let us stand close together. Some friend of Caesar may happen to be here... (*to do some mischief*).

Bru. O, do not talk of standing together. Be cheerful, Publius; no harm is going to be done to you and to your body or to any other Roman. Publius, you go and tell this to all the people.

Cas. You leave us, Publius; otherwise the people rushing at us may do some harm to your weak, old body.

Bru. Yes, do that, Publius, go away ; let no men, except we, who have done this deed, suffer for it (*let only the doers of this deed pay the penalty for it*).

Re-enter Trebonius

Cas. Where is Antony ?

Treb. He has run away to his house in a state of great panic and confusion. Men, women and children shout and rush about as if it were the day of Last Judgement.

Bru. We certainly want to know what fate has in store far us. We know that we all must die. But people attach importance to the exact time of death, and they want to prolong life as far as possible (*We will die, but let us live as long as we can*).

Casca. If a man dies twenty years earlier, he is saved from fearing death for twenty years. (*if he lives for twenty years it would mean living under fear of death for twenty years. Early death means freedom from the fear of death*)

The time—the time of death. **Drawing...out**—prolonging the period of life. **Stand upon**—attach importance to ; consider important. **Puts off**—delays [here it means—is saved from].

Bru. Grant that, and then is death *a benefit.*
So are we Caesar's friends, that have *abridged.*
His time of fearing death–*Stoop* Romans, stoop,
And let us *bathe* our hands in Caesar's blood.
Up to the elbows, and *besmear* our swords :
Then *walk we forth,* even to the market-place,
And, waving our *red* weapons o'er hands,
Let's all cry, "Peace, freedom, and liberty !"

Cas. Stoop then, and wash. *How many ages hence*
Shall this our *lofty* scene be acted over,
In *states unborn,* and *accents* yet unknown!

Bru. How many times shall Caesar *bleed in sport,*
That now *on Pompey's basis lies along,*
No worthier than the dust !

Cas. So oft as that shall be
So often shall the *knot of us* be call'd
The men that gave their country liberty.

Dec. What, shall we forth ?

Cas. Ay, every man away ;
Brutus shall lead ; and we will *grace his heels*
With the most boldest and best hearts of Rome.

Enter a Servant

Bru. *Soft* ! who comes here ? A friend of Antony's.

Serv. Thus, Brutus, did my master *bid me* kneel ;
Thus did Mark Antony bid me fall down,
And, *being prostrate. thus* he *bade me* say :
Brutus is noble, wise, *valiant,* and *honest* ;
Caesar was *mighty,* bold, royal, and loving :
Say I love Brutus, and I honour him :
Say I fear'd Caesar, honour'd him and loved him,
If Brutus will *vouchsafe* that Antony

A benefit—a blessing ; a good thing. **Abridged**—cut short. **Stoop**—bend down ; bow down. **Bathe**—wash ; dip. **Besmear**—dip in ; stain with. **Walk...forth**—let us go down to. **Red**—blood stained. **How many...hence**—how many centuries after this (i.e. times to come). **Lofty**—grand. **States unborn**—states that are not existing now but will be born in future. **Accents**—languages. **Bleed**—be killed. **In sport**—in a play (drama) on the stage. **Pompey's basis**—on the foot of Pompey's statue. **Lies along**—lies flat ; lies stretched out. **No...dust**—not more worthier and important than the dust on which his dead body is lying. **Knot of us**—our groups. **Grace his heels**—follow him obediently. **Soft**—be silent ; stop for a while. **Bid me**—ordered me. **Being prostrate**—lying flat on the ground. **Thus**—in this

Bru. If we admit that, death, then, must be considered a blessing. In that case we have been kind and friendly to Caesar, because by killing him we have saved him from living under the fear of death for a longer time. Bend down my countrymen, and let us dip our hands up to the elbow in Caesar's blood ; let us stain our swords with it. Let us, then, move on and go to the market place. There we should wave our blood-stained swords in the air, and shout "Peace, Liberty and freedom."

Cas. Yes, let us bend down and dip our hands. Think how in times to come this grand scene of Caesar's murder will be re-enacted in new languages that are not yet born, and in new states that are not yet in existence.

Bru. Caesar's body which is as worthless as dust, now, lies flat at the foot of Pompey's statue. This murder of Caesar will be staged in theatres in future.

Cas. Whenever this incident will be enacted on the stage, our group (*we*) will be called the liberators of Rome.

Dec. What ! shall we move ?

Cas. Yes, let us all move. Brutus will lead us, and we who are noble and brave will do him honour by following him.

Enter a Servant

Bru. Wait a bit (*keep silent*), someone comes here. He appears to be some friend of Antony.

Serv. O, Brutus, my master (*Antony*) ordered me to fall at your feet, and after falling down at your feet, to say that Brutus is noble, wise, brave and honourable; that Caesar was powerful, bold and kind; that he (*Antony, my master*) loves and respects Brutus. My master has asked me to tell you that he (*Antony*) honoured and loved Caesar, but he also feared him. He has also ordered me to say that if Brutus kindly guarantees that no harm will be done to him (*to Antony*), and that.......

---

way. **Bade me**—ordered me. **Valiant**—brave. **Honest**—honourable. **Mighty**—powerful. **Vouchsafe**—kindly allow ; kindly permit.

May safely come to him, and be *resolved*
How Caesar *hath* deserved to lie in death,
Mark Antony shall not love Caesar dead
So well as Brutus living: but will follow
The fortunes and affairs of noble Brutus
Thorough the hazards of this *untrod state,*
With all true faith. So says my master Antony.

Bru. Thy master is a wise and valiant Roman ;
I never thought him worse.
Tell him, so *please him come* unto this place,
He shall be *satisfied* ; and, by my honour,
Depart untouched.

Serv. I'll *fetch* him *presently* [Exit.

Bru. I know that we shall have him well to *friend.*

Cas. I wish he may : but yet have I a *mind*
That fears him much : and my *misgiving still* always.
Falls shrewdly to *the purpose.*

Re-enter Antony

Bru. But here comes Antony. Welcome, Mark Antony,

Ant. O mighty Caesar! dost thou *lie so low*?
Are all thy conquests, glories, triumphs, *spoils,*
Shrunk to this *little measure*? Fare thee well.
I know not, gentlemen, what you intend
Who else must be *let blood,* who else is *rank* :
If I myself, there is no hour so fit
As Caesar's death's hour ; nor no instrument
Of half that worth as those your swords, made rich
With the most noble blood of all this world.
I do *beseech ye,* if you *bear me hard* ;
Now, whilst your *purpled* hands do *reek* and *smoke.*
Fulfil your pleasure. *Live a thousand years,*
I shall not find myself so *apt* to die :
No place will please me so, no *mean* of death,
As here by Caesar, and *by* you cut off,
The *choice* and *master spirits* of this age.

Resolved—convinced ; satisfied. **Hath**—has. **Through**—through ; all through. **Hazards**—dangers. **Untrod state**—unknown state of affairs ; uncertain state of affairs. **So...come**—if it pleases him to come. **Satisfied**—convinced. **Depart**—leave us. **Untouched**—unharmed ; without any harm to him. **Fetch**—bring. **Presently**—immediately ; at once. **To friend**—as a good friend. **A mind**—a feeling ; a foreboding. **Misgiving**—fear. **Still**—always. **Falls...purpose**—proves to be unpleasantly true. **Shrewdly**—unpleasantly. **Lie so low**—have fallen so low. **Spoils**—gains, wealth you brought to Rome after your victories. **Shrunk**—reduced. **Little measure**—this handful of dust, that is, your dead body ; the little space where his dead body is lying. **Let blood**—killed. **Rank**—diseased, and so, fit to be cut down or cured through blood-letting. **Beseech ye**—request you. **Bear me hard**—have any grudge

......if he comes here and is convinced that Caesar really deserved death, then Mark Antony will admit that living Brutus deserves his devotion more than dead Caesar. Then, Antony will throw his lot with noble Brutus, and will faithfully follow him through all dangers of this uncertain and unsettled state of affairs. This is the message that Antony, my master, has sent to you.

Bru. Your master is a noble and brave Roman. I have always had this high opinion of him. Tell him that, if he is pleased to come here, I will give him convincing reasons for Caesar's death, and on my honour, I say that he will leave this place unharmed [*No harm will be done to him, here.*]

Serv. I will bring him here at once.

[The servant goes.

Bru. I am sure that he will be our friend.

Cas. I wish, he may. But I have a feeling that makes me afraid of him. And my fears have always proved to be unpleasantly true.

Re-enter Antony

Bru. Well, here he is, I am pleased to see you, Mark Antony.

Anto. O Caesar, have you fallen so low from your high position ? Have all your victories, glories and great gains for Rome been reduced to this poor dead body (*a handful of dust*). I bid you good bye, Caesar. Now, sirs, I do not know what you intend doing now. After Caesar who else is to be killed. If I am the man to be killed after Caesar, then the time of Caesar's death will be the most appropriate time for my death also. No other weapons than your swords stained with the blood of Caesar, the noblest man of Rome, will be more desirable weapons to kill me. If you have any ill-will against me. I pray you to fulfil your desire by killing me right now when your hands are still red and streaming with Caesar's hot blood. Even if I were to live for a thousand years, I would never be as ready and willing to die as I am now. Caesar's side would be the best place for me to die at and fall by. No other way would be better than being killed at your hands, because at present you are the noblest and most respected men of Rome.

(ill-will) against me. **Purpled**—red with Caesar's blood (blood stained). **Reek**—give out the smell of fresh blood. **Smoke**—let the blood go up as steam. **Live...years**—if I live a thousand years. **Apt**—willing and ready. **Mean**—means ; manner. **By**—near. **Choice**—the noblest ; the choicest (selected). **Master spirits**—most honourable men.

Bru. O Antony, beg not your death of us.
Though now we must appear *bloody* and cruel,
As, by our hands and this our *present act*
You see we do, yet see you but our hands
And *this the bleeding business they* have done.
Our *hearts* you see not ; they are *pitiful* ;
And pity *to the general wrong of Rome—*
As fire drives out fire, *so pity pity—*
Hath done this deed on Caesar. *For your part.*
To you our swords have *leaden points,* Mark Antony :
Our arms, in strength of malice ; and our hearts,
Of brothers' temper, do *receive you in*
With all kind love, good thoughts and *reverence.*

Cas. Your *voice* shall be as strong as any man's
In the *disposing of* new *dignities.*

Bru. Only be patient, till we have *appeased*
The *multitude beside themselves with fear,*
And then we will *deliver you* the cause,
Why I, that did love Caesar when I struck him,
Have thus *proceeded.*

Ant. I doubt not of your wisdom,
Let each man render me his bloody hand.
First, Marcus Brutus, will I *shake with* you ;
Next, Caius Cassius, do I take your hand ;
Now, Decius Brutus, yours ; now yours, Metellus ;
Yours, Cinna ; and, *my valiant* Casca, yours ;
Though last, not least in love, yours good Trebonius.
Gentlemen all,—alas, what shall I say ?
My *credit* now stands on such *slippery ground*
That one of two bad ways must *conceit* me,
Either a coward or a flatterer.
That I did love thee, Caesar, O, 'tis true ;
If then thy spirit look upon us now,
Shall it not grieve thee, *dearer* than thy death,
To see thy Antony *making his peace,*
Shaking the bloody fingers of thy *foes.*

Bloody—blood thirsty, with our hands stained with Caesar's blood. **Present act**—this murder of Caesar. **This the bleeding business**—this bloody business of Caesar's murder. **They**—our hands. **Hearts**—our real motives. **Pitiful**—full of pity. **To the general wrong of Rome**—for the sufferings of the common people of Rome. **Pity pity**—pity for the sufferings of the people of Rome has driven out our pity for Caesar. **For your part**—as for you ; so far as you are concerned. **To you**—for you. **Leaden points**—blunt edges. **Our...malice**—our arms (hand) which, bathed in Caesar's blood, may appear to you full of great ill-will or enmity. **Of...temper**—full of brotherly love. **Receive you in**—are ready to receive you. **Reverence**—respect. **Voice**—vote ; authority. **Disposing of**—conferment of ; distribution of. **Dignities**—high offices and honours. **Appeased**—pacified ; calmed. **Multitude**—mob.

Bru. O, Antony, do not ask us to kill you, though now we may appear to be blood thirsty and cruel, because you see only our hands stained with Caesar's blood ; you see this bloody business of Caesars murder which our hands have done. You do not see our hearts ; our hearts are full of pity. Just as fire drives out fire, so our pity for the sufferings of Roman people drove out our pity for Caesar [*our pity for the suffering Romans was greater than our pity for Caesar. So we killed him to save the people of Rome suffering under Caesar's tyranny*]. As for you, Mark Antony, our swords have blunt edges, our swords will do no harm to you. Our bloody hands which appear to be full of great ill-will (*hatred*) and our hearts which are full of brotherly love for you are all ready to welcome you with love, kindness and great regard and respect.

Cas. In distribution of new offices and honours, your vote (consent) will have as much weight as that of any one of us.

Bru. Only be patient till we have calmed the mob who are almost mad with terror. After that we will tell you why I, who loved Caesar so much, have behaved in such a way as to stab him (*Caesar*).

Ant. I have no doubts about your wisdom. Let each one of you give me his blood-stained hand. I will, first, take your hand Marcus Brutus ; next I will shake hands with you, Caius Cassius ; now Decius Brutus, let me have your hand ; now, yours, Metellus ; I will now shake hands ; and now Trebonius, your hand, though I take your hand last, but that does not mean that I love you less than I love any one else. Now gentlemen, alas, I do not know what to say. Just now, I stand in a very uncertain position. You may form any one of the two bad opinions about me. You may think that I am either a coward or a flatterer O, Caesar, I admit that you were so dear to me. If your spirit is watching us now, O, most noble, it will certainly give you deep pain. It will give you deeper pain than even your own death to see that your friend, Antony, is making friends with those who bore you ill-will, and he is shaking hands with those whose hands are red with your blood.

Beside...fear—almost mad with fear. **Deliver you**—tell you ; communicate to you. **Proceeded**—acted. **Shake with you**—shake hands with you. **My valiant**—my brave (Antony is ironical). **Credit**—reputation as friend of Caesar. **Slippery ground**—uncertain position. **Conceit**—judge. **Dearer**—more deeply. **Making...peace**—making friends with. **Foes**—enemies.

Most noble, in the presence of thy *corse* ?
Had I as many eyes as thou hast wounds,
Weeping as fast as *they stream forth* thy blood,
It would *become me* better than to *close*
In terms of friendship with thine enemies.
Pardon me, Julius ! Here wast thou *bay'd* brave *hart* ;
Here didst thou fall ! and here thy hunters stand,
Sign'd in thy spoil and *crimson'd* in thy *lethe,*
O world, thou wast the forest to this hart ;
And this indeed, O world, the *heart of thee.*
How like a deer, *striucken* by many princes,
Dost thou here lie !

Cas. Mark Antony,—

Ant. Pardon me, Caius Cassius ;
The enemies of Caesar shall say this ;
Then, in a friend, it is *cold modesty.*

Cas. I blame you not for praising Caesar so ;
But what *compact* mean you to have with us ?
Will you be *pricked in number of our friends ;*
Or shall we *on* and not depend on you ?

Ant. Therefore I took your hands, but was, indeed,
Swayed from the point by looking down on Caesar
Friends am I with you all and love you all,
Upon this hope, that you shall give me reasons
Why, and *wherein,* Caesar was dangerous.

Bru. *Or else were this a savage spectacle.*
Our reasons are so *full of good regard,*
That were you, Antony, the son of Caesar,
You should be satisfied.

Ant. That's all I seek ;
And *am moreover suitor* that I may
Produce his body to the market-place ;
And in the *pulpit*, as becomes a friend,
Speak *in the order of his funeral.*

Bru. You shall, Mark Antony.

Corse—dead body. **Had I...wounds**—if I had as many eyes as there are wounds on the dead body of Caesar. **They**—wounds. **Stream forth**—let flow. **Become me**—be more proper for me. **Close**—to come to an agreement. **Bay'd**—brought to bay like a hunted animal; made helpless by your murderers. **Hart**—deer. **Signed in...spoil**—stained with your blood; tainted with your murder. **Crimsoned**—coloured red. **Lethe**—life blood, **Heart of thee**—the source and centre of the very life of the world. **Stricken**—struck dead. **Cold modesty**—Antony, even being a friend of Caesar, has been modest in his praise of Caesar. **Modesty**—moderation. **Compact**—agreement; contract. **Pricked**—marked. **In number...friends**—in the list of our friends. **On**—go on without you. **Swayed**—carried

O most noble Caesar, it would really grieve you to see me doing all this in the very presence of your dead body. If I had as many eyes as you have wounds, if these eyes let flow tears as your wounds are flowing with blood, it would be better for me than making friends with your enemies like this. Forgive me, Julius Caesar. Here were you surrounded by your enemies, here they held you at bay just as hounds hold a hart (*deer*) at bay. Here you dropped dead, and here stand your murderers stained with your blood, coloured red with your life blood. This world was a forest where you (*Caesar*) used to roam freely like a deer. You were really the very heart (*source and centre of all life and energy*) of this world. Now you lie here like a deer hit (*hunted*) by many princes.

Cas. Mark Antony,—

Ant. Forgive me, Caius Cassius ; even the enemies will say this much about Caesar, and in a friend of Caesar like me, saying this much is only moderation (*I, a friend of Caesar should have said much more in praise of Caesar*).

Cas. I do not blame you for praising Caesar so, But, what sort of an agreement do you want to have with us ? Shall we count you as one of our friends, or shall we go on with our business without depending on your cooperation ?

Ant. I shook hands with you because I wish to be numbered among your friends. I was, of course, carried away by my emotions at the sight of Caesar's dead body. I wish to be a friend to you all, but I hope that you will give me reasons why and in what you thought Caesar to be dangerous.

Bru. If we do not satisfy you in this respect, this act of ours, then, would be a brutal murder. But we have such sound reasons for our action that you would be convinced of the justness of our action even if you were the very son of Caesar.

Ant. That is all I desire, I also request you to allow me to take Caesar's dead body to the market place, and to speak a few words, as is proper for a friend, during Caesar's funeral ceremony.

Bru. You will have our permission to do that, Mark Antony.

---

away; moved. **Wherein**—in what. **Or else**—otherwise; if we do not satisfy you. **Were**—would be. **Savage spectacle**—brutal sight. **Or else were this a savage spectacle**—otherwise this act of ours would be a brutal murder. **Full...regard**—sound consideration. **Am...suitor**—and further request. **Produce**—take away and show. **Pulpit**—raised platform or stage for making a speech. **In...funeral**—in the course of his funeral ceremony.

Cas. Brutus, a word with you,—
[*Aside to Brutus*] You know not what you do ; *do not consent*
That Antony speak in his funeral.
Know you how much the people may be *moved*
By that which he will *utter* ?

Bru. *By your pardon,—*
I will myself into the pulpit first.
And show the reason of our Caesar's death ;
What Antony shall speak, I will *protest*
He speaks by leave and by permission ;
And that we are contented Caesar shall
Have all *true rites* and lawful ceremonies,
It shall *advantage* more than do us wrong.

Cas. I know not what may *fall* ; I like it not.

Bru. Mark Antony, here, take you Caesar's body.
You shall not in your funeral speech blame us.
But speak all good you can *devise* of Caesar,
And say, you do't by our permission ;
Else shall you not have any *hand* at all
About his funeral : and you shall speak
In the same pulpit *whereto* I am going,
After my speech is ended

Ant. Be it so ;
I do desire no more.

Bru. Prepare the body then, and follow us.

[Exeunt all but Antony.

Ant. O, pardon me thou *bleeding piece of earth.*
That I am *meek and gentle* with these *butchers* !
Thou art the *ruins* of the noblest man
That ever lived in the *tide of times.*
Woe to the hand that shed this costly blood.
[Over thy wounds now do I prophesy,
Which like *dumb mouths*, do *ope* their *ruby lips.*
To beg the voice and utterance of my tongue—]
A curse shall *light* upon the *limbs* of men ;
Domestic fury and *fierce civil strife.*

Do not consent—don't allow Antony to speak at Caesar's funeral. **Moved**—excited; roused. **Utter**—say. **By...Pardon**—with your permission; excuse me. **Protest**—proclaim; declare. **True**—Proper; due. **Rites**—ceremonies. **Advantage**—do good. **Fall**—happen. **Devise**—think of. **Else**—otherwise. **Hand**—part; share. **Whereto**—to which. **Bleeding...earth**—dead body bathed in a pool of blood (earth here means dead-body). **Meek and gentle**—helplessly soft and silent. **Butchers**—murderers. **Ruins**—remains. **Tide of times**—course of ages. **Woe...hand**—cursed be the hand. **Dumb mouths**—wounds on Caesar's

Cas. Brutus, I want to speak a word to you (*Aside to Brutus*). You do not know what you are doing. Do not allow Antony to speak at Caesar's funeral. Don't you know what he may speak and how his words may excite the people?

Bru. Excuse me ; I will myself first go to the stage and address the people, and tell them why we have killed Caesar. I will also declare that whatever Antony says is said with our consent and by our permission, and that Caesar shall be honoured with proper funeral ceremonies. It will do us more good than harm.

Cas. I do not know what may happen, But I do not like the idea of Antony addressing the people.

Bru. Mark Antony, here is Caesar's body, take it to the market place. In your funeral speech you must not put any blame on us. Say all you can in praise of Caesar, and also tell the people that you speak with our permission. Otherwise you shall have no share in Caesar's funeral. Moreover, you will speak from the same pulpit (*stage*) from which, I will first address the people. You will speak after me.

Ant. Let it be so. I do not desire anything more.

Bru. Prepare the body for the funeral, and, then, follow us.

[They all go, except Antony

Ant. Forgive me, O blood covered body of my murdered friend, that I have been gentle and humble with these cruel murderers. There lie the remains of the noblest man of all ages. May a curse fall on the hands that have shed the noble blood of Caesar. Your open wounds are like red lips which are asking me to speak on their behalf. Here, in the presence of these wounds, I make this prophecy ; a curse will fall on the bodies of men ; a horrible civil war......

---

dead body are like mouths that can't speak. **Ope**—open. **Ruby lips**—red lips. **Light**—fall. **Limbs**—bodies. **Domestic fury**—demestic riots. **Fierce**—terrible. **Civil strife**—civil war.

Shall *cumber* all the parts of Italy ;
Blood and destruction shall be so *in use,*
And *dreadful objects* so familiar
That mothers shall *but* smile when they behold
Their infants *quarter'd with the hands of war* ;
All *pity choked* with *custom of fell deeds* !
And Caesar's spirit, *ranging* for revenge,
With *Ate* by his side *come hot from hell.*
Shall in these *confines* with a *monarch's voice*
Cry Havoc and *let slip* the *dogs of war,*
That this foul deed shall smell above the earth.
With *carrion men, groaning for burial.*

Enter a Servant

You serve Octavius Caesar, do you not ?
Serv. I do, Mark Antony.
Ant. Caesar did write for him to come to Rome.
Serv. He did receive his letters, and is coming :
And bid me say to you by word of mouth,—
O Caesar ! [Seeing the body
Ant. *Thy heart* is *big,* get thee apart and weep,
Passion, I see, is *catching ;* for mine eyes,
Seeing those *beads of sorrow* stand in thine,
Began to water. Is thy master coming ?
Serv. He *lies* to-night within seven leagues of Rome.
Ant. *Post back* with speed, and tell him what hath *chanced* :
Here is a mourning Rome, a dangerous Rome,
No Rome of safety for Octavius yet :
Hie hence, and tell him so. Yet, stay awhile :
Thou shalt not *back.* till I have *borne* this *corse*
Into the market-place ; there shall I try,
In my *oration*, how the people take
The cruel *issue* of these bloody men :
According to the which thou shalt *discourse*
To young Octavius of the state of things.
Lend me your hand [Exeunt, with Caesar's body.

Cumber—burden; harass; ravage. **So in use**—so common ; so frequent. **Dreadful**—terrible. **Objects**—sights, scenes. **But**—only. **Quartered**—cut to pieces. **With...war**—bloody hands of soldiers. **Pity choked**—pity and compassion crushed (by cruel customs). killed with suffocation; extinguished. **Custom...deeds**—familiarity with cruel deeds; becoming accustomed to cruel deeds. **Ranging**—wandering(in search of prey). **Ate**—goddess of revenge. **Come...hell**—come in hot haste from hell. **Confines**—regions. **Monarch's voice**—the tone and authority of a king. **Cry havoc**—give order for death and destruction. **Let slip**—let loose. **Dogs of war**—diseases, famines, fire etc; fire and sword. **That**—so that. **Carrion men**—dead bodies. **Groaning...burial**—crying for burial and so that they may be saved

...... will ravage all parts of Italy. Acts of violence and bloodshed will be so common, and dreadful sights so familiar that mothers shall only smile to see their children cut to pieces by the bloody hands of cruel soldiers. All pity in their hearts will be killed by their familiarity with cruel deeds (*Frequent acts of cruelty will make people so accustomed to it that all pity in their hearts will die*). The spirit of Caesar will wander about in search of vengeance (बदला). His spirit will move in the company of Ate, the goddess of revenge who will come in hot haste from hell to move with Caesar's spirit and will give order for death and destruction. It will let loose famine, fire and sword to create havoc. The foul smell from the dead bodies rotting on the earth will rise up and spoil the whole atmosphere (*dead bodies will remain rotting in the open, and no one will be there to bury them*). They will cry for their burial.

Enter a Servant

You are a servant of Octavius Caesar, are you not ?

Serv. Yes, Mark Antony.

Ant. Caesar sent him a letter asking him to come to Rome.

Serv. He did receive his letter, and he is coming. He ordered me to say to you personally.

[Seeing the body of Caesar

Alas, Caesar !

Ant. Your heart is full of grief ; so go aside and weep, Sorrow, I find, is infectious, seeing the tears of grief in your eyes, my eyes are also filled with tears. Is your master coming ?

Serv. He is staying tonight within seven leagues (*25 miles*) of Rome.

Ant. Go back as quickly as possible and tell your master all that has happened. Tell him that Rome is plunged in grief, and that at present he will not be safe in Rome. But, you stay here for a while you must not go back till I have carried this dead body to the market place, because there, through my funeral speech, I will try to find out how people react to this cruel murder of Caesar. Then, you will be able to tell Octavius all about the state of affairs in Rome. Help me lift up this dead body.

---

from rotting in the open. **Thy...big**—your heart is full of grief. **Passion**—sorrow, grief. **Catching**—infectious. **Beads of sorrow**—tears of grief. **Beads**—tears. **Began to water**—began to shed tears. **Lies**—stays. **Post back**—go back very quickly. **Chanced**—happened. **Hie hence**—go quickly from here. **Post back**—go back and give the news. **Back**—return. **Borne**—carried. **Corse**—dead body. **Oration**—speech. **Issue**—result ; outcome. **Discourse**—speak. **Lend...hand**—help me in lifting the body.

Scene II—The Forum

Enter Brutus and Cassius and a *throng* of Citizens

Cit. *We will be satisfied* : let us be satisfied.

Bru. Then follow me, and *give me audience,* friends,
Cassius, go you into the other street,
And *part the numbers.*
Those that will hear me speak, let'em stay here ;
Those that will follow Cassius go with him ;
And public *reasons shall be rendered*
Of Caesar's death.

1 Cit. I will hear Brutus speak.

2 Cit. I will hear Cassius : and compare their reasons.
When *severally* we hear them rendered.

[*Exit. Cassius, with some of the Citizens, Brutus goes into the pulpit.*

3 Cit. The noble Brutus *is ascended,* silence !

Bru. Be patient *till the last*
Romans, countrymen, and *lovers* ! hear me for my cause ; and be silent, that you may hear : believe me for mine honour ; and have respect to mine honour that you believe. *Censure* me *in your wisdom,* and *awake your senses,* that you may the better judge. If there be any in this *assembly,* any dear friend of Caesar's, to him I say that Brutus' love to Caesar was no less than his. If then that friend demand why Brutus rose against Caesar, this is my answer :—Not that I loved Caesar less, but that I loved Rome more. *Had you rather* Caesar were living, and die all slaves, than that Caesar were dead, to live all free men ? As Caesar loved me, I weep for him ; as he was fortunate, I rejoice at *it* ; *as* he was *valiant,* I honour him ; but, as he was ambitious, I slew him. There is tears for his love; joy, for his fortune; honour, for his *valour*, and death, for his ambition. Who is here so *base*, that would be a *bondman* ? If any, speak ; for him have I *offended.* Who is here so *rude,* that would not be a Roman ? If any, speak ; for him have I offended. Who is here so *vile,* that will not love his country ? If any, speak ; for him have I offended. I *pause* for a reply.

All. None, Brutus, none

Throng—crowd. **We...satisfied**—we want satisfactory reasons for Caesar's murder. **Give me audience**—listen to me. **Part**—divide in two. **Numbers**—crowd of people. **Reasons...rendered**—reasons will be given why Caesar was murdered. **Rendered**—given. **Severally**—separately. **Ascended**—has gone upon the stage. **Till the last**—till the speech is ended. **Lovers**—good friends. **Censure**—judge or criticise. **In your wisdom**—wisely. **Awake your senses**—be intelligent ; awaken your intelligence. **Assembly**—crowd ; gathering. **Had you rather**—would you prefer ; if you had desired Caesar to live. **It**—Caesar's good fortune. **Valiant**—brave. **Valour**—bravery. **Base**—low, mean. **Bondman**—slave. **Offended**—done an offence. **Rude**—ignorant ; barbarous. **Vile**—wicked ; worthless. **Pause**—wait.

Scene II—Rome, The Forum

Enter Brutus and Cassius and a crowd of Roman Citizens

Cit. We must be given satisfactory explanation why Caesar has been killed. Give us good reasons to satisfy us.

Bru. Follow me, then, and listen to me, friends. Cassius, you go to the other street and divide the crowd into two. Let those who want to listen to me stay here, and those who wish to listen to Cassius may go with him. We will give a public explanation of Caesar's murder.

1 Cit. I will listen to Brutus' explanation.

2 Cit. I will listen to Cassius ; and when we have heard them separately, we shall compare the reasons given by them.

[Cassius goes with some of the citizens.
Brutus goes upon the pulpit.

3 Cit. Be silent, noble Brutus is on the stage.

Bru. Listen to me patiently till I end my speech. Citizens of Rome, my countrymen and friends, listen to me for the sake of the cause that I have to plead, and be silent so that you may be able to listen. Remember that I am an honourable man, and so believe what I say to be true. Judge me wisely ; rouse your intelligence so that you may judge me rightly. If there is any one in this gathering, any dear friend of Caesar, let me tell him that my love and regard for Caesar was not less than his. If, then, this friend of Caesar asks me why I rose against Caesar, my answer is this—I rose against Caesar because my love for Rome was greater than my love for Caesar. Would you like to see Caesar alive and live like his slaves all your life ? Or, would you rather like to see Caesar dead and live as free citizens of Rome ? As Caesar loved me, I weep over his death ; Caesar was fortunate and I was happy about it. As he was brave, I respected him ; but as he was ambitious (*wanted more and more power*) I killed him. I weep because he loved me ; I am happy that he was fortunate, I respected his bravery, but I killed him for his ambition (*hunger for power*). Is there anyone here so mean that he would willingly become a slave ? If there is any such man, let him speak. I must have surely offended such a man. Is there any-one so ignorant and barbarous that he would not feel proud of being a true Roman ? If there is any such man, let him speak. I must have surely offended such a man. Is there any one here, so worthless that he has no love for his country ? If there is any, let him speak, I have surely injured his feelings.

All. There is none Brutus, there is none.

Bru. Then none have I offended. I have done no more to Caesar than you shall do to Brutus. The *question of his death* is *enrolled* in the Capitol ; his glory not *extenuated,* wherein he was worthy, nor his offences *enforced,* for which he suffered death.

Enter Antony and others, with Caesar's body

Here comes his body, mourned by Mark Antony ; who though he *had no hand in* his death, shall receive the benefit of his dying, a place in the *commonwealth* ; as which of you shall not ? *With this* I depart,—that, as I slew my best love for the good of Rome, I have the same dagger for myself, when it shall please my country to *need* my death.

All. Live, Brutus ! live ! live !
1 Cit. Bring him *with triumph* home unto his house.
2 Cit. Bring him a statue with his ancestors.
3 Cit. Let him be Caesar.
4 Cit. Caesar's *better parts.*
Shall be crown'd in Brutus.
1 Cit. We'll bring him to his house with shouts and *clamours.*
Bru. My countrymen,—
1 Cit. Peace, ho !
2 Cit. Peace ! silence ! Brutus speaks.
Bru. Good countrymen, let me depart alone,
And, for my sake, stay here with Antony,
Do grace to Caesar's corpse, *and grace his speech*
Tending to Caesar's glories, which Mark Antony,
By our permission, is allowed to make
I do *entreat* you, not a man depart,
Save I alone, till Antony have *spoke.* [Exit
1 Cit. Stay, ho ! and let us hear Mark Antony
3 Cit. Let him go up into the *public chair* ;
We'll hear him. Noble Antony, go up—
Ant. For Brutus' sake I am *beholding to* you
[*Goes into the pulpit.*
4 Cit. What does he say of Brutus ?
3 Cit. He says, for Brutus' sake,
He finds himself beholding to us all,
4 Cit. 'T were best he speak no harm of Brutus here.
1 Cit. This Caesar was a tyrant.

Question...death—the considerations which led to his death ; considerations which made his death necessary. **Enrolled**—is recorded. **Extenuated**—belittled. **Enforced**—exaggerated ; unduly stressed.

Had no hand—took no part ; was not responsible for. **Commonwealth**—government of the people. **With this**—with these words. **Need**—require. **With triumph**—in a victory procession. **Better parts**—better qualities. **Shall be crowned**—shall become perfect ; will find fulfilment. **Clamours**—cheers ; shouts of applause. **Do grace**—pay respect to. **And**

Bru. In that case I have not injured anybody's feelings. I have done to Caesar what you will do to me if I grow ambitious. (*If I grow ambitious you will be justified in killing me, just as I am justified in killing Caesar who had grown ambitious*) *The considerations leading to Caesar's death have been duly recorded in the Senate House. In those records his glory which he deserves, has not been minimised, nor have the faults, for which he died, been exaggerated.*

Enter Antony and others with Caesar's body.

See, his body is being brought here, accompained by Antony who is the chief mourner. Antony, though he took no part in murdering Caesar, yet he will share, as all of you will also share, the advantages that will follow Caesar's death. He will have a place in the government of the country, and, in fact, every one of you will have a share in it. I now take leave of you with these words that just as I killed my dearest friend for the good of Rome, so shall I kill myself with the same dagger whenever my country will require my death.

All. You must live, Brutus ; you must live.

1 Cit. Let us take him to his house in a victory procession.

2 Cit. Make a statue in his honour, by the side of the statue of his ancestors.

3 Cit. Let us give him that high office which Caesar held.

4 Cit. Nobler qualities of Caesar will find perfection in Brutus.

1 Cit. We will take him home with loud cheers all the way.

Bru. Fellow citizens,

1 Cit. silence, let everybody be quiet.

2 Cit. Be quiet, Brutus is speaking.

Bru. My good countrymen, let me go alone. For my sake, please stay here with Antony, and pay your respects to Caesar's dead body, and give a respectful hearing to Antony's speech in Caesar's praise. Antony will make this speech with our permission. I request you that no one, except me, should leave this place until Antony has finished his speech.

1 Cit. All of you wait ; let us listen to Mark Antony.

3 Cit. Let him go on the public platform, and we will listen to him. Noble Antony, go up.

Ant. I am indebted to you on behalf of Brutus, for you have granted his request and have stayed to listen to me.

[*Goes into the pulpit.*

4 Cit. What remark did he make about Brutus ?

3 Cit. He said that he was obliged to us all on behalf of Brutus because we granted Brutus's request and allowed him to go up the stage.

4 Cit. It would be in his own interest not to say anything against Brutus here.

1 Cit. This Caesar was a cruel dictator.

---

grace his speech—give respectful hearing to Antony's speech. **Tending to**—related to. **Entreat**—request ; appeal to. **Save I**—except me. **Spoke**—spoken. **Public chair**—public platform ; pulpit. **Beholding**—obliged ; indebted.

3 Cit. Nay, that's certain ;
We are blest that Rome is *rid of him,*
2 Cit. Peace ! let us hear what Antony can say,
Ant. You gentle Romans,—
All. Peace, ho ! let us hear him.
Ant. Friends, Romans, countrymen, *lend me your ears* ;
I come to bury Caesar, not to praise him,
The evil that men do *lives after them ;*—
The good is oft *interred* with their *bones* ;
So let it be with Caesar. The noble Brutus
Hath told you Caesar was ambitious
If it were so, it was a *grievous fault.*
And *grievously* hath Caesar *answer'd it.*
Here, *under leave* of Brutus and the rest,—
For Brutus is an honourable man,
So are they all, all honourable men
Come I to speak in Caesar's funeral.
He was my friend, faithful and *just* to me ;
But Brutus says he was ambitious ;
And Brutus is an honourable man.
He hath brought many *captives* home to Rome,
Whose *ransoms* did the *general coffers* fill !
Did this in Caesar seem ambitious ?
When that the poor have cried, Caesar hath *wept* ;
Ambition should be made of sterner stuff ;
Yet Brutus says he was ambitious ;
And Brutus is an honourable man
You all did see, that *on the Lupercal*
I thrice presented him a kingly crown
Which he did thrice refuse ; was this ambition ?
Yet Brutus says he was ambitious ;
And, sure he is an honourable man;
I speak not to *disprove* what Brutus spoke,
But here I am to speak what I do know,
You all did love him once, *not without cause* ;
What cause *withholds* you then to mourn for him ?
O *judgement* ! thou art fled to *brutish beasts*
And men have lost their reason ! *Bear with me* ;
My heart is in the coffin there with Caesar,
And I must *pause* till it come back to me.

Rid of him—freed from Caesar's tyranny. **Lend...ears**—listen to me attentively. **Lives after them**—is remembered even after their death. **Interred**—buried ; forgotten. **Bones**—dead bodies. **Grievous fault**—serious fault. **Grievously**—heavily ; tragically. **Answer'd it**—has paid the penalty for it ; has suffered death for it. **Under leave**—after taking permission (from Brutus). **Just**—fair and honest. **Captives**—imprisoned and conquered princes. **Ransoms**—prices paid for the release of prisoners of war, or other prisoners. **General coffers**—treasury of the state. **Wept**—in sympathy for the sufferings of the poor or weaker

3 Cit. There is no doubt in it. We are fortunate that Rome has been freed from Caesar's tyranny.

2. Cit. Silence ! Let us hear what Antony can rightly say in Caesar's praise.

Ant. You gentle Romans,—

Cit. Let us all be silent. Let us hear him.

Ant. Friends, Romans and my fellow countrymen, listen to me I am here not to praise Caesar, but only to perform the funeral ceremonies (*and bury Caesar's dead body*). Evil deeds done by men are remembered long after their death, but the good deeds done by them are forgotten as soon as they are dead and buried. Let it be so with Caesar, too (*Let Caesar's good deeds be forgotten, as he is dead now*) Noble Brutus has told you that Caesar was ambitious. (*Caesar was power hungry*). If it was so, it were certainly a serious fault in Caesar and he has paid a heavy penalty for that fault (*by suffering death for that*). I have come to speak to you by the permission of Brutus and Brutus is a noble man, in fact, they are all noblemen. I have come to speak at Caesar's funeral. He was my friend, sincere and just to me. But Brutus says that Caesar was ambitious, and may be there is some truth in it, because Brutus is an honourable man. Caesar brought many prisoners of war to Rome, and huge sums of money received as price for their release enriched the public treasury. Was that a sign of any ambition in Caesar ? Caesar was all love and sympathy for the poor. He often wept in sympathy for their suffering. An ambitious man should not be so tender hearted ; he should be made of some harder stuff. Yet, Brutus tells us that Caesar was ambitious, and Brutus is, after all, a noble man. You yourselves saw that on the day of the feast of Lupercalia, I offered him the crown three times and every time he declined to accept it. Was that a proof of Caesar's ambition ? Yet Brutus says that he was ambitious, and Brutus no doubt, is an honourable man. I speak to you not to disprove what Brutus has said, but only to tell you what I myself know. There was a time when Caesar was loved by you all, and there were sufficient reasons for you to love him. Is there any reason now that prevents you from mourning his death ? O, Reason, it appears that you have left human beings and have flown away to live in the breast of wild beasts, for men have lost the power of judgement (*They cannot judge what is right and what is wrong*). Friends, be patient with me. For the moment I am sad and shocked at the sight of Caesar's dead body lying in the coffin, and I must wait a while till I recover my balance of mind.

---

ones. **Ambition...sterner stuff**—ambitious persons are not so kind-hearted but made up of harder and cruel hearts. **Sterner stuff**—harder material ; a harder heart. **It**—my heart. **On the Lupercal**—on the day of the Lupercalia. **Disprove**—prove wrong ; prove false. **Not without cause**—not without sufficient reasons ; you had your own reasons for loving him. **Withholds**—prevents ; checks. **Judgement**—intelligence ; power of reasoning ; discrimination. **Brutish beasts**—wild animals. **Bear with me**—have patience with me ; tolerate me. **Pause**—stop speaking for a while.

1 Cit. *Methinks* there is much reason in his sayings,
2 Cit. If thou consider rightly of the matter,
Caesar has had great wrong.
3 Cit. Has he, *masters ?*
I fear, there will *a worse* come in his place,
4 Cit. Mark'd ye his words ? He would not take the crown ;
Therefore 'tis certain he was not ambitious.
1 Cit. If it be found so, some will *dear abide it.*
2 Cit. Poor soul ! his eyes are red as fire with weeping,
3 Cit. There's not a nobler man in Rome than Antony.
4 Cit. Now mark him, he begins again to speak.
Ant. *But yesterday* the word of Caesar might
Have *stood* against *the world* : now lies he there,
And none so poor to do him reverence,
O masters, if I were *disposed to stir*
Your hearts and minds to *mutiny* and *rage,*
I should do Brutus wrong, and Cassius wrong,
Who, you all know, are honourable men :
I will not do them wrong ; I rather choose
To wrong the dead, to wrong myself and you,
Then I will wrong such honourable men
But here's a *parchment,* with the seal of Caesar ;
I found it in his *closet,* 'tis his will :
Let but the *commons* hear this *testament,*—
Which pardon me, I do not mean to read,—
And they would go and kiss dead Caesar's wounds,
And *dip their napkins* in his sacred blood,
Yea, beg a hair of him *for memory,*
And, dying, mention it within their wills,
Bequeathing it, as a rich *legacy*
Unto their issue.
4 Cit. We'll hear the will : read it, Mark Antony.
All. The will, the will ! we will hear Caesar's will,
Ant. Have patience, gentle friends, I must not read it ;
It is not *meet* you know how Caesar loved you
You are not wood, you are not stones, but men ;
And, being men, hearing the will of Caesar,
It will *inflame* you, it will make you mad,
'Tis good you know not that you are *his heirs* ;
For, if you should, O, *what would come of it* !

Methinks—I think. **Caesar...wrong**—a great wrong (injustice) has been done to Caesar. **Masters**—good people. **A worse**—a man worse than Caesar. **Dear abide it**—pay very dearly (heavily) for it ; they will have to suffer heavily. **But yesterday**—till yesterday. **Stood against the world**—Caesar's word was law which no one in the whole world could oppose or challenge. **And...reverence**—and now even the lowest (meanest, poorest) of men is not ready to respect Caesar. **Disposed**—inclined. **Stir**—excite ; move. **Mutiny**—riot ; rebellion. **Rage**—anger ; fury. **Parchment**—document. **Closet**—private room ; study

First Cit. I think there is much reason in what he says,

Sec. Cit. If you think over this matter rightly, you will agree that a great injustice has been done to Caesar.

Third Cit. Has he been unjustly treated, gentlemen ? I fear that now there may come a man in Caesar's place, and he may prove worse than Caesar.

Fourth Cit. Did you note what he said ? Caesar declined to accept the crown ; it is, therefore, clear that he was not ambitious.

First Cit. If that is proved, some people will have to pay heavily for Caesar's murder. (*Some people will have to pay a heavy penalty for Caesar's murder.*)

Sec. Cit. Poor Antony! He has wept so bitterly that his eyes are red like fire.

Third Cit. Antony is certainly the noblest man in Rome.

Fourth Cit. Now see. He begins speaking again.

Antony. Only yesterday, Caesar's word was law, and no one in the whole world could question it; but now he lies dead in his coffin, and even the poorest man in Rome is not ready to pay his respects to dead Caesar. O gentlemen, if I had any wish to incite you to revolt, or fill you with fury, I should, then, be doing great wrong to Brutus and Cassius. And you all know that they both are honourable men. So I would do no harm to them. I would rather do injustice to Caesar and to myself and to you than do any harm to such honourable men (*as Brutus and Cassius*) But I have here a document bearing Caesar's seal. I found it in his private room. It is his will. You will forgive me because I don't intend reading it to you, but if the common people hear it read, they would be so moved that they would go and kiss Caesar's wounds, and dip their hankerchiefs in Caesar's sacred blood; yes, they would each beg for a strand of his hair, to keep it as a sacred memorial, and, before their death, they will mention it in their will that they are leaving the sacred hair of Caesar as a rich heritage for their children.

Fourth Cit. We must hear the will; read it Mark Antony

All. The will! read it; we will all hear Caesar's will.

Antony. Be patient, gentle friends, I must not read it out. It is not proper that you should know how much Caesar loved you. You are not lifeless and soulless things like woods and stones. You are human beings. And since you are capable of thinking and feeling as human beings, hearing Caesar's will read, you will be filled with fury (*great anger*); it will make you mad with anger; it is better that you do not know that he (*Caesar*) has left all his property to you (*that you are to inherit all his property*); I cannot foretell what terrible things may happen if you know this (*that you are the inheritors of Caesar's property*).

Commons—the common people. **Testament**—Caesar's will. **Dip**—wet. **Napkins**—handkerchiefs. **Yea**—yes. **For memory**—as a holy relic ; as a memorial. **Bequeathing**—leaving some thing through a will. **Legacy**—heritage ; thing left by will to some body. **Unto their issue**—to their children. **Meet**—proper. **You...stones**—you are not insensible things ; lifeless and soulless things like woods and stones. **Inflame**—excite ; fill with fury. **His heirs**—inheritors of his property. **What would come of it**—what would be the result.

4 Cit. Read the will ! we'll hear it, Antony ;
You shall read us the will, Caesar's will.
Ant. Will you be patient ? Will you *stay awhile* ?
I have *o'ershot myself* to tell you of it.
I fear, I wrong the honourable men
Whose daggers have stabb'd Caesar ; *I do fear* it.
4 Cit. They were *traitors* : honourable men !
All. The will ! the testament !
2 Cit. They were villains, murderers : the will ! read the will !
Ant. You will compel me, then, to read the will ?
Then *make a ring* about the *corpse* of Caesar,
And let me show you him that made the will,
Shall I *descend* ? and will you give me *leave* ?
All. Come down.
2 Cit. *Descend.*
3 Cit. You shall have leave. [He comes down.
4 Cit. A ring ! Stand round
1 Cit. Stand *from* the hearse, stand from the body.
2 Cit. Room for Antony, most noble Antony.
Ant. Nay, *press not* so upon me ; stand far off.
Citizens. Stand back ! Room ; *Bear back* !
Ant. If you have tears, prepare to shed them now,
You all do know this *mantle* ; I remember
The first time ever Caesar put it on ;
'Twas on a summer's evening, in his tent,
That day he overcame the *Nervii*
Look, in this place ran Cassius' *dagger through* :
See, what a *rent* the *envious* Casca made ;
Through this, the well-beloved Brutus stabb'd ;
And, as he *plucked* his cursed *steel* away,
Mark how the blood of Caesar follow'd it,
As rushing out of doors, *to be resolved*
If Brutus so *unkindly knock'd* or no ;
For Brutus, as you know, was Caesar's *angel*

Stay awhile—wait for a short time. **O'ershot myself**—gone further than I meant ; have said more than I intended to say. **I do fear it**—I do fear that I have done a wrong to these honourable men (Caesar, Cassius and others, [Note Antony's cleverness in praising the conspirators in an ironical tone. What he says means just the opposite of its literal meaning.] **Traitors**—faithless men ; men who betrayed Caesar and their country, Rome. **Make a ring**—stand in a circle round. **Corpse**—dead body. **Descend**—come down (the pulpit from where he was addressing the crowd.) **Leave**—permission. **Press not**—don't crowd around me. **Bear back**—get back. **Mantle**—cloak ; gown. **Nervii**—Name of a brave and war-like people (Caesar had the toughest battle against them. Caesar's victory over Nervii was one of his greatest victories.) **Dagger through**—dagger pierced through Caesar's body. **Rent**—deep cut ; a gash ; deep wound. **Envious**—malicious ; full of ill-will. **Plucked**—pulled out. **Steel**—dagger. **Mark**—notice ; see. **To be resolved**—to ascertain ; to feel certain that.

Fourth Cit. Read the will ; we must hear it, Antony. You shall have to read Caesar's will, so that we may hear it.

Antony. Will you be patient ? Will you wait for a short time ? I fear, in telling you about the will. I have gone further than I meant [*I have said and done more than I intended to say or do*). I am afraid I am doing an injustice to those honourable men whose daggers stabbed Caesar to death. I am really afraid I have wronged them.

Fourth Cit. They were traitors. You call them honourable men ?

All. Read the will, we must hear the will.

Second Cit. They were traitors and murderers. We want the will ; read the will.

Antony. Do you, then, compel me that I should read the will ? Well, then stand in a circle round the dead body of Caesar. Let me show you the man who made this will. Shall I step down the pulpit ? Will you permit me to do that ?

All. Yes, come down.

Second Cit. Come down.

Third Cit. You have our permission.

Fourth Cit. Make a circle round Caesar's body.

First Cit. Stand from the coffin, stand from the body.

Second Cit. Make room for Antony, for most noble Antony.

Antony. Not that, do not stand so closely crowded round me. Stand farther away.

All. Stand farther away. Make some room : get back.

Antony. If you are capable of weeping and shedding tears, be prepared to shed them now [*because the sight I am going to show you will move you to tears*]. You all know this cloak (*of Caesar*) very well. I still distinctly remember the first occasion on which Caesar put on this cloak. He put on this cloak for the first time in his tent. It was a summer evening, and on that day the dagger of Cassius pierced the cloak ; see, what a big hole (*gash*) was made by the dagger of malicious Casca. This is the point (*hole*) through which the dagger of his beloved Brutus stabbed Caesar. When Brutus pulled out his damned dagger, see how blood rushed through the wound to make certain whether it was really Brutus who had struck that cruel blow. You all know that Brutus was Caesar's darling (*dearest friend or guardian angel*).

Unkindly—cruelly [but it also means unnaturally. It was unnatural on Brutus' part to stab Caesar, his dear friend]. **Knocked**—struck ; stabbed. **Angel**—darling ; dearest friend (or guardian angel).

Judge, O you gods, how dearly Caesar loved him !
This was the *most unkindest cut of all* ;
For when the noble Caesar saw him stab,
Ingratitude, more strong than traitors' arms,
Quite *vanquish'd him* ; then *burst* his mighty heart ;
And, in his mantle *muffling up* his face,
Even at the base of Pompey's statue,
Which all the while ran blood, great Caesar fell.
O, what a fall was there, my countrymen !
Then I, and you, and all of us fell down,
Whilst bloody *treason flourished* over us
O, now you weep, and I *perceive you feel*
The dint of pity : those are gracious *drops*.
Kind souls, what, weep you, when you but behold
Our Caesar's *vesture* wounded ? Look you here !
Here is himself, *marr'd,* as you see *with traitors.*

1 Cit. O *piteous* spectacle !
2 Cit. O noble Caesar !
3 Cit. O *woeful* day !
4 Cit. O traitors ! villains !
1 Cit. O most bloody sight !
2 Cit. *We will be revenged.*
All Cit. Revenge ! *About* ! *Seek* ! Burn ; Fire !
Kill ! Slay ! Let not a traitor live !
Ant. Stay, countrymen,
1 Cit. Peace there ! hear the noble Antony.
2 Cit. We'll hear him, we'll follow him, we'll die with him.
Ant. Good friends, sweet friends, let me not stir you up
To such a sudden *flood* of *mutiny.*
They that have *done this deed* are honourable,
What *private griefs* they have, alas, I know not,
That made them do it. They are wise and honourable,
And will, no doubt, with reasons answer you,
I come not, friends to *steal away your hearts.*

Most...of all—the cruellest and most unexpected (unnatural) stab (thrust of the danger). **Ingratitude**—treachery (of a dear friend ; ungratefulness). **More...arms**—stronger than the hands and daggers of the traitors. **Vanquished him**—defeated him ; overpowered him. **Burst**—broke. **Muffling up**—covering. **Treason**—treachery (of the murderers of Caesar) here it means the traitorous murderers of Caesar ; conspiracy. **Flourished**—triumphed ; waved their swords in triumph ; were victorious. **Perceive**—see. **Drops**—drops of tears in your eyes. **Vesture**—garment ; cloak. **Marr'd**—mangled ; stabbed at many places. **With traitors**—by the traitors with their daggers. **Piteous**—pitiful. **Woeful**—sad. **We will be revenged**—we shall take revenge on the conspirators. **About**—go about ; rush about. **Seek**—search out. **Flood**—outburst. **Mutiny**—riots ; rebellion. **Done this deed**—performed this terrible deed or murder. **Private griefs**—personal grievances ; personal grudge. **Steal...hearts**—win you over by appealing to your emotions and passions.

And only heaven knows how deeply Caesar loved Brutus ! This was the most cruel and most unexpected of all the stabs. For, when noble Caesar saw that Brutus was also among his killers, he was completely overpowered. He was shocked by Brutus' ungratefulness which proved stronger than the hands and daggers of the traitors. Then, his noble heart broke, and covering up his face with his cloak, great Caesar fell at the very foot of Pompey's statue. His blood had been flowing down that statue all the time. O, my countrymen, it was a terrible fall, indeed ! Caesar's fall was my fall, your fall and a fall of us all ; it meant the ruin of all of us. The murderers, traitors (*the killers of Caesar*) at that time triumphed over us and brandished (*waved*) their swords in triumph. O, now I can feel there are tears in your eyes, I see that pity has moved your hearts. These are gracious tears of kindness and sympathy. But, kind-hearted friends, do you weep to see only the cloak of Caesar torn and wounded ? Now, see, here is Caesar himself, wounded and mangled, as you see, by the traitors with their daggers.

1 Cit. Oh ! what a pitiable sight !

2 Cit. O, noble Caesar ! (*It is a pity that he lies dead*).

3 Cit. It is indeed a very sad day !

4 Cit. O, the treacherous villains !

1 Cit. O, most bloody sight !

2 Cit. We must take revenge.

All. Yes, revenge. Let us go about in search of the traitors. Set fire to their houses and kill and slaughter all of them. Let not a traitor escape.

Ant. Wait, my countrymen.

1 Cit. Be silent. Listen to what noble Antony has to say.

2 Cit. We will listen to him, we will follow him, we will, if need be, even die with him.

Ant. My good and dear friends, let me not incite you to such a sudden out-burst of riot (*rebellion*). People who have done this deed are men of honour. I do not know what personal grievances against Caesar made them do this deed. But as they are wise and honourable men, they will, I am sure, give good reasons for this deed of theirs. My friends, I am not here to win you over by making an appeal to your emotions and passions.

I am no *orator,* as Brutus is,
But as you know me all, a *plain blunt* man,
That love my friend ; and that they know full well
That gave me *public leave to speak* of him.
For I have neither *wit,* nor *words,* nor *worth,*
Action, nor *utterance,* nor the power of speech
To stir men's blood ; I only speak *right on* :
I tell you that which you yourselves do know ;
Show you sweet Caesar's wounds, *poor poor dumb mouths*
And *bid them* speak for me ; but were I Brutus,
And Brutus Antony, *there were an Antony,*
Would ruffle up your *spirits, and put a tongue* :
In every wound of Caesar that should move
The stones of Rome to rise and *mutiny.*

Cit. We'll mutiny,
1 Cit. We'll burn the house of Brutus.
3 Cit. Away, then ! come, seek the conspirators.
Ant. Yet hear me countrymen ; yet hear me speak,
Cit. Peace, ho ! Here Antony, Most noble Antony,
Ant. Why, friends you go to do you know not what ;
Wherein hath Caesar thus deserved your loves ?
Alas, you know not,—I must tell you then :
You have forgot the will I told you of,
Cit. Most true : the will ! Let's stay and hear the will.
Ant. Here is the will, and under Caesar's seal :—
To every Roman citizen he gives,
To every *several* man, *seventy-five drachmas*
2 Cit. Most noble Caesar ! We'll *revenge his death,*
3 Cit. O royal Caesar !
Ant. Hear me with patience.
Cit. Peace, ho !

Orator—a powerful and effective speaker. **Plain**—plain spoken ; straight-forward. **Blunt**—straight-forward utterly frank. **Public leave to speak**—permission to speak in public. **Wit**—intelligence ; intellectual cleverness. **Words**—fluency of speech. **Worth**—prestige ; standing. **Action**—gesture and manners. **Utterance**—art of speaking ; elocution. **To...blood**—to excite the feelings and passions of men. **Right on**—straight ; without any preparation. **Poor...mouths**—the open wounds on Caesar's body are like open mouths which want to say something, but these are dumb, for they cannot speak. **Bid them**—ask them (the wounds of Caesar's body). **There...Antony**—then he would be an Antony. **Would**—who would. **Ruffle**—provoke ; fill with fury. **Spirits**—souls, hearts. **Put a tongue**—give words ; give the power of speaking. **Mutiny**—revolt. **Wherein**—in what way. **Several**—individual. (**Seventy five drachmas**—about three pounds). **Drachmas**—a Greek coin of the value of 9 or 10 pence. **Revenge...death**—take a revenge for Caesar's death ; avenge Caesar's death.

I am not as good and great a speaker as Brutus. I am, as you all know, a plain-spoken and straight-forward man and I loved my friend Caesar. This fact is well-known to those also who gave me permission to speak in public, I have neither intelligence nor fluency of speech nor any prestige or standing. I have neither good gestures nor any art of speaking to excite the feelings and passions of men. I speak without any thought or preparation [*I speak out whatever comes to my tongue's end*] I am simply telling what is already known to you. I am showing you gentle Caesar's wounds which are like open but dumb (*speechless*) mouths, and I ask these wounds (*these dumb mouths*) to speak on my behalf (*I hope that instead of my weak words these wounds will excite you to revolt*). But if an orator like Brutus were here in my place, he would, then excite your hearts and fill them with fury. He would give every wound of Caesar the power of speaking so forcefully that they (*wounds of Caesar*) would move even the stones of Rome to rise up and revolt against the murderers of Caesar. (*If I were a powerful speaker like Brutus, I would describe the wounds of Caesar and the details of his murder so forcefully that not only you Romans but even the stones of Rome would rise and revolt against Caesar's murderers*).

All. We will all rise and revolt against them

1 Cit. We will set fire to the house of Brutus.

3 Cit. Let us move, then. Come, let us find out the conspirators.

Ant. But, listen to me, my countrymen. Let me say a few words more.

All. Silence, listen to most noble Antony,

Ant. Look here, my friends, you do not know what you are going to do. In what way does Caesar deserve this love of yours ? (*What has he done to be loved by you so deeply ?*)

Ah, you do not know this. This I must tell you, then, You have forgotten the will about which I spoke to you.

All. Perfectly true, we will stay here to hear the will.

Ant. Well, here is the will, and it bears Caesar's seal. To every individual Roman citizen, Caesar leaves an amount of seventy five drachmas.

2 Cit. O, most noble Caesar ! we will take a revenge for his murder.

3 Cit. Oh most generous and kingly Caesar !

Ant. Listen to me patiently.

All. Silence, everybody !

Ant. Moreover, he hath left you all his *walks,*
His private *arbours,* and new-planted *orchards,*
On this side Tiber ! he hath left them you,
And to your *heirs* for ever ; *common pleasures,*
To walk abroad and *recreate* yourselves.
Here was a Caesar ! when comes such another ?

1 Cit. Never, never ! Come, away, away !
We'll burn his body in the holy place,
And with the *brands fire* the traitors' houses,
Take up the body,

2 Cit. Go, fetch fire,

3 Cit. *Pluck down* benches,

4 Cit. Pluck down forms, windows, anything,

[*Exeunt Citizens, with the body*

Ant. Now let it work, *Mischief,* thou art *afoot,*
Take thou what *course thou wilt* !

Enter a Servant

How now, fellow ?

Serv. Sir, Octavius is already come to Rome.

Ant. Where is he ?

Serv. He and Lepidus are at Caesar's house.

Ant. And *thither will I straight* to visit him ;
He comes *upon a wish*. Fortune *is merry* :
And in *this mood will give us anything.*

Serv. I heard *him* say, Brutus and Cassius
Are rid like madmen through the gates of Rome

Ant. *Belike* they *had some notice of* the people,
How I had *moved* them, *Bring* me to Octavius

[*Exeunt*

Scene III—Rome, A street

Enter, Cinna the Poet

Cin. In dreamt *to-night* that I did feast with Caesar,
And *things unlucky charge my fantasy,*
I have no will to *wander forth of doors,*
Yet *something leads me forth.*

Walks—paths through which Caesar used to walk privately. **Arbours**—shady places in a garden ; bowers. **Orchards**—gardens. **On this side Tiber**—on the forum side of River Tiber. **Heirs**—children, descendants. **Common pleasures**—as common pleasure grounds to be enjoyed equally by all. **To walk abroad**—to walk about. **Recreate**—refresh. **Brands**—burning sticks ; torches. **Fire**—set fire to. **Pluck down**—pull down. **Mischief**—evil passion, ill-will of the masses. **Afoot**—have started ; have been roused. **Course**—direction, path. **Thou wilt**—you will. **Thither**—there. **Will I straight**—will I go straight. **Upon a wish**—exactly according to my wish ; just a right moment. **Is merry**—is favourable ; is in a good mood. **This mood...anything**—such favourable conditions can reward us as we wish. **Him**—Octavius. **Are rid**—have ridden their horses and run away like mad men. **Belike**—it seems likely ; perhaps. **Some notice**—some idea.

Ant. Besides that, he has left to you all his private walks, his shady bowers and his fruit gardens on this side of the River Tiber. He has left there to you and to your descendants for ever to be enjoyed equally by all. You can move about in them freely and refresh yourselves. Such a man this Caesar was ! When will we find another man, noble and generous like Caesar ? [*Will another man like Caesar be ever born in the world* ?]

1. *Cit.* No, never, never again. Let us move. We will go and cremate Caesar's body in the holy grounds, and with burning sticks we will set fire to the houses of traitors. Let us carry the body.

2. *Cit.* Bring some burning sticks,

3. *Cit.* Pull down some of the branches (*to make fire*).

4. *Cit.* Pull down frames, windows, anything that will catch fire.

[*All the citizens go with the dead body.*]

Ant. Now let this poison of fury and hatred work in their mind. Evil passion (*fury ; hatred ; ill-will*), I have set you moving. Now I don't bother what course of action you take. (*You may now do whatever you like to do*).

Enter a Servant

What is the matter, fellow ?

Serv. Sir, Octavius has already come to Rome.

Ant. Where is he?

Serv. He and Lepidus are at Caesar's home.

Ant. I will go straight to Caesar's house to meet them He has come just at the right time [*just when I wished him to be here*]. Fortune seems to be in a cheerful mood and in this mood she would grant us anything we may desire,

Serv. I heard him say that Brutus and Cassius have ridden their horses and have rushed out of the gates of the city of Rome. They were rushing at a mad speed.

Ant. Perhaps they got some information about the way in which I had *moved* and excited the people (*against them*).

Now, you take me to Octavius

Scene III—Rome, A Street

Enter Cinna, the Poet.

Cin. Last night I dreamt that I was enjoying a feast with Caesar. Ominous and unlucky things weigh upon (*fill*) my imagination. (*My mind is full of evil forebodings*), I have no desire to move out of the house, yet some unknown power is driving me out of my house.

Had..........notice —they had got some notice how I had moved the people; they had got some information about how and etc. **Notice of** — information about. **Moved**—incited, agitated. **Bring**— take. **Tonight**—last night. **Things unlucky**— unlucky, ominous things, **Charge**—burden; weigh upon; fill. **Fantasy**—imagination. **Wander..........doors**—go out of my house. **Something**—some strange force ; some mysterious power. **Leads..........forth**—drives me out or drags me out of doors.

Enter Citizens

1. *Cit*. What is your name ?

2. *Cit* Whither are you going ?

3. *Cit*. Where do you dwell ?

4. *Cit*. Are you a married man, or a bachelor?

2 *Cit*. Answer every man *directly*.

1 *Cit*. *Ay* and briefly.

4 *Cit*. Ay. and wisely.

3 *Cit*. Ay, and truly, *you were best*.

Cin. What is my name? *Whither* am I going ?

Where do I dwell ? Am I a married man, or a bachelor? Then to answer every man directly and briefly, wisely and truly : wisely I say, I am a bachelor.

2 *Cit*. *That's as much as to say,* they are fools that marry: *you'll bear me a bang* for that, I fear. *Proceed, directly*.

Cin. Directly, I am going to Caesar's funeral.

1 *Cit* As a friend, or an enemy ?

Cin. As a friend,

2 *Cit*. That matter is answered directly.

4 *Cit*. For your dwelling, briefly.

Cin. Briefly, I dwell by the Capitol.

3 *Cit*. Your name, sir, truly.

Cin. Truly, me name is Cinna.

1 *Cit*. Tear him to pieces ; he is a conspirator.

Cin. I am Cinna the poet, I am Cinna the poet.

4 *Cit*. Tear him for bad *verses*, tear him for his bad verses.

Cin. I am not Cinna, the conspirator.

4 *Cit*. It is no matter, his name's Cinna; pluck but his name out of his heart, and *turn him going*.

3 *Cit*. Tear him, tear him ! Come, brands ho ! fire-brands : to Brutus', to Cassius' ; burn all. Some to Decius' house, and some to Casca's : some to Ligarius'. Away ! go ! [Exeunt.

ACT IV

Scene I—Rome, A Room in Antony's House

Antony, Octavius, and Lepidus seated at a table

Ant. These many, then, shall die; their names are *pricked*.

Directly—straight-forwardly. **Ay** — yes. **You..........best** — it would be best for you. **Whither**—whereto; where. **That's..........say**—that is equal to saving. **Yu'll..........bang**—you will get a heavy blow from me. **Proceed directly**—answer in a straight-forward manner. **Verses** — poems; poetry. **Turn..........going**—send him off, and then let him go about his business. **Pricked**—ticked; marked off.

Enter Citizens

1 *Cit.* What is your name ?

2 *Cit.* Where are you going ?

3 *Cit.* Where do you live ?

4 *Cit.* Are you a married man or a bachelor ?

2 *Cit.* Reply to each of us straight-forwardly.

1 *Cit.* Yes, and be brief.

4 *Cit.* Yes, and answer intelligently.

3 *Cit.* Yes, and it would be best for you if you answer truthfully.

Cin. What is my name? Where am I going ? Where do I live ? Am I married or a bachelor ? These are the questions I have to answer. And I am to answer every man straight-forwardly and briefly, intelligently and truly. So, intelligently, I tell you that I am not married.

2 *Cit.* This is equal to saying that those who are married are fools. I fear that for this answer of yours you will get a blow from me. Go on, answer us in a straight-forward manner.

Cin. To answer straight-forwardly, I say that I am going to attend Caesar's funeral.

1 *Cit.* Are you going there as a friend or as an enemy?

Cin. As a friend.

2 *Cin.* Well, that is really a straight-forward answer.

4 *Cit.* Now, tell us where you live, and be brief.

Cin. To be brief, I live near the Capitol.

3 *Cit.* Now, Sir, tell us your name truthfully.

Cin To tell you the truth, my name is Cinna.

1 *Cit.* Tear him to pieces He is a conspirator.

Cin. I am Cinna, the poet, I am not a conspirator.

4 *Cit.* Well, then, tear him to pieces for his bad poetry (*or poems*)

Cin. I am not that Cinna who is a conspirator.

4 *Cit.* It does not matter who he is. His name is Cinna, after all. Just tear his name out of his heart and then let him go about his business.

3 *Cit.* Tear him, tear him to pieces. Come, bring burning sticks. Let us rush to the houses of Brutus and Cassius. Set fire to all their houses. Let some of us rush to the house of Decius, and some to the house of Casca, some to the house of Ligarius. Let us rush at once.

ACT IV

Scene I—Rome, A Room in Antony's House.

Antony, Octavius and Lepidus, seated at a table.

Ant. All these men, whose names are marked down (off) in the list, must be killed.

Oct. Your brother too must die; *consent you*, Lepidus?
Lep. I do consent—
Oct. *Prick him down,* Antony.
Lep. *Upon condition* Publius shall not live,
Who is your sister's son, Mark Antony.
Ant. He shall not live. Look, *with a spot* I *damn him.*
But, Lepidus, go you to Caesar's house ;
Fetch the will hither, and we shall determine
How to *cut off* some *charge in legacies.*
Lep. What, shall I find you here ?
Oct. *Or* here or at the Capitol. [Exit, Lepidus
Ant. This is a *slight unmeritable* man,
Meet to be sent on errands : is it fit,
The three-fold world divided, he should *stand*
One of the three to share it?
Oct. So you thought him,
And *took his voice* who should be prick'd to die,
In our *black sentence* and *proscription.*
Ant. Octavius, I *have seen more days than you*:
And though we lay these honours on this man.
To *ease* ourselves of *divers slanderous loads*,
He shall but bear *them as the ass bears gold*,
To groan and *sweat* under the *business*,
Either led or driven as we point the way;
And having brought our *treasure where we will*,
Then *take we down his load*, and *turn him off*,
Like to the empty ass, so shake his ears,
And graze in *commons.*
Oct. You may do your will :
But he's a *tried* and *valiant* soldier.

Consent you—do you agree to it? **Prick him down**—put a mark against his name as one to be killed. **Upon condition**—according to this condition. **With a spot**—with a tick ; by putting a mark against his name on the list. **Damn him** — condemn him to death. **Cut off**—reduce. **Charge**—amounts to be paid. **In legacies**—in the form of gifts left for the people in Caesar's will. **Or**—either. **Slight**—insignificant. **Unmeritable**—having no merit ; undeserving ; worthless. **Meet**—fit. **To be sent on errands**—to be used for odd jobs. **Three-fold world**—three parts of Roman Empire.— (1) Spain (2) France and Belgium (Gaul) (3) Africa. **Stand**—be, **Took his voice**—took his opinion ; took his vote. **Black sentence**—sentence of death. **Proscription**—list of the persons to be killed. **I have..........you** — I am older and more experienced than you, **Ease**—relieve; to lighten. **Diverse..........loads**—burden of various kinds of disgrace and condemnation by the people. [With these honours, Lepidus would be sharing the part of the blame that people may put upon them.) **Them** — the burden of these honours. **As..........gold**— these honours would be only a burden to Lepidus, just as gold borne by an ass is only a burden ; it is, after all, used only by the master, not by the ass [Antony means that these honours would he borne only as a burden by Lepidus. At the right time they (Antony and Octavius, will deprive him of these honours ; then, he will be

Oct. Your brother should also be killed, Lepidus, Do you agree to it ?

Lep. Yes, I do agree.

Oct. Then Antony, Mark him down as one to be killed.

Lep. But on this condition, Mark Antony, that Publius who is your nephew also dies.

Antony. He shall also die; see I put a mark against his name on the list, and condemn him to death. But now, Lepidus, you go to Caesar's house and bring his will here. We will, then, decide how we can reduce the amount that is to be paid in legacies.

Lep. What do you say? Will you be here when I return?

Oct. Yes, we will be either here or at the Capitol.

[Lepidus goes.]

Ant. He is an insignificant creature, a worthless, fellow deserving no respect. He is fit only to do odd jobs like an errand boy [*a servant who is sent out to do odd jobs*] Is it proper that he should get the share of the one-third of the Roman empire when we divide it.

Oct. A short while ago you did think him to be worthy of this honour. When we made the list of people who were to be sentenced to death, you took his vote as to who should be marked out to be killed or exiled.

Ant. Octavius, let me tell you that I am older and more experienced than you We confer these honours on this man so that by sharing it he may relieve us of some of the burden of blame and condemnation from the people. He will carry the burden of these honours and titles just as an ass bears the burden of gold. He will sweat and suffer under the weight and go wherever we lead him. But as soon as he has served our purpose, we will deprive him of his titles and powers. Then, we will let him loose to go like an unloaded donkey to shake his ears and graze in the common pastures.

Oct. You may do as you please. But, remember that he is a tried, tested and brave soldier.

---

like an ass unloaded of the gold borne by it)]. **Sweat**—suffer; work hard; perspire. **Business**—the job of carrying the load. **Treasure** — the valuable work. **Where we will** — where we want. **Take..........load** — we will deprive him of his rights and titles. **Turn him off**—Let him loose ; let him go. **Commons**—common pasture lands; grassy field where cattle of all the people graze. **Tried**—experienced; one who has been tested. **Valiant**—brave.

Ant. So is my horse, Octavius ; and for that
I do *appoint* him *store* of *provender,*
It is a creature that I teach to fight,
To wind, to stop, to run *directly* on,
His corporal motion govern'd by my spirit.
And, *in some taste*, is Lepidus but so ;
He must be taught, and train'd, and *bid go forth*;
A *barren-spirited* fellow ; *one that feeds*
On objects, orts, and imitations,
Which, *out of use* and *staled by other men*,
Begin his fashion ; do not talk of him
But as a *property*. And now, Octavius,
Listen great things. Brutus and Cassius
Are *levying powers* : we must *straight make head* :
Therefore let our *alliance be combined*,
Our best friends made, our best means *stretch'd out*;
And let us presently go sit in council
How *covert* matters may be best *disclosed.*
And *open perils surest answered,*

Oct. Let us do so : for we are *at the stake*,
And *bayed about* with many enemies;
And some that smile have in their hearts, I fear,
Millions of *mischiefs*. [Exeunt.

Scene II—Before Brutus's Tent, in the Camp near Sardis

Drum. Enter Brutus, Lucillius, Lucius and Soldiers ;
Titinius and Pindarus meet them

Bru. *Stand, ho* !

Lucil. Give the *word*, ho ! and stand.

Bru. What now, Lucillius ? Is Cassius near ?

Lucil. He is at hand ; and Pindarus is come
To do you salutation from *his master.*

Bru. He *greets me well.* Your master, Pindarus,
In *his own change*, or, *by ill officers*,
Hath given me some *worthy cause* to wish
Things done, undone ; but *if he be at hand*,
I shall be *satisfied*

Appoint—provide for. **Store**—sufficient. **Provender** — food (for cattle or farm animals). **To wind**—to turn ; to wheel about quickly. **Directly**—straight. **Corporal**—physical: bodily. **His......spirit**—his (horse's) physical movements controlled by my mind. **Spirit**—mind. **In......taste**—in some measure; to some extent. **Bid......forth**—ordered to move. **Barren-spirited**—stupid; having no ideas of his own ; having no originality. **One......imitations**—a fellow who fills his mind with second-hand things, thoughts and ideas. **Imitations**—always copying ; having no originality. **Out of use**—out of fashion ; out-dated. **Staled by other men**—used and cast away by other people ; made cheap and common place through long use by other people. **Property**—only as a tool : a thing to be used for our purpose. **Levying powers**—raising troops. **Straight**—at once. **Make head**—raise t... **lliance**—

Ant. Octavius, that way my horse is also tested, tried and brave. But, for that I provide him with sufficient food. My horse is a creature whom I have taught to turn swiftly and run straight, as I wish. And to some extent this Lepidus is also such a creature. He must be taught and trained and ordered to run, and do what we want him to do. He is stupid and has no ideas of his own. He fills his mind with second-hand thoughts and ideas. He copies the ways of others and uses things which have become cheap and out of date through the long use by others. Things gone out of fashion become a fashion for him. Let us not talk of him. We should now speak of more important things, Octavius, Brutus and Cassius are raising troops. And it is necessary that we should also raise a force to meet them. Let us, therefore, unite all those who are on our side. Let us make as many friends as we can, and use our resources to the utmost (*make our means to go as far as possible*). Let us at once sit in conference to decide how hidden dangers may be discovered, and how we can safely meet the dangers which are openly threatening us.

Oct. Let us do so, because we are like bears tied to a stake (*pole*) and barked at and snapped by our enemies who are like hounds. We are cornered like some hunted animals and must turn and give a fight. I am afraid, that some, who smile outwardly, have many injuries in their hearts [*and so they may do much harm to us*] [They leave

Scene II—Before Brutus's tent, in the Camp near Sardis

Drum. Enter Brutus, Lucius, and soldiers;
Titinius and Pindarus meet them.

Bru. Halt.

Lucil. Give the password. Halt.

Bru. What is it, Lucillius? Is Cassius near ?

Lucil. Yes, he is quite near ; and he has sent Pindarus to pay respects to you.

Bru. He sends his greetings through a good man. Your master, Pindarus, has given me sufficient reasons to feel that such things done by him should not have been done. I do not know whether it is the result of his changed feelings for me, or the result of the actions of his bad officers.

---

supporters ; those who are on our side. **Be combined**— united ; gathered together. **Stretched**—made to go as far as possible ; exploited fully ; made best use. **Covert** — secret. **Disclosed**—discovered. **Open**—openly, well known. **Perils**—dangers. **Surest answered**—safely met ; most effectively faced. **At the stake**—tied to a stake (pole) like a bear at whom dogs are barking and snapping. **Bayed about**—surrounded by enemies who are like barking hounds rushing at us. **Mischiefs**—injuries. **Stand, ho**—halt. **Word**—pass-word. **To..........salutation**—to pay you respects ; to greet you. **His master**—that is, Cassius. **Greets me well** —sends his greetings through a good man. **His own change**—through some change in his feelings for me. **By ill officers**—or due to the actions of his bad officers. **Hath**—has. **Worthy cause**—sufficient reason. **If..........at hand**—near me; with me. **Satisfied**—get a satisfactory or convincing explanation.

Pin. I do not doubt,
But that my noble master will appear
Such as he is, *full of regard and honour.*
Bru. *He is not doubted.* A word, Lucillius :
How he received you, let me be *resolved.*
Lucil. With courtesy and with respect enough ;
But not with such *familiar instances,*
Nor with such free and friendly *conference,*
As *he hath used of old.*
Bru. Thou hast described
A *hot friend cooling.* Ever note, Lucillius,
When love begins to sicken and *decay,*
It *useth* an *enforced ceremony.*
There are no tricks in plain and simple faith;
But *hollow* men, like horses *hot at hand,*
Make *gallant show* and promise of their *mettle,*
But when they should endure the bloody spur,
They *fall* their *crests* and, like-deceitful *jades*
Sink in the trial. Comes his army on ?
Lucil. They mean this night in Sardis to be *quarter'd* :
The greater part, the *horse in general,*
Are come with Cassius.

[Low march within.

Bru. Hark ! he is arrived.
March gently on to meet him

Enter Cassius and his Powers.

Cas. Stand, ho !
Bru. Stand, ho ; *Speak the word along.*
1 *Sol.* Stand !
2 *Sol.* Stand !
3 *Sol.* Stand !
Cas. Most noble brother, you have done me wrong.
Bru. Judge me, you gods ! *wrong I mine enemy* ?
And, if not so, how should I wrong a brother ?
Cas. Brutus, this *sober form* of yours *hides wrongs* ;
And when you do them—

Regard—respect. **Full..........honour**—worthy of respect and honour. **He..........doubted**—I do not suspect him. **Resolved**—freed from uncertainty. **Familiar instances**—marks of friendship ; gestures of friendship. **Conference** — conversation. **He hath used of old**—as he used to do in the past. **Hot friend**— warm-hearted friend. **Cooling**—becoming indifferent, **Decay**—decline. **Useth**—uses. **Enforced ceremony**—unnatural formality; forced politeness. **Tricks**—artificiality ; unnatural pretensions. **There..........tricks**—there is no need of any artificiality or formal behaviour. **Hollow**—insincere. **Hot at hand**—active and spirited at the start. **Gallant show**—brave display. **Mettle**—spirit; courage. **Fall**—let fall. **Crests**—ridge on a horse's neck ; the part of the neck which has long hair (mane) [high crest is considered the quality of a good horse]. **Jades**—worn-out and worthless horses.

Pin. I am sure you will still find my noble master worthy of all respect and honour.

Bru. I do not suspect him or his motives. Tell me how Cassius received you, Lucillius. I want to be free from uncertainty.

Lucil Well, he received me with great politeness and respect, but not with those marks of friendship nor with that frank and friendly conversation, as he used to do in the past.

Bru. You have described a warm-hearted friend becoming cold and indifferent [*that shows that Cassius does not have that warmth and love for me as he used to hove*] You always see, Lucillius, these people act with forced politeness and formality when their love begins to cool down. Simple and faithful people do not require any artificial show or formality. But insincere men are like those horses which show great spirit, endurance and courage when they start moving, but they become crest-fallen (*they let their crests fall and give way under the strain*), when they are spurred on and put to the real test. [*They have little endurance. So, under strain of a test , they prove worthless like worn-out and old horses*). Is his army approaching, Lucillius ?

Lucil. They intend camping at Sardis, to-night. The main body of cavalry (*soldiers on horseback*) have already arrived and are here with Cassius.

Bru. Listen, here he comes. [A low marching sound within.
Let us gently march on to meet him.

[Enter Cassius and his forces]

Cas. Halt.

Bru. Halt there. Pass the order to the soldiers.

First Sol. Halt.

Second Sol. Halt.

Third Sol. Halt.

Cas. My noble brother, you have done a great wrong to me.

Bru. Judge me, O gods ! I do not do any wrong (*injustice*) even to my enemies, and if it is true, how then can I do any wrong to my dear friend ?

Cassius. Brutus, your calm and serious appearance very often hides the wrongs done by you [*You look so calm and dignified that people just fail to see the wrongs you do*] and when you do such wrongs......

Sink in the trial—fail when put to the test. **Quarter'd**—camped. **Horse In general**—the main body of cavalry. **Speak..........along**—give order to the soldiers to halt. **Wrong I mine enemy**—I can't do any wrong even to my enemy. **Wrong**—do injustice. **Sober form**—calm and grave appearance. **Hides wrong**—your calm and serious exterior hides many wrongs done by you.

Bru. Cassius, *be content* ;
Speak your griefs softly : I do know you well.
Before the eyes of both our armies here.
Which should *perceive* nothing but love from us.
Let us not *wrangle*: bid them move away;
Then in my tent, Cassius, *enlarge your griefs.*
And I will *give you audience.*

Cas. Pindarus,
Bid our commanders lead their *charges* off
A little from this ground.

Bru. Lucillius. *do you the like*, and let no man
Come to our tent till we have *done* our *conference.*
Let Lucius and Titinius guard our door. [Exeunt.

Scene III—Within the Tent of Brutus

Enter Brutus and Cassius

Cas. That you have wrong'd me, doth appear in this.
You have condemn'd and *noted* Lucius Pella
For taking bribes here of the Sardians;
Wherein my letters, praying on his side,
Because I knew the man, was *slighted off.*

Bru. You wrong'd yourself to write in such case,

Cas. In such a time as this it is not *meet*
That every *nice offence* should *bear his comment*

Bru. Let me tell you, Cassius, yourself
Are much *condemn'd to have an itching palm* :
To sell and *mart* your *offices* for gold.
To *undeservers.*

Cas. *I, an itching palm?*
You know that you are Brutus that speaks this,
Or, by the gods, this speech *were else* your last.

Bru. The name of Cassius *honours* this corruption,
And *chastisement* does therefore *hide his head*

Cas. *Chastisement* !

Be content—calm yourself. **Speak your griefs softly**—express your grievances quietly. **Softly**—calmly ; quietly. **Before the eyes**—in the presence of. **Perceive**—see, **Wrangle**—quarrel. **Enlarge your griefs**—fully express your grievances. **Give you audience**—give you a patient hearing **Charges**—troops. **A little from**—at a little distance from this place. **Do you the like**—you do the same. **Done**— finished. **Conference**— talks; discussion. **Noted**—branded with disgrace. **Wherein**—in respect of which; regarding which. **Slighted off** — were treated with neglect and contempt. **Meet**—proper. **Nice offence**—small offence; trifling mistake. **Bear his comment**—should be criticised or be commented upon. **Condemned..........itching palm**—are accused of exacting bribes ; are accused of having greed for bribes. **Mart**—trade in. **Offices**—higher posts. **Undeservers**—undeserving persons. **I, an itching palm?**—I, do I take bribes? **Were else**—would otherwise be. **Honours**—makes it appear honourable. **Hide his head**—keep itself hidden. **Chastisement**—punishment.

Bru. Cassius. be calm. Express your grievances gently. (*Do not get excited. Speak softly*). I understand you very well. Let us not quarrel in the presence of our troops. They should see nothing but love between us. Order the troops to move away for the present. Then, in my tent you can fully express your grievances, and I will give you a patient hearing.

Cas. Pindarus, give orders to our officers to lead their soldiers a little farther away from this place.

Bru. Lucilius, you do the same, and see that no one approaches our tent till we have finished our discussion. Let Lucius and Titinius stand guard at the door of our tent. They leave

Scene III—Brutus's Tent

Enter Brutus and Cassius

Cas. That you have done a great wrong to me is proved by these facts. You have branded Lucius Pella with disgrace for taking bribe from the people of Sardis I wrote you some letters in defence of Pella, because I know his honourable character; but you treated those letters with neglect and contempt.

Bru. It was wrong on your part to have written in defence of such an offence.

Cas. At such a time, it is not proper to criticise or condemn every petty offence.

Bru. Let me tell you, Cassius, that you yourself stand accused of being greedy and exacting bribes You gave higher posts to undeserving and incompetent persons, and accepted bribes from them [*you have thus traded and sold these posts for money*]

Cas. What ! Do you accuse me of greed and exacting bribes ? You know that you are Brutus whom I love and respect so much, otherwise I would have killed you right here for saying such a thing. And this would have been your last speech.

Bru. It is your great name, Cassius, which makes this crime appear honourable, and saves you from proper punishment.

Cas. Punishment !

Bru. Remember March, the Ides of March remember :
Did not great Julius bleed for justice' sake?
What villain touch'd his body, that did stab,
And not for justice? What, shall one of us,
That struck the foremost man of all this world
But for supporting robbers, shall we now
Contaminate our fingers with *base* bribes,
And sell the *mighty space of our honours*
For so much *trash* as may be *grasped thus*?
I had rather be a dog and *bay* the moon
Than such a Roman.
Cas. Brutus, *bay not* me,
I'll not endure it : you forget yourself
To *hedge me in* ; I am a soldier, I,
Older in practice, abler than yourself
To make conditions.
Bru. *Go to* ; you are not, Cassius.
Cas. I am.
Bru. I say you are not.
Cas. *Urge* me no more, I shall forget myself ;
Have mind upon your health tempt me no farther.
Bru. Away. *slight man* !
Cas. Is't possible?
Bru. Hear me, for I will speak.
Must I *give way and room* to your rash *choler ?*
Shall I be frighted when a madman *stares* ?
Cas. O ye gods, ye gods ! Must I endure all this ?
Bru. All this? ay, more ; *fret*, till your proud heart break ;
Go, show your slaves how *choleric* you are,
And make your *bondmen tremble*. Must I *budge* ?
Must I *observe* you ? Must I stand and *crouch*
Under your *testy humour* ? By the gods,
You shall *digest the venom of your spleen*,
Though it do *split you* ; for, *from this day forth*,

What villain...justice?—nobody who stabbed Caesar was a villain as everyone struck him for the cause of justice. **Touched**—stabbed. **But for**—simply for. **Contaminate**—corrupt; pollute. **Base** — mean; disgraceful. **Mighty..........honours**—high offices of honour which we can give to others. **Trash**—worthless coins (money). **Grasped**—held in hand; caught. **Thus**—in this way [here Brutus closes his fist to show how it can be held,] **Bay**—bark at, **Bay not**—do not harass; trouble. **Hedge me in**—limit my freedom of action ; put restrictions on my freedom of action. **To make conditions**—to manage affairs; or to decide the qualifications for various offices; to decide who are fit for various posts or offices. **Go to**—an expression of impatience or incredulity (oh, it is the limit 1). **Urge**—provoke, take care of your own welfare (safety) (lest I should injure you.) **Have mind upon your health**—think of your poor health and safety. **Slight man**—worthless man. **Give way**

Bru. Remember what happened on fifteenth of March. Was not great Julius Caesar killed for the sake of justice ? Was anyone of those who stabbed him a villain ? Did anyone stab him for another motive than justice ? Did we kill Caesar, the noblest man of this world, only to support robbers ? Shall we, now, pollute our hands by accepting bribes ? Shall we now sell for money the high offices of honour which we have the power to give to others ? I would rather be a dog barking at the moon than be a Roman of such a low character.

Cas. Brutus, do not harass me any further. I will not tolerate it. You forget your own position when you put limits to my freedom of action. I am an older and more experienced soldier than you. And so, I am far more competent to decide which persons are fit for which jobs (*or I am far abler than you to manage such affairs*).

Bru. Oh, it is the limit No! Cassius, you are not (*what you say you are*).

Cas. I am.

Bru. I say, you are not.

Cas. Do not provoke me any more, or I will lose all control over myself (*and may do you some injury*). Think of your own safety and do not provoke me any further.

Bru. Get out of my tent, you worthless man.

Cas. Is it possible that you should treat me like this ?

Bru. Listen to me. For I must speak Should I bow before your anger and give it a free scope ? Do you think that I will feel frightened if a madman like you looks at me with anger ?

Cas. O, gods, must I bear all this insult ?

Bru. Yes, all this and much more. Go on being irritated till your proud heart breaks. Go away and show your anger to your slaves and make them tremble out of fear. Must I bow down to your ill temper ? I swear by gods that you will yourself suffer from the poison of your anger (*you will yourself swallow the poison of your own anger*) and it will make you burst out ; from today onwards..........

---

and room—surrender to; allow it to flow freely. **Choler**—anger. **Stares**—looks angrily. **Fret**—go on worrying ; get irritated. **Choleric**—short-tempered; ill-tempered. **Bondmen** —slaves. **Tremble**—tremble out of fear of your anger. **Budge**—give way. **Observe**—perform courtesies. **Crouch**—bow before. **Testy humour**—touchy temper; irritable temper. **Digest..........spleen**—suffer from the poison of your own anger. **Venom**—poison. **Spleen** —anger. **Split you**—make you burst out. **From this day forth**—from this day onwards.

I'll use you for my mirth yea, for my laughter,
When you are *waspish.*

Cas. *Is it* come to this ?

Bru. You say, you are a better soldier :
Let it appear so, make your *vaunting* true,
And it shall please me well : for mine own part,
I shall *be glad to learn of noble men,*

Cas. You wrong me every way ; you wrong me, Brutus :
I said, an elder soldier, not a better :
Did I say, better ?

Bru. If you did, I care not

Cas. When Caesar lived, he *durst not* thus have *moved* me.

Bru. Peace, peace ! you durst not so have *tempted* him

Cas. I durst not !

Bru. No.

Cas. What ? durst not tempt him ?

Bru. *For your life you durst not.*

Cas. Do not *presume too much upon my love* ;
I may do that I shall be sorry for.

Bru. You have done that you should be sorry for.
There is no terror, Cassius, in your threats :
For I am *arm'd so strong in honesty*
That *they* pass by me as the *idle* wind,
Which I *respect not*. I did send to you
For certain sums of gold which you denied me.
For I can raise no money by *vile means*:
By heaven I had rather *coin my heart*
And *drop my blood for drachmas*, than to *wring*
From the *hard* hands *of* peasants their vile trash
By any *indirection* : I did send
To you for gold to pay my *legions*,
Which you denied me: was that done like Cassius ?
Should I have answer'd Caius Cassius so ?
When Marcus Brutus grows so *covetous*,
To *lock* such *rascal counters* from his friends.

I'll......mirth—use you as an object of mirth and ridicule (I will just laugh at you). **Waspish**—irritated ; in an Irritable mood. **Is it**—has it ? **Vaunting**—boast, **Be glad to......noble men**— be glad to learn from, take lessons from men who are truly noble. **Durst not**—dared not. **Moved**—irritated; provoked, **Tempted**—provoked. **For......not**—for fear of your life you would never have had the courage to do that. **Presume......love**—do not take undue advantage of my love for you ; do not depend on it so much, **Arm'd......honesty**—my integrity of character makes me so strong ; honesty and integrity are his strongest weapons. **They**—your threats. **Idle**—ineffective, harmless. **Respect not**—do not pay any heed to, **Vile means**—corrupt methods. **Coin my heart**—change my heart into coins. **Drop my blood**—let my blood flow. **For drachmas**—to be changed into coins. **Wring**—take by force; 'exact.

whenever you will be in such an irritated state of mind, I shall take you as a source of merriment, and a thing to be laughed at.

Cas. Have matters come to such a pass [*that you can ridicule me or laugh at me* ?]

Bru. You say that you are a better soldier; prove that you are ; prove your boast of being a better soldier true, and I will be pleased if you prove that. So far as I am concerned, I will always be glad to learn something from people who are truly noble.

Cas. You do me great injustice in every way. You, Brutus, do me a great wrong ; I said that I was a more experienced soldier, not that I was a better soldier. Did I call myself a better soldier ?

Bru. I do not care even if you have said that.

Cas. When Caesar was alive, he could not dare to irritate and provoke me as you are doing now.

Bru. Be calm, have patience ! You know, you did not have the courage to provoke him in such a way.

Cas. I did not have the courage?

Bru. No, you did not.

Cas. Do you mean to say that I did not have the courage to provoke Caesar ?

Bru. No, you did not, because of the fear of your life [*You knew that if you had done that, Caesar would have killed you. So, you never provoked him.*]

Cas. Do not overwork on my love for you. Do not insult me so much. I may do you some harm which I shall afterwards repent of [*Do you think that I love you so much, that I shall allow you to continue insulting me like this* ? *I may do something to you for which I will be sorry later on.*]

Bru. You have already done things for which you should feel sorry. Your threats, Cassius, do not frighten me. My honesty (*integrity of character*) has made me so strong that your threats pass by me like the puffs of ineffective wind. I pay no heed to your threats. I requested you to send me some money, but you did not do that. I cannot raise money through corrupt means. By gods of Rome, I would change my heart into pieces (*coins*) of money, and let my drops of blood be changed into drachmas, but I would not collect money by force from the poor hard-working farmers in an unjust and irregular manner. I asked you to send me some money, so that I might pay my soldiers, but you refused to do that. Was it a thing to be done by a friend like Cassius ? Could I ever have done this to Cassius ? If Marcus Brutus grows so greedy as to deny his friends some worthless pieces of metal (*coins*).

Hard—hardened by hard labour. **Indirection**—irregular means; bad means. **Legions**—soldiers. **Covetous**— greedy. **Lock**—keep back ; keep locked. **Rascal counters**—worthless coins.

Be ready, gods, with all your thunderbolts:
Dash him to pieces !

Cas. I denied you not.

Bru. You did.

Cas. I did not : he was but a fool
That brought my answer back. Brutus hath *rived* my heart :
A friend should bear his friend's *infirmities,*
But Brutus makes mine greater than they are.

Bru. I do not, till you *practise* them *on me*

Cas. You love me not.

Bru. I do not like your faults.

Cas. A friendly eye could never see such faults.

Bru. *A flatterer's* would not, though *they* do appear.
As *huge* as high Olympus.

Cas. Come, Antony and young Octavius, come,
Revenge yourselves alone on Cassius
For Cassius is *aweary* of the world ;
Hated by one he loves, *braved* by his brother ;
Checked like a *bondman* ; all his faults observed
Set in a note-book, learn'd and *conn'd by rote*,
To *cast into my teeth.*, O, I could weep
My spirit from mine eyes ! There is my dagger,
And here my naked breast ; within, a heart
Dearer than *Plutus'* mine, richer than gold :
If that thou *be'st* a Roman, take it forth ;
I, that denied thee gold, will give my heart ;
Strike, as thou didst at Caesar ; for, I know,
When thou didst hate him worst, thou lovedst him better
Than ever thou *lovedst* Cassius.

Bru. *Sheathe* your dagger ;
Be angry when you will, it shall have *scope* ;
Do what you will, *dishonour shall be humour.*
O Cassius, you are *yoked with a lamb.*
That carries anger as the flint bears fire,
Who, much *enforced* shows a *hasty spark*,
And *straight* is cold again.

Dash him to pieces—destroy him completely. **Rived**—tore through ; cut open ; broke. **Infirmities**— faults ; weaknesses. **Practise**—use them, **On me**—against me **A flatterer's**—the eye of a flatterer. **They**—Cassius' faults. **Huge**—big; high, **Aweary**—tired of ; sick of. **Braved**—questioned ; defied; treated with contempt. **Checked**—rebuked. **Bond man**— slave. **Set..........note book**—carefully recorded. **Conn'd by rote**—learnt by heart : memorised. **Cast...teeth**—to be flung at my face; to reproach me with. **My spirit from my eyes !**—let my soul weep through my eyes. **Dearer**—more precious. **Plutus'**—god of wealth. **Be'st**—are. **Lovedst**—loved. **Sheathe**—put the dagger back into its sheath (scabbard) **Scope**—

I pray to gods that they should blow him to pieces with their thunderbolts (*they should destroy him completely*).

Cas. I did not refuse to send you money.

Bru. You did.

Cas. I did not. The man who brought my message to you was a fool. Brutus, you have broken my heart. A friend ought to tolerate the failings and faults of a friend. But you exaggerate my weaknesses.

Bru. I do not exaggerate your weaknesses until you begin to practise them on me.

Cas. You do not love me.

Bru. I do not like your faults.

Cas. A true friend would never take note of such minor faults.

Bru Only an insincere man, a flatterer would not notice your faults, even if they were as big as mount Olympus.

Cas. Antony and young Octavius come ; take a terrible revenge only on Cassius. Cassius is now sick of this world and this life. Now that friend whom I love most, hates me most. My brother, now, treats me with contempt. All my faults and failings have been noted and learnt by heart, so that at times they (*faults*) may be flung in my face. Oh, I wish I could weep and let my very life flow through my eyes (*in the form of tears*) ! There is my dagger, and here is my bare breast. Within this breast of mine, there is my heart more valuable and precious than all the wealth of Pluto, the god of wealth. My heart is richer than gold. If you are a true Roman, take out my heart with that dagger. You accuse me that I denied you money; now I will give you my heart. Stab me with this dagger just as you stabbed Caesar. Because I know that even when you hated him most, you still loved him more than you have ever loved me.

Bru. Put your dagger back into its sheath. Be angry whenever you please. I will allow your anger to have a free play Do what you please. Even if you insult me, I will consider it only a passing whim of the moment. O, Cassius, you will find that your friend is a man as gentle as a lamb. I carry anger just as a flint carries fire. A flint gives out a spark when it is struck hard, and becomes cold after the flash. I also burst into anger when I am irritated, but soon I become cold.

---

free play ; free outlet. **Dishonour**—insult from you. **Humour**—only a whim ; a caprice ; just a sudden silly impulse. **Dishonour...humour**—even I will endure your insults considering them as your passing mood or whim. **Yoked with**—befriended with ; thrown in the company of ; have as a friend or companion **A lamb**—as gentle as a lamb. **Enforced**—provoked; rubbed against. **Hasty spark**—a sudden spark or flash of anger. **Straight**—at once; immediately.

Cas. Hath Cassius lived
To be *but mirth and laughter* to his Brutus.
When grief and *blood ill-temper'd vexeth* him ?
Bru. When I spoke that, I was ill-temper'd too.
Cas. Do you confess so much? Give me your hand.
Bru. And my heart too.
Cas. O Brutus !
Bru. What's the matter ?
Cas. Have not you love enough to *bear with me.*
When that *rash humour* which my mother gave me.
Make me forgetful ?
Bru. Yes, Cassius, and *from henceforth.*
When you are *over-earnest* with your Brutus,
He'll think your mother *chides*, and *leave you so*
[Noise within

Poet (*within*). Let me go in to see the generals;
There is some *grudge* between 'em ; 'tis not *meet*
They be alone.
Lucil (*within*). You shall not come to them.
Poet (*within*). Nothing but death shall *stay* me.

Enter Poet, followed by Lucilius, Titinius and Lucius

Cas. How now ! What's the matter ?
Poet. For shame, you generals ! What do you mean ?
Love and be friends, as two such men should be :
For I have seen more years, I am sure, than *ye*.
Cas. Ha, ha ! how *vilely* doth this *cynic* rhyme !
Bru. Get you *hence*, sirrah *Saucy* fellow, *hence*!
Cas. Bear with him, Brutus; 'tis his *fashion.*
Bru. I'll know his *humour*, when he knows his time:
What should the wars do with these *jigging fools*?
Companion, hence !
Cas. Away, away, be gone ! [Exit poet.
Bru. Lucilius and Titinius, bid the commanders
Prepare to *lodge* their companies to-night.
Cas. And come yourselves and bring Messala with you
Immediately to us. [Exeunt, Lucilius and Titinius.
Bru. Lucius, a bowl of wine. [Exit Lucius.
Cas. I did not think you could have been so angry.
Bru. O Cassius, I am *sick of many griefs*.

But—only. **Mirth and laughter**—an object of ridicule ; a thing to be laughed at. **Blood ill-tempered**—a disturbed mind; unbalanced disposition. **Vexeth**—troubles; upsets. **Bear with me**—to put up with my ill-temper; to put up with my anger. **Rash humour**—short temper; irritable temper, **From henceforth**—from now onwards. **Over earnest**—hot-tempered; use hard words. **Chides**—rebukes. **Leave you so**—leave the matter there; leave it at that, **Grudge**—ill-feeling. **Meet**—proper. **Stay**—prevent. **Ye**—you. **Vilely**—badly. **Cynic**—rude

Cas. Have I lived only to be an object of ridicule and mockery to my dear Brutus whenever ill-temper or my grief overpowers and troubles me?

Bru. When I spoke like that, I was also in a fit of ill-temper

Cas. Do you admit that much? Give me your hand (*let us forget it all*).

Bru. Here is my hand and my heart, too.

Cas. O Brutus !

Bru. What is the matter ? Why are you so much moved ?

Cas. If you really love me, you should have patience with me when my ill-temper, which I have inherited from my mother, makes me forget good manners and lose self-control.

Bru. Yes, Cassius, from now onwards whenever you lose your temper with me, I will think it is your mother's ill-temper that rebukes me, and so, I will leave it at that.

[Noise within.

Poet (*within*) Let me go in. I must meet the commanders. There is some ill-feeling between them, and it is not safe to leave them alone with each other.

Lucil. You cannot go in.

Poet. Only death shall prevent me from going in.

Enter—Poet, followed by Lucilius, Titinius and Lucius.

Cas. What is this? What is the matter ?

Poet You, generals, should feel ashamed of yourselves for quarrelling in this way. You should love each other and be friends. You should follow my advice, because I am older and more experienced than you.

Cas. Ha, ha ! how badly do the lines of this rude fellow rhyme (*sound* !)

Bru. You, rude fellow, get out at once.

Cas. Do not lose your patience with him, I know, it is his usual way.

Bru. I will he patient with his moods (*or his ways*) only if he chooses the right time to show them What these foolish fellows, writing cheap poems, have to do in times of war ? Go away, you fellow,

Cas. Go away at once Be gone ! [Poet goes

Bru. Lucilius and Titinius, tell the officers to provide quarters to their troops for the night-stay.

Cas. And come yourselves and bring Messala with you.

[Lucilius and Titinius go.

Bru. Bring me a bowl of wine. Lucius [Lucius goes.

Cas. I never thought that you could ever be so angry.

Bru. Alas, Cassius, I am troubled by many sorrows.

---

fellow. **Hence**—go away from here; get out. **Saucy**—rude; impudent fellow. **Fashion**—way. **Humour**—mood. **Jigging fools**—foolish writers of silly rhymes or poems. **Companion**—you fellow. **Lodge**—provide quarters for the night stay. **Sick..........griefs**—troubled by many sorrows.

Cas. Of your philosophy you make no use,
If you *give place to accidental evils.*
Bru. No man bears sorrow better. Portia is dead.
Cas. Ha ! Portia ?
Bru. She is dead.
Cas. How *'scaped* I killing when I *cross'd* you so ?—
O *insupportable* and *touching* loss !—
Upon what sickness ?
Bru. *Impatient of* my absence,
And grief, that young Octavius with Mark Antony
Have made themselves so strong ; — *for with her death.*
That tidings came : with this she *fell distract*,
And, her attendants absent, swallowed fire.
Cas. And died so ?
Bru. Even so.
Cas. O ye immortal gods ?

Re-enter Lucius with wine and taper

Bru. Speak no more of her—Give me a bowl of wine.
In this I *bury* all *unkindness*, Cassius [Drinks
Cas. My heart is thirsty for that noble *pledge.*
Fill, Lucius, till the wine *o'erswell* the cup ;
I cannot drink too much of Brutus' love [Drinks.
Bru. Come in Titinius. [Exist Lucius

Re-enter Titinius with Messala.

Welcome, good Messala,
Now sit we close about this taper here,
And *call in question* our *necessities.*
Cas. Portia. art thou gone ?
Bru. No more, I pray you.
Messala, I have here received letters,
That young Octavius and Mark Antony
Come down upon us with a mighty *power*,
Bending their expedition towards Philippi.
Mes. Myself have letter of the *selfsame tenor.*

Give place to—surrender ; bow down to, **Accidental evils**—misfortunes brought by chance. **'Scaped**—escaped ; how did I escape being killed? **Cross'd**—provoked ; made you angry. **Insupportable**—unbearable. **Touching**—tragic ; grievous. **Upon**—because of ; owing to. **Upon what sickness?**—of what disease she died. **Impatient of**—unable, to bear. **Tidings**—news. **For..........came**—I received this news of (Octavius and Antony becoming strong) along with the news of Portia's death. **Fell distract**—lost all balance of mind. **Bury**—drown. **Unkindness**—ill-feeling. **Pledge**—oath. **O'erswell**—overflows, **Call in question**—discuss; examine, **Necessities**—pressing needs. **Power**—army. **Bending their expedition**—directing their march; marching towards, **Self-same**—this very ; the same. **Tenor**—purpose.

Cas. If you surrender to the misfortunes brought by chance, it means that you make no use of your philosophy of stoicism (*a stoic is one who takes pleasure and pain indifferently*).

Bru. No man can bear pain better than I. Do you know, Portia is dead?

Cas. What ! is Portia dead ?

Bru. Yes, she is dead.

Cas. I really wonder why you did not kill me when I provoked you so much. O, what an unbearable and tragic loss ! What was the cause of her death ?

Bru. She was unable to bear my absence, and she heard that Antony and Octavius had become very powerful. My absence and this news made her lose all her self-control. When her attendants were away, she swallowed burning coals.

Cas. Did she die that way ?

Bru. Yes, that is how she died,

Cas. O, you immortal gods !

Re-enter Lucius with wine and candles.

Bru. Let us not talk about her any more—give me a glass of wine. In this cup of wine, Cassius, I will drown all my ill-will.

[He drinks]

Cas. I am also very much eager to fulfil this pledge of reconciliation. Lucius, fill this cup of wine till it overflows. I am so thirsty for Brutus's love that I can never drink too much of it. [*I am so thirsty for Brutus's love that my thirst can never be quenched, however much I may drink of his love* (*in the form of this wine*)]. [He drinks]

[Lucius goes.

Bru. Come in, Titinius !

Re-enter Titinius with Messala.

Welcome, good Messala. Now we will sit close together round this candle and discuss what is necessary for us to do.

Cas. Portia ! Are you really dead?

Bru. I request you not to talk about her any more Messala, I have received letters which tell me that young Octavious and Mark Antony are ready to attack us with a strong army. They are swiftly marching towards Philippi.

Mes. I have also received the same information.

Bru. With what *addition* ?
Mes. That by *proscription* and bills of outlawry,
Octavius. Antony and Lepidus,
Have put to death a hundred senators.
Bru. Therein our letters do not well agree.
Mine speak of seventy senators that died.
By their proscriptions, Cicero being one.
Cas. Cicero one ?
Mes. Cicero is dead,
And by that order of proscription.
Had you your letters from your wife, my lord?
Bru. No, Messala.
Mes. Nor nothing in your letters *writ of her*?
Bru. Nothing, Messala
Mes. That, methinks is strange.
Bru. Why ask you? Hear you *aught* of her in yours?
Mes. No, my lord.
Bru. Now, as you are a Roman, tell me true.
Mes. Then like a Roman bear the truth I tell:
For certain she is dead, *and by strange manner.*
Bru. Why, farewell, Portia. We must die. Messala.
With *meditating* that she must die *once*,
I have the patience to endure *it* now.
Mes. Even so great men great losses should endure.
Cas. I have as much of this *in art* as you,
But yet my nature could not bear it so.
Bru. Well, *to our work alive*. What do you think
Of marching to Philippi *presently*?
Cas. I do not think it good.
Bru. Your reason?
Cas. This it is :
'Tis better that the enemy seek us :
So shall he *waste his means*, *weary* his soldiers'
Doing himself *offence* whilst we, lying still,
Are full of rest, defence, and *nimbleness.*

Addition—more news; further details. **Proscription**—a list of persons declared as dacoits or undesirable persons. **Writ of her**—written about her. **Aught**—anything **And.........manner**—and she died in a strange manner. **Meditating**—thinking. **Once**—at some time or the other.

It—Portia's death. **In art**—theoretically; in theory. **To.........alive**—let us attend to our business which concerns- those who are still living [let us forget the deads (Cicero and Portia)]. **Work alive**—let us attend to the present work. **Presently**—immdiately. **Waste.........means**—wastes his resources. **Weary**—tires. **Offence** harm. **Nimbleness**—energy; swiftness to act.

Bru. What other news have you received in your letters ?

Mes. I have received this information also that Octavius, Antony and Lepidus prepared a list of persons condemned to death, and they have put hundred senators to death.

Bru. In that respect our letters differ *slightly*. My letters say that seventy senators have been put to death, and Cicero is one of them.

Cas. Is Cicero also one of them ?

Mess. Yes, Cicero has been killed according to that list of condemned persons. Did you receive any letters from your wife, my lord ?

Bru. No, I have heard nothing from her, Messala.

Mess. It is rather strange.

Bru. But, why do you ask all this ? Have you heard anything about her in your letters ?

Mess. No, my lord :

Bru. Come, you are a true Roman, tell me the truth.

Mess. Then with the courage of a true Roman bear the news, I am going to break to you. Because it is certain that Portia, your wife, is dead, and she died in a strange and unnatural manner.

Bru. Well, then, I bid you farewell, Portia. We must all die. The thought that she was also to die someday gives me the courage to bear the news of her death.

Mess. This is really the way in which great men should bear great losses.

Cas. In theory I am a stoic like you, but I myself could never bear such a loss so patiently.

Bru. Well, let us no more talk of the dead. Let us attend to the business that concerns those who are living. What do you think of marching to Philippi immediately ?

Cas. I think that it will be an unwise move.

Bru. What is your reason for thinking so ?

Cas. My reason is simply this that it will be better for us that we stay here and our enemies come searching for us. In this way they will exhaust their supplies, tire out their soldiers and do a lot of harm to themselves. We, on the other hand, shall stay where we are, and thus, we will be fresh and full of energy and swiftness for action.

Bru. Good reasons must *of force give place to* better.
The people '*twixt* Philippi and this ground
Do stand but in a *forced affection* ;
For they have *grudged us contribution :*
The enemy, marching along *by them*,
By them *shalt make a fuller number up*,
Come on refresh'd *new-added*, and encouraged :
From which advantage shall we cut him off,
If at Philippi we do face him there,
These people at our back.

Cas. Hear me, good brother.

Bru. *Under your pardon*. You must note *beside*,
That we have *tried the utmost of our friends*.
Our *legions* are *brimful*, our cause is ripe :
The enemy increaseth every day ;
We, at the *height*, are ready to *decline*.
There is a tide in the affairs of men,
Which *taken at the flood*, leads on to fortune
Omitted all the voyage of their life
Is bound in *shallows,* and in miseries.
On such a full sea are we now *afloat* ;
And we must *take the current* when it serves,
Or lose our *ventures*.

Cas. Then *with your will*, go on ;
We'll along ourselves, and meet them at Philippi.

Bru. The *deep of night is crept upon our talk*,
And nature must obey *necessity*;
Which we will *niggard* with a little rest,
There is no more to say ?

Cas. No more, Good night
Early to-morrow will we rise and hence.

Bru. Lucius ! [Re-enter Lucius,] —My gown.
[Exit Lucius] Farewell, good Messala
Good night Titinius, noble, noble Cassius,
Good night, and good *repose.*

Cas. O my dear brother !
This was an *ill beginning* of the night :
Never come such *division* 'tween our souls !
Let it not, Brutus.

Of force—of necessity ; perforce ; due to compulsion of circumstances. **Give place to**—yield. **'twixt**—between. **Forced affection**—they show love for us only under compulsion ; really they do not have any regard for us. **Grudged us contribution**—have given money unwillingly. **By them**—through their territory **Shall..........up**—reinforce their troops ; recruit new soldiers and increase their number. **New-added**—fully reinforced. **Under..........pardon**—with your permission. **Beside**—in addition to this ; moreover. **Tried..........friends**—have received maximum help from our friends. **Legions**—troops.

Bru. Your reasons are good, no doubt, but mine are better. So, good reasons must yield to better ones. The people living between Philippi and this place (*Sardis*) show love for us only under compulsion, (*they have no real love for us*) ; because they give us the supplies that we need, quite unwillingly Our enemy passing through this region (*area*) will recruit new soldiers and increase the number of his soldiers. They will, then, attack us refreshed, reinforced and encouraged. But if we march to Philippi and meet them there, we shall leave these unsympathetic people at our back, and thus we will deprive our enemy of taking advantage of these people.

Cas. Listen to me, my good brother.

Bru. Excuse me for a moment. You must also remember that we have already received as much help from our friends as they could possibly afford. Our plans are fully matured, and the power of our enemy is increasing everyday. We are, now, at the height of our power, and if we wait, our strength will decrease There is a tide (*opportunity*) in the life of human beings. Just as ships must sail when the tide is high, similarly men should make the best of the opportunity when it comes. If men miss the right opportunity, they get stuck up in the sand banks of the sea of life, Just as a ship missing the tide gets stuck up in the shallow, sand banks in the sea. We have now, such a golden opportunity ; we must either make use of it or should be prepared to face failure and loss.

Cas. Then, if it is so, do as you desire. We will march and meet them (*our enemies*) at Philippi.

Bru. The darkness of the night has come down upon us while we were talking. It would be better if we obey the call of sleep, which is necessary. Let us rest only for a short while. Is there any thing more to be said ?

Cas. Nothing more, Good night We get up early tomorrow and march.

Bru. Lucius, (Re-enter Lucius) my night gown. (Lucius goes) Farewell, good Messala, Good night Titinius. Good night, noble Cassius. may you enjoy a sound sleep.

Cas. O, my dear brother, this evening began very badly. In future, let there be no such conflict between us, Brutus. (*Let our hearts not be divided by such conflicts*).

Brimful—as many as they should be. **Height**—height of our power. **Decline**—fall down. **Taken..........flood**— used when the tide is high. **Omitted**—missed : neglected. **Shallows**—shallow waters : sand banks in the sea. **Afloat**—floating. **Take the current**—make use of the high tide : take advantage of the proper opportunity. **Ventures**—enterprise ; missions. **With..........will**—as you desire. **Deep..........night**—darkness of the night. **Is..........talk**—fell as we were talking. **Necessity**—the call of sleep ; sleep which is necessary. **Niggard**—manage sparingly, manage with, a short allowance. **Repose**—rest. **Ill beginning**—bad beginning. **Division**—difference.

Bru. Everything is well.
Cas. Good night, my lord.
Bru. Good night, good brother,.
Tit. Mes. Good night, Lord Brutus
Bru. Farewell, every one.

[Exeunt Cassius, Titinius, and Messala.

Re-enter Lucius, with the gown]

Give me the gown. Where is thy *instrument ?*
Luc. Here in the tent.
Bru. What, thou speak'st *drowsily* ?
Poor *knave*, I blame thee not ; thou art o'*erwatch'd.*
Call Claudius, and some other of my men;
I'll have them sleep on cushions in my tent.
Luc. Varro and Claudius !

[Enter Varro and Claudius]

Var. Calls my lord ?
Bru. I pray you, sirs, lie in my tent and sleep :
It may be, I shall *raise* you *by and by*
On business to my brother Cassius.
Var. *So please you, we will stand and watch your pleasure,*
Bru. I will not have it so; Lie down, good sirs ;
It may be I shall otherwise *bethink me.*
Look Lucius here's the book *I sought for so* ;
I put it in the pocket of my gown.
[Varro and Claudius, lie down]
Lus. I was sure your lordship did not give it me.
Bru. *Bear with me*, good boy. I am much forgetful.
Canst thou hold up thy heavy eyes awhile,
And *touch* thy instrument a *strain* or two ?
Luc. Ay, my lord, an't please you.
Bru. It does, my boy :
I trouble thee too much, but thou art willing

Instrument—harp; musical instrument. **Drowsily**—in sleep. **Knave**—boy. **Overwatched**—tired with keeping awake or keeping a watch late in the night. **Raise**—wake you up. **By and by**—so on. **On business to**—to carry some message to. **So please you**—if it pleases you. **We..........pleasure**—we will keep standing and watch for anything you may wish us to do. **Bethink-me**—may change my mind. **I sought for so**—looked for. **Bear with me**—to mind what I say ; have patience with me. **Touch**—play upon. **Strain**—tune.

Bru. Now all is well, there is no conflict between us.

Cas. Good night, my lord.

Bru. Good night, my good brother.

Tit., *Mess*. Good night, lord Brutus.

Bru. I wish you all good night.

[Cassius, Titinius and Messala go

Re-enter Lucius with the gown]

Give me the dressing gown. Where is your musical instrument ?

Lus. It is here in the tent.

Bru. What ! you are speaking in a sleepy voice. Poor boy, I do not blame you for being sleepy. You are tired of keeping awake late in the night. Call Claudius and some other of my guards ; I will ask them to sleep on cushions in my tent.

Lus. Varro and Claudius !

[Enter Varro and Claudius]

Var. Did you call us, my lord ?

Bru. I pray you gentlemen to lie in my tent and sleep here. Most probably I may have to wake you up very soon to carry some message to my brother, Cassius.

Var. If it pleases you. Sir, we will stand waiting for anything you may wish us to do.

Bru. No, I do not wish you to do that. Lie down, gentlemen.

I fear, otherwise I may change my mind. Well Lucius, here is the book I was looking for. I had put it in the pocket of my gown.

[Varro and Claudius lie down

Lus. I was sure that your lordship had not given this book to me.

Bru. Have patience with me, my good boy. I have grown very forgetful these days. But can you keep awake for a while, and play a tune or two on your instrument ?

Luc. Yes Sir, if it pleases you.

Bru. It will please me, my boy I am sorry that I give you so much trouble, but you are always willing to serve me.

Luc. It is my duty, sir.
Bru. I should not *urge* thy duty *past thy might*;
I know *young bloods* look for a time of rest.
Luc. I have slept, my lord, already.
Bru. It was well done : and thou shalt sleep again :
I will not *hold* thee long : if I do live.
I will be good to thee. [Music and a song.
This is a *sleepy tune*: O *murderous slumber*,
Lay'st thou thy *leaden mace* upon my boy,
That plays thee music? Gentle knave, good night ;
I will not do thee much wrong to wake thee.
If thou dost *nod*, thou *break'st* thy instrument ;
I'll take it from thee ; and, good boy, good night,
Let me see. let me see ; is not the leaf *turn'd down*
Where I left reading ? Here it is, I think
[He sits down.

[Enter the Ghost of Caesar]

How *ill* this *taper* burns I Ha ! who comes here?
I think, it is the weakness of my eyes
That *shapes* this *monstrous apparition*
It *comes upon* me—Art thou *anything* ?
Art thou some god, some angel, or some devil,
That makest my blood cold, and my hair *to stand* ?
Speak to me, what thou art.
Ghost. Thy evil spirit, Brutus.
Bru. Why comest thou ?
Ghost. To tell thee thou shalt see me at Philippi.
Bru. Well, then I shall see thee again ?
Ghost. Ay, at Philippi
Bru. Why, I will see thee at Philippi, then.
[Ghost vanishes.
Now I have *taken heart*, thou *vanishest* :
Ill spirit, I would hold more talk with thee
Boy Lucius ! Varro ! Claudius ! Sirs, awake !
Claudius' !

Urge—press. **Past.......might**—beyond your capacity. **Young bloods**—young men who are strong and full of energy. **Hold**—detain. **Sleepy tune**—a sleep-inducing tune. **Murderous slumber**—sleep which kills each day [each day's life dies with sleep at night]. **Leaden**—heavy; dull. **Mace**—rod or staff of authority. **Nod**—feel sleepy. **Breakest**—will surely break. **Turned down**—folded. **Ill**—dimly. **Taper**—candle. **Shapes**—gives shape to : creates, **Monstrous**—horrible. **Apparition**—ghost ; phantom. **Comes upon**—advances towards. **Anything**—a real thing ; any thing real. **To stand**—to stand on end out of terror. **Taken heart**—get back my lost courage. **Vanishest**—disappears. **Ill**—evil.

Luc. It is my duty. Sir.

Bru. But I should not press upon you work beyond your capacity. [*I should not burden you with over-work*]. I know, young people require greater rest and sleep. They anxiously wait for the time of rest.

Luc. I have already slept, my lord.

Bru. You did well ; and you shall soon go to sleep. I will not detain you for long. If I live longer, I will look after your welfare.

[Lucius plays on the instrument and sings.

It is a soft sleep inducing tune. O Sleep ! the killer of days, have you overpowered the senses of my boy-servant who was entertaining you with music and song ? Good night, my gentle boy, I will not be cruel to keep you awake any longer. If in your sleepiness you nod, you will surely let fall your instrument, and break it. I will take it (*instrument*) from you. Good night, my dear boy. Let me see where I left off reading; Did I not fold the leaf to mark it ? Here It is, I think.

[He sits down

[Enter the Ghost of Caesar]

How dimly does this candle burn ! But, who is this ? I think it is the dimness of my sight which gives shape to this horrible phantom. It is advancing towards me. Are you anything real, or only an illusion ? Are you some god, or some angel or some devil (*evil spirit*) ? You make my blood freeze. You make my hair stand on end. Tell me what you really are.

Ghost I am your evil spirit, Brutus.

Bru. Why have you come here ?

Ghost. I have come just to tell you that I will meet you again at Philippi.

Bru, Well, then, will I see you again ?

Ghost. Yes, at Philippi.

Bru. Very well, then, I will meet you again at Philippi.

[Ghost disappears

Now, when I have recovered my courage, you have disappeared. O, you evil spirit, I would like to have more talk with you. Lucius ! Varro ! Claudius ! wake up, all of you, Claudius!

Luc. The strings, my lord, are *false*

Bru. He thinks *he still is at* his instrument.
Lucius, awake !

Luc. My Lord ?

Bru. Didst thou dream, Lucius, that thou so criedst out ?

Luc. My Lord, I do not know that I did cry.

Bru. Yes, that thou didst. Didst thou see anything ?

Luc. Nothing, my lord.

Bru. Sleep again, Lucius, *Sirrah* Claudius !
[To Varro] Fellow thou, awake !

Var. My lord ?

Clau. My lord ?

Bru. Why did you so cry out, sirs, in your sleep ?

Var. Clau. Did we, my lord ?

Bru. Ay : saw you any thing ?

Var. No, my lord, I saw nothing

Clau. Nor I, my lord.

Bru. Go, and *commend me* to my brother Cassius ;
Bid him *set on his powers betimes* before,
And we will follow.

Var & Clau. It shall be done, my lord. [Exeunt

ACT V

Scene I—The Plains of Philippi

Enter Octavius, Antony, and their army.

Oct. Now, Antony, our hopes are *answered* :
You said the enemy would not come down,
But *keep* the hills and upper regions
It proves not so ; their *battles* are at hand ;
They mean to *warn* us at Philippi here,
Answering before we do demand of them.

Ant. *Tut, I am in their bosoms*, and I know
Wherefore they do it. They *could be content*
To visit other places, and come down
With *fearful bravery*, thinking by this *face*
To fasten in our thoughts that they have courage ;
But 'tis not so.

False—out of tune. **He..........at**—he is still playing on. **Sirrah**—fellow. **Commend me**—convey my greetings to. **Set..........powers**—order his troops to march. **Betimes**—early in the morning. **Answered**— carried out : fulfilled. **Keep**—stay on. **Battles**—armies ; troops. **Warn**—challenge. **Answering..........them**—accepting our challenge before we have called them to fight. **Tut**—nonsense. **I..........bosoms**—I know all their secrets; I know that they plan to do. **Wherefore**—what for ; why. **Could be content**—they would gladly go to other places. **Fearful bravery**—mere show, of courage to cover up their fear or with a frightening show of splendour **Face**—outward show. **To fasten..........thoughts**—to impress upon us ; to make us think.

Luc. My lord, the strings of the instrument are out of tune.

Bru. He thinks that he is still playing on his instrument. Wake up, Lucius.

Luc. My lord

Bru. Did you have a dream Lucius ? You cried in your sleep.

Luc. My lord, I do not know if I cried.

Bru. Yes, you did cry. Did you see any thing ?

Luc. Nothing my lord.

Bru. You go to sleep again, Lucius, you fellow, Claudius (*to Varro*) and you fellow, wake up.

Varro. Yes my lord.

Claudius. Did you call me, Sir ?

Bru. Why, Sirs, did you cry out so loud in your sleep ?

Varro. Claus. Did we cry out my lord ?

Bru. Yes, you did. Did you see any thing ?

Varro. No, my lord, I saw nothing,

Claudius. Nor did I see any thing, Sir.

Bru. Go, and convey my greetings to my brother, Cassius Ask him to order his troops to march early in the morning. My troops will follow them

Var. Clau. It shall be done, my lord. [They go

ACT V

Scene I—The Plains of Philippi

Enter Octavius, Antony and their Army.

Oct. Now, Antony, what we were wishing for has happened after all. You said that the enemy would not come down ; he would stay on the hills and the higher areas. But your reading has proved to be wrong, because their armies are very near. They intend accepting your challenge before we actually call them to fight.

Ant. Nonsense ! I know all their secret plans and intentions. They would very gladly shift to their places; but they come down to attack us only with a show of courage to cover up their fear. They think that by this outward show, they would impress upon us that they have courage, which they do not have. [*They are really afraid of us; they are only putting up a show of bravery or courage*)

Enter a Messenger.

Mess. Prepare you generals ;
The enemy comes on in *gallant show* :
Their *bloody sign of battle* is *hung out*
And something to be done immediately.
Ant. Octavius, lead your *battle softly on*
Upon the left hand of the *even field.*
Oct. Upon the right hand I ; keep thou the left,
Ant. Why do you *cross me* in this *exigent* ?
Oct. *I do not cross you ; but will do so* [March

Drum Enter Brutus, Cassius and their Army ;
Lucilius, Titinius, Messala and others

Bru. They stand, and would have *parley.*
Cas. Stand fast, Titinius ; we must *out* and talk ;
Oct. Mark Antony, shall we give *sign of battle* ?
Ant. No, *Caesar,* we will *answer on their charge.*
Make forth; the generals would have some words.
Oct. *Stir not* until the signal.
Bru. Words before blows. *is it so*, countrymen ?
Oct. Not that we love words better as you do
Bru. Good words are better than bad strokes, Octavius.
Ant. In your bad strokes, Brutus, you give good words.
Witness the hole you made in Caesar's heart,
Crying "Long live ! hail, Caesar !"
Cas. Antony !
The *posture of your blows* are yet unknown ;
But for your words, they rob the *Hybla bees*
And leave them honeyless.
Ant. Not *stingless* too.
Bru. O, yes, and *soundless* too ;
For you have stol'n their buzzing, Antony ;
And very wisely threat before you *sting.*

Gallant show—military splendour ; a great display of courage and bravery. **Bloody..........battle**—red flag. **Hung out**—is unfurled ; is flying and fluttering. **Battle**—troops : army. **Softly on**—gently forwarding. **Even field**—level field. **Cross me**—oppose me ; thwart me. **Exigent**— crisis ; emergency. **I do not..........do so**—I am not merely thwarting you ; but I will do as I said. **Parley**—conference. **Out**—go out. **Sign of battle**—signal. **Answer on their charge**—meet them when they attack us. **Make forth**—go forward. **Stir not**—do not attack ; do not move. **Is it so**—do you wish that. **Posture**—manner. **Posture... blows**—what kind of blows you can strike. **Hybla bees**—bees found in Hybla, a mountain, and a town of Sicily. **Stingless**—without a sting ; harmless and helpless. **Soundless**—without the noise of humming. **Sting**—prick; strike.

Enter a Messenger.

Mess. Generals, get ready for fighting. The enemy is advancing with a great show of courage and military splendour. Their red flag is flying. We must do something immediately.

Ant. Octavius, you take your troops slowly to the left of the level field.

Oct. I shall keep to the right hand, you keep to the left.

Ant. Why do you oppose me at this time of crisis?

Oct. I not only oppose you but will do as I said.

[The troops are heard marching

[The beating of a drum. Enter Brutus, Cassius and their Army, Lucilius, Titinius, Messala and others].

Bru. They are standing, and it looks that they would like to have a conference.

Cas. You remain here, Titinius ; we must go forward and talk.

Oct. Mark Antony, shall we give the signal for the fight ?

Ant. No, Octavius Caesar, we will meet them when they attack. Let us go forward, their commander would like to talk to us.

Oct. (*to his troops*) Do not move till the signal for the fight is given.

Bru. You want to exchange words before exchanging blows ? Is it so, countrymen?

Oct. But that does not mean that we prefer words to blows as you do.

Bru. Good words are better than bad blows., Octavius

Ant. Brutus, you speak kind words and give cruel blows [*Your kind words often go* with *cruel blows*] Remember the wound you gave to Caesar's heart even while you greeted him with good words, crying "Long live Caesar ; I offer my greetings to Caesar"

Cas. It is not yet known what kind of blows you can strike, Antony ; but as for your words, they are very sweet. It seems that your words have stolen all the honey of the bees of Hybla mountain, and have left them without honey.

Ant. Have my words not stolen the stings of those bees also? And thus have left them stingless? [*Don't you feel the sting of my words? My words*, *in fact, are not so sweet as stinging.*]

Bru. O, yes ; you have left those bees soundless also, because you have stolen their power of buzzing also. You are now buzzing like a bee, and are very wisely giving us warning before stinging

Ant. Villains, you did not so, when your *vile* daggers
Hack'd one another in the sides of Caesar ;
You *show'd your teeth* like apes, and *fawn'd like hounds.*
And bow'd like *bondmen,* kissing Caesar's feet ;
Whilst damned Casca, like a *cur*, behind
Struck Caesar on the neck. O, you flatterers !

Cas. Flatterers ! Now, Brutus, thank yourself.
This tongue had not *offended* so to-day,
If Cassius might have ruled.

Oct. Come, come, *the cause* : if *arguing* make up sweat
The proof of it will turn to *redder drops.*
Look ;
I draw a sword against conspirators ;
When think you that the sword *goes up* again ?
Never, till Caesar's three and thirty wounds
Be well avenged or till *another Caesar*
Have added slaughter to the sword of traitors

Bru. Caesar, thou canst not die by traitors' hands.
Unless thou bring'st them with thee.

Oct. So I hope ;
I was not born to die on Brutus' sword.

Bru. O, if thou wert the noblest of thy *strain.*
Young man, thou could'st not die more *honourable.*

Cas. A *peevish* school-boy, *worthless* of such honour.
Joined with a *masker* and a *reveller* !

Ant. Old Cassius still !

Oct. Come, Antony. away !
Defiance, traitors, *hurl* we *in your teeth* :
If you dare fight today, come to the field ;
If not, when you have *stomachs.*

[Exeunt Octavius, Antony and their Army

Vile—dirty; hateful. **Hack'd one another**—clashed with one another. **Show'd......teeth**—grinned like monkeys. **Fawned......hounds**—crawwed at Caesar's feet, just as faithful dogs do at the feet of their master. **Bondmen**—slaves. **Cur**—dog. **This tongue**—tongue of Antony. **Offended**—insulted. **If Cassius......ruled**—if Cassius had had his way [Cassius had asked Brutus to kill Antony along with Caesar] ; if the will of Cassius had prevailed. **The cause**—the business in hand. **Arguing**—mere wordy quarrel; exchange of hot words. **The proof**—the, practical test [*i.e.*, that fighting with swords]. **Redder drops**—drops of blood. **Goes up**—goes back into its sheath. **Another Caesar**—Octavius Caesar himself. **Have......traitors**—has also been killed by the traitors [murderers of Julius Caesar]. **Have added slaughter**—one more Caesar, (Octavius Caesar) is killed by the conspirators. **Strain**—race. **Honourable**—honourably. **Peevish**—silly; childish. **Worthless**—unworthy. **Joined with**—Octavius joined with Antony. **Masker**—one fond of theatrical performances, dances & etc. **Reveller**—merry maker ; a mere pleasure-seeker given to drinking, dancing and other sensual pleasures. **Defiance**—challenge, **Hurl**—throw; fling. **In your teeth**—in your face. **Stomachs**—a desire for fighting.

Ant. Villains, you gave no such warning before your dirty daggers clashed with one another as they pierced Caesar's body. (*You stabbed Caesar without a warning*). You showed teeth (*grinned*) like monkeys. Like faithful dogs you crawled at Caesar's feet. You fell on your knees and kissed his feet as if you were his slaves, while cursed Casca, struck at his back very much like a street dog which had no courage to attack from the front. You are all a pack of flatterers and hypocrites.

Cas. Flatterers ! you see Brutus, how Antony's tongue has insulted us. You alone are responsible for it. If you had followed my advice (*of killing Antony along with Caesar*), Antony would not have been living to insult us like this.

Oct. Come ! come, let us waste no time in this exchange of bitter words. Let us get down to business (*start fighting* ; *start to act*). If our arguments make us perspire, the drops of perspiration will change into red drops of blood as soon as we put our arguments to the practical test of fighting. [*Our arguing (exchange of hot words) has made us sweat, but when we begin fighting we will then, receive and give wounds. And so instead of watery drops of perspiration, red drops of blood would flow from our bodies*] See, I have drawn out my sword to be used against the conspirators. When, do you think, will my sword be sheathed again? It will not be sheathed until I have taken revenge on the conspirators for all the thirty three wounds on Caesar's body, or until a second Caesar (*i.e., Octavius Caesar*) is also murdered by the conspirators [*I will either take a terrible revenge for each wound given to Caesar's body or die at the hands of the conspirators*].

Bru. Octavius Caesar, we are no traitors. You cannot die at the hands of traitors unless you have traitors in your ranks. [*The only possibility of your dying at the hands of traitors is that you have some traitors with you. Because no one from among us is a traitor*].

Oct. I hope so. I was not born to die at the hands of Brutus.

Bru. O, even if you were the noblest man of your race, no death would be more honourable for you than the death at my hands and with my sword.

Cas. He is a silly young chap and is unworthy of the honour of dying at Brutus's hands. He is a companion of an equally worthless merry maker and pleasure seeker (*i.e. Antony*).

Ant. Oh, Cassius is still the same ill-tempered fellow as he used to be.

Oct. Come Antony, let us move away. We throw challenge. In your face, you traitors. If you have the courage today, come to the battle field. If you have no courage now, come whenever you have the courage and inclination to fight.

[Octavius, Antony and their army go away

Cas. Why, now, blow wind, *swell billow*, and swim *bark*
The storm is up and all is *on the hazard*
Bru. Ho Lucilius ! hark, a word with you.
Lucil. [Standing forth] My Lord?
[Brutus and Lucilius talk apart
Cas. Messala !
Mes. [Standing forth]. What says my general ?
Cas. Messala,
This is my birthday ; *as* this very day
Was Cassius born. Give me thy hand, Messala ;
Be thou my witness that against my will,
As Pompey was, am I compell'd to *set*
Upon one battle all our liberties.
You know that I *held Epicurus strong.*
And his opinion : now I change my mind,
And partly *credit things* that do *presage.*
Coming from Sardis, on our *former ensign*
Two mighty eagles *fell ;* and there they *perch'd,*
Gorging and feeding from our soldiers' hands,
Who to Philippi here *consorted us ;*
This morning are they fled away and gone,
And in their *stead* do *ravens, crows, and kites,*
Fly o'er our heads, and downward look on us,
As we were sickly prey : their shadows seem
A *canopy* most *fatal*, under which
Our army lies, ready to *give up the ghost.*
Mes. Believe not so.
Cas. I but believe it partly:
For I am fresh of spirit and resolved
To meet all perils very *constantly*
Bru. Even so, Lucilius–
Cas. Now, most noble Brutus,
The *gods to-day stand friendly*, that we may,
Lovers in peace, lead on our days to age !

Swell—rise high. **Billow**—waves. **Bark**—ship; boat. **On the hazard**—at stake. **As**—on. **Set upon one battle**—staked on one battle ; risked on one battle. **All our liberties**—everything ; all our freedom of action, strategy and decision. **Held Epicurus strong**—was a follower of Epicurus the great philosopher. He believed that gods are not interested in human affairs and so they send no warnings in the form of omens. Cassius says that as a follower of Epicurus, he did not believe in omens. **Credit things**—believe in things. **Presage**—fore-shadow ; foretell. **Former ensign**—foremost standard bearer (soldier carrying the flag. **Fell**—pounced, **Perch'd**—sat. **Gorging**—feeding greedily. **Consorted us**—accompanied us. **Stead**—place **Ravens..........kites**—these are birds of ill omen, they fly over their prey when it is sick and about to die. **As we were**—as if we

Cas. Well, let the wind blow, let the waves rise high ; and let our ship sail. The storm has risen, and now everything is at stake.

Bru. Listen, Lucilius, I want to speak to you.

Lucil. (Standing forth) yes, my lord.

[Brutus and Lucilius talk separately to each other,

Cas. Messala.

Mes. (Standing forth) What is your order, general.

Cas. Messala, today is my birthday ; on this day was I born, Give me your hand Messala. You shall bear witness to it that like Pompey I have also been compelled to risk everything, all our freedom, on the result of a single battle. I am doing it as unwillingly as Pompey had done in his case. You know that I have always been a firm follower of the philosophy of Epicurus, and so never before have I believed in omens. But now, I have changed my mind. Now, I partly believe in omens and portents which foreshadow future. During our march from Sardis, two big eagles pounced and sat on our foremost standard bearer. They kept on feeding and eating greedily from the hands of our soldiers, They accompanied us to Philippi. This morning they have flown away and disappeared, and in their place there appear ravens, crows and kites They hover over our heads and look down upon us as if we were like sick animals ready to die and become their prey. Their shadows over our heads ar~ like a covering which presages death. It looks as if our armies were marching under the very wings of death, and were to die very soon.

Mes. Do nor believe such things.

Cas. I believe all this only partly because I am fresh in my spirits. And, I am determined to face all dangers with great firmness.

Bru. Yes, that is so Lucilius.

Cas. Now, most noble Brutus, may the gods be friendly to us today, so that after the war is over and there is peace, we may live long as loving friends.

---

were. **Sickly prey**—sick and ready to die to become their prey. **Canopy**—a covering over a bed, on resting on poles to shelter many people. **Fatal**—foreshadowing death. **Give..........ghost**—die. **Constantly**—firmly. **Gods to-day..........friendly**—may gods stand friendly to-day. **Lovers**—friends.

But since the affairs of men rest *still incertain*.
Let's reason with *the worst that may befall* :
If we do lose this battle, then is this
The very last time we shall speak together :
What are you then determined to do ?

Bru. Even by the rule of that philosophy
By which I did blame *Cato* for the death
Which *he did give himself*, I know not how
But I do find it cowardly and vile.
For fear of what might *fall*, so to *prevent*
The time of life; arming myself with patience
To stay the *providence of some high powers*
That govern us below.

Cas. Then, if we lose this battle.
You are contented to be led in triumph
Through the streets of Rome ?

Bru. No, Cassius no : think not thou noble Roman,
That ever Brutus will go *bound* to Rome ;
He bears too great a mind. But this same day
Must end that work the Ides of March begun;
And whether we shall meet again I know not.
Therefore our *everlasting farewell* take;
For ever and for ever, farewell, Cassius !
If we do meet again, why, we shall *smile* :
If not, why then this parting was well made.

Cas. For ever, and for ever, farewell, Brutus !
If we do meet again, we'll smile indeed ;
If not, 'tis true this parting was well made

Bru. Why then, *lead on*,—O, that a man might know :
The *end* of this day's business, *ere* it come !
But it sufficeth, that the day will end,
And then the end is known. *Come, ho* ! *away* !

[Exeunt

Still—always. **Incertain**—uncertain. **Reason**—consider. **Let's**...........**befalls**—let us consider what we shall do if the worst happens. **Cato**—Cato the younger who had joined Pompey against Caesar. When whole of Africa surrendered to Caesar, Cato committed suicide. **He**...........**himself**—inflicted upon himself the suicide that he committed. **Fall**—happen, **Time of life**—life-span. **Prevent**...........**life**—to anticipate natural end of life, by ending life unnaturally through suicide. **To stay**—to wait for ; live. **Providence**—fate ordained by. **To stay**...........**us below**—to wait for the fate ordained by bigher powers who govern the fate of men living on the earth below them (the higher powers). **Us below**—mortal men of this world. **Through**—from end to end. **Bound**—bound in chains as a prisoner of war. **Everlasting farewell**—farewell for ever. **Smile**—smile at our victory. **Lead on**—advance, **End**—the final result, **Ere**—before. **Come, ho ! away**—order given to the troops.

But as all affairs of men are always uncertain, we should, therefore, consider what we will do if the worst happens. If we lose this battle then, this will be our last meeting. We will never meet and talk again in case we are defeated. What do you intend doing, in case we are defeated ?

Bru. I will act according to that philosophy which made me condemn Cato for committing suicide. Somehow I consider it a cowardly act to put an end to the natural duration of life, by committing suicide. It is really an act of cowardice to commit suicide because of the fear of the worst that might happen. Armed with patience, I am determined to wait for the fate ordained by higher powers who govern the fate of mortal men on the earth below. [*I will not commit suicide, I will wait for the hour of death fixed by gods who govern the fate of men*].

Cas. Then, if we are defeated in this battle, will you be prepared to be led as a prisoner through the streets of Rome ? Will you like to be chained to the chariot of the victorious commander for a victory procession ?

Bru. No Cassius, no : do not think, you noble Roman, that Brutus will ever go to Rome as a prisoner bound in chains. I have a mind too proud and noble to suffer such a humiliation. This very day, we should finish the work we began on 15th of March. May be that it is our last meeting. Let us therefore, bid eaeh other farewell for ever. Good bye, Cassius, good bye for ever ! If we do meet again, we shall smile. But if we do not meet again, then this our parting from each other would be the best and fittest farewell.

Cas. Good bye for ever, Brutus ! If we do meet again we will surely smile joyfully : but if we do not meet again, it is true that we are parting in the best and fittest manner.

Bru. If it is so, lead your forces. I wish we could know before hand the result of this day's business. But it is enough to know that this day will end, and the end of the day will bring us the final result. Come, let us move away. [They leave

Scene II—Plain of Philippi, The field of battle

Alarum Enter Brutus and Messala

Bru. Ride, ride, Messala ride and give these *bills*.
Unto the *legions* on *the other side*. [Loud alarum
Let them *set on* at once ; for I perceive.
But *cold demeanour* in *Octavius' wing*,
And sudden *push* gives them the *overthrow*.
Ride, ride, Messala : let them all come down. (Exeunt

Scene III—Another part of the field

Alarum. Enter Cassius and Titinius

Cas. O look, Titinius, look, the *villains fly* !
Myself have to *mine* own turn'd enemy ;
This *ensign* here of mine was *turning back* :
I *slew* the coward, and did take *it* from him.
Tit. O Cassius, Brutus gave *the word* too early ;
Who, having *some advantage* on Octavius,
Took it too eagerly : his soldiers *fell to spoil,*
Whilst we by Antony are all *enclosed*

Enter Pindarus

Pin. Fly further off, my lord, fly further off;
Mark Antony is in your tents, my lord ;
Fly, therefore, noble Cassius, fly far off !
Cas. This hill is far enough. Look, look Titinius ;
Are those my tents where I *perceive* the fire ?
Tit. They are, my lord.
Cas. Titinius, if thou lovest me,
Mount thou my horse and *hide thy spurs in him*.
Till he have brought thee up to yonder troops.
And here again : that I may rest assured,
Whether yond troops are friend or enemy.
Tit. I will be here again, *even with a thought*. [Exit.
Cas. Go Pindarus, get higher on that hill ;
My sight was *ever thick* ! *regard* Titinius,
And tell me what thou *notest* about the field.

[Pindarus *ascends* the hill.

Bills—written orders. **Legions**—troops. **The other side**—the other side commanded by Cassius. **Set on**—attack. **Cold demeanour**—lack of warmth and courage in fighting. **Octavius' wing**—on the side commanded by Octavius **Push**—attack. **Overthrow**—defeat **Alarum**—orders to take up arms, and fight **Villains**—Cassius' own troops. **Fly**—run away from the field. **Mine**—my own soldiers. **Ensign**—standard bearer ; flag bearer. **Turning back**—retreating; going back. **Slew**—killed. **It**—the flag. **The word**—the order. **Some advantage**—slight edge over ; partial victory. **Fell to spoil**—started plundering ; started

Scene II—Plains of Philippi, The Battle-field

Noise of trumpets calling soldiers to take up arms
Enter Brutus And Messala

Bru. Ride, Messala, Ride with all speed and give these written orders to the troops commanded by Cassius on the other side. (*loud noise of battle*). Tell them to attack at once. I see a Jack of spirit and courage in the troops of Octavius, and it is possible that a sudden attack might give them a crushing defeat. Ride with all speed, Messala and let all the troops of Cassius make an attack at once. [They leave

Scene III—Another part of the field

Noise of battle. Enter Cassius and Titinius

Cas. Look Titinius, look, how these villains: our soldiers, are running away. I had to act as an enemy to some of my own soldiers (*I had to kill some of them*). My flag bearer was running away, so I killed him and took this flag from him.

Tit. O Cassius, Brutus gave the signal for attack too early. Having gained some advantage over Octavius, he became too eager to get complete victory. His soldiers stopped fighting and started looting and plundering. The result of all this is that we are surrounded by Antony's troops

Enter Pindarus

Pin. Run away, my lord, run farther away. Mark Antony has reached the tents of your camp ; therefore, fly from here, noble Cassius.

Cas. This hill on which we stand is far enough from our tents (*so we need not fly any farther*). Look Titinius, are those my tents, where I see a fire burning?

Tit. Yes, my lord, they are (*our tents*).

Cas. Titinius, if you have any love for me, ride my horse and spur hard to make it run at its highest speed, so that it takes you to that place where those troops are, and, then come back fast enough. I want to be certain whether those troops are ours or our enemy's.

Tit. I shall return with the speed of thought (*I will be as quick as a thought*). [He goes

Cas. Go, Pindarus, climb higher on that hill. My eye-sight has always been dim (*weak*). Keep an eye on Titinius, and tell me all that you see around the battle-field. [Pindarus climbs up the hill

---

looting the people and the wounded soldiers, **Enclosed**—surrounded. **Perceive**—see. **Mount**—ride. **Hide**...........**in him**—spur the horse hard, so that it may run as fast as possible. **Even**...........**thought**—as quick as thought [the speed of thought is faster than that of light Thought can reach anywhere in no time.] **Ever thick**— always dim. **Regard**— observe; watch carefully. **Notest**—find; see. **Ascends**—climbs up.

This day I breathed first. Time is come round,
And where I did begin, there shall I end :
My life is run his compass. Sirrah, what news ?

Pin. [*Above*] O my lord !

Cas. What news ?

Pin. [*Above*] Titinius is *enclosed round about*
With horsemen that *make to him on the spur* ;
Yet he spurs on, Now they are almost on him.
Now, Titinius ! Now *some light* O, he lights too
He's *ta'en* [*Shout*]
And, hark ! they shout for joy,

Cas. Come down, behold no more.
O, coward that I am, to live so long,
To see my best friend ta'en before my face !,
[Pindarus descends.
Come hither, *sirrah* :
In Parthia did I take thee prisoner ;
And then I *swore thee, saving of thy life*;
That whatsoever I did bid thee do.
Thou shouldst *attempt it*. Come now, keep thine oath ;
Now be a freeman : and with this good sword.
That ran through Caesar's bowels *search* this bosom
Stand not to answer : here, take thou the *hilts*
And, when my face is cover'd as 'tis now,
Guide thou the sword. [Pindarus stabs him].
Caesar, thou art revenged,
Even with the sword that kill'd thee

Pin. So, I am free; yet would not so have been,
Durst I have *done my will*. O Cassius !
Far from this country Pindarus shall run.
Where never Roman shall *take note of* him. [Exit

Re-enter Titinius with Messala

Mes. It is but *change*, Titinius ; for Octavius
Is overthrown by noble Brutus' power.
As Cassius' legions are by Antony.

Tit. These *tidings* will well comfort Cassius.

Mes. Where did you leave him ?

This..........first—I was born on this day. **Time..........round**—the time of life has completed its circle [my life will end just where it began.] **My life..........compass**—my life has completed its full course [my life has reached the point where it will end]. **Enclosed.........about**—surrounded on all sides. **Make to him**—rush towards him **On the spur**—riding fast. **Some**—some of the soldiers. **Light**—alight ; dismount their horses. **Ta'en**—

This is the day I was born. The circle of my life has become complete. My life shall end on the day on which it began. My life has run its full course. Fellow, what news have you to give?

Pin. (*Above*) O my lord I

Cas. What is the news?

Pin. (From the hill top) Titinius is surrounded on all sides by soldiers on horse backs. They are rushing towards him at a fast speed. But Titinius is also rushing on (he has not turned back) Now they have almost reached him. O Titinius ! now some of them have dismounted. O ! Titinius also gets down his horse. He has been taken prisoner (*shout*). Listen, they are shouting out of joy.

Cas. Come down ; do not see all this any more. O, what a coward I am to live so long, and to see any friend taken prisoner in my very presence !

[Pindarus comes down the hill]

Come here, fellow. I took you prisoner in Parthia. And then sparing your life to you, I made you swear that you would do whatever I might order you to do. Now is the time for you to keep your oath. Become a free man, Take this sword. With this I killed Caesar. Thrust it into my chest. Hold the handle of the sword, and run it through my body when my face is covered like this.

[Pindarus stabs him

Pin. So, I am free now (*by killing my master*). But, if I could follow my own will I would not have killed my master to become a free man. O Cassius, I will go away to some far-off country where no Roman will ever see me. [He goes

Re-enter Titinius with Messala

Mes. It is only one of the exchanges of fortune, Titinius for Brutus' forces have defeated the troops under Octavius, and Cassius' troops have been defeated by Antony's.

Tit. Cassius will be glad to hear it.

Mes. Where did you leave Cassius ?

---

taken prisoner. **Sirrah**—fellow. **Swore thee**—made you swear. **Saving..........life**—sparing your life. **Attempt it**—do it now. **Search**—penetrate ; thrust into. **Stand**—wait. **Hilts** — handle of the sword. **Guide..........sword**—thrust the sword into my chest ; guide the sword into my body. **Done..........will**—acted according to my will. **Take note of**—see. **Change**—change of fortune ; exchange of fortune. **Tidings**—news.

Tit. All *disconsolate,*
With Pindarus, his *bondman*, on this hill
Mes. Is not that he that lies upon the ground ?
Tit. He lies not like *the living*, O my heart
Mes. Is not that he?
Tit. No. this was he, Messala,
But Cassius is no more. O setting sun,
As in thy red rays thou dost *sink* to-night,
So in his red blood *Cassius' day* is set ;
The sun of Rome is set ! Our day is done ;
Clouds, dews and dangers come ; our deeds are done !
Mistrust of my success hath done this deed.
Mes. Mistrust of good success hath done this deed.
O hateful error, *melancholy's child,*
Why dost thou show to the *apt* thoughts of men
The *things that are not* ? O *error*, soon *conceived,*
Thou never comest unto a happy birth,
But kill'st the *mother* that *engender'd* thee !
Tit. What Pindarus! Where art thou, Pindarus?
Mes. Seek him, Titinius, whilst I go to meet
The noble Brutus, *thrusting this report*
Into his ears : I may say thrusting it ;
For piercing *steel* and *darts envenomed,*
Shall be as *welcome* to the ears of Brutus,
As *tidings* of this *sight*.
Tit. *Hie* you Messala,
And I will seek for Pindarus *the while*. [Exit Messala.
Why didst thou send me forth, brave Cassius ?
Did I not meet thy friends ? and did not they
Put on my *brows* this *wreath* of victory.
And bid me give it thee ? Didst thou not hear their shouts ?
Alas, thou hast *misconstrued* everything !
But *hold thee*, take this garland on thy brow;
Thy Brutus bid me give it thee, and I
Will *do his bidding*. Brutus, come *apace*,
And see how I *regarded* Caius Cassius
By your leave, gods : this is a *Roman's part* :
Come, Cassius' sword, and find Titinius' hear.
[Kills himself.

Disconsolate—disappointed ; dejected. **Bondman**—slave. **The living**—one alive. **Sink**—set. **Cassius' day**—the sun of Cassius' life. **Mistrust..........success**—fear of the result of my mission. **Good success**—good result. **Melancholy's child**—product of sadness or grief [People suffering from melancholy (sadness) imagine dangers which do, not really exist). **Apt**—willing or ready to be deceived. **Things..........not**—things and dangers which really do not exist. **Error**—mistake ; misunderstanding. **Conceived**—born in the mind. **Mother**—melancholy which gives birth to this misunderstanding ; the

Tit. I left him here on this hill, all sad and disappointed. He was in the company of Pindarus, his slave.

Messala. Is not that Cassius who lies upon the ground there ?

Titinius He does not look to be alive. Alas ! my heart !

Mes. But, he is not Cassius?

Tit. No Messala, he was Cassius, but now he is not [because now it is only his dead body]. O, setting sun, just as you are sinking in the red glow of your red rays, similarly the sun of Cassius' life has sunk in the pool of his red blood. Glory of Rome has gone with Cassius ; now there is nothing but darkness for us all. Now it is a period of darkness, dews, misfortunes and dangers. Our work has ended. Fear of the bad result of my mission made him commit suicide.

Mes. Yes, doubt about good results has made him do this. O, hateful misunderstanding, you are a product of sadness. Why do you fill the minds of people with foolish fear of dangers which really do not exist ? O, misunderstanding, you are easily born in the minds of men, but your birth is evil, because you kill the person who gives you birth [*melancholic men give birth to fear of imaginary dangers, and this, misunderstanding, product of his own mind, kills him*]

Tit. But, where is Pindarus ? Pindarus !

Mes. You search for him. Titinius, and I go to see noble Brutus and break this news to him or thrust this news into his ears. I say thrust, because this bad news of Cassius' death will be as welcome to Brutus as daggers or poisoned arrows thrust into his body.

Tit. Hurry up Messala, and I will, in the meantime, search for Pindarus.
[Messala goes.

Brave Cassius, why did you send me away ? Did you not see that I had met your friends ? They had put this garland on my forehead as a token of their victory. Did you not know that they had asked me to give this garland to you? Did you not hear their shouts of joy ? Alas ! you misunderstood all that happened. But, wait, let me put this garland on your head. Your beloved Brutus ordered me to give this garland to you. Now I am carrying out his orders. Brutus, reach here quickly, and see how much respect and love I have for Cassius. Forgive me O gods ; I am now going to do what a brave Roman should do. I will thrust Cassius' sword into my heart.
[Titinius kills himself.

---

melancholy person. **Engender'd**—gave birth to; produced. **Thrusting..........report**—breaking this news **Steel**—dagger ; sword. **Darts**—arrows. **Envenomed**—poisoned. **Welcome**—pleasant **Tidings**—news. **Sight**—the scene of Cassius's dead body. **Hie**—make haste. **The while**—in the mean time. **Brow**—forehead. **Wreath**—garland. **Misconstrued**—misunderstood. **Hold thee**—stop. **Do..........bidding**—carry out his order. **Apace**—quickly. **Regarded**—respected. **Roman's part**—what a Roman should do.

Alarum. Re-enter Messala, with Brutus, young Cato, Strato, Volumnius, Lucillius.

Bru. Where, where, Messala, doth his body lie ?
Mes. Lo, *yonder*, and Titinius mourning it.
Bru. Titinius' face is *upward*.
Cato. He is *slain*.
Bru. O Julius Caesar, thou art *mighty* yet !
Thy spirit walks abroad and turns our swords
In our *own proper entrails*. [Low alarums.
Cato. Brave Titinius !
Look, whether he have not crown'd dead Cassius !
Bru. Are yet two Romans living such as these ?
The, last of all the Romans, fare thee well
It is impossible that ever Rome
Should *breed thy fellow*, Friends, I owe *moe* tears.
To this dead man then you shall see me pay.
I shall find time, Cassius, I shall find time.
Come, therefore, and to Thasos send his body;
His *funerals* shall not be in our camp.
Lest it *discomfort us*. Lucillius, come ;
And come young Cato : let us to the field.
Labeo, and Flavius, set our *battles* on :—
'Tis three o'clock; and, Romans, yet ere night
We shall *try fortune* in a second fight. [Exeunt

Scene IV—Another Part of the Field

Alarum. Enter fighting, Soldiers of both armies, then Brutus, young Cato, Lucillius and others.

Bru. Yet countrymen ; O, *yet hold up your heads* !
Cato. What *bastard* doth not ? Who will go with me ?
I will proclaim my name about the field :
I am the son of Marcus Cato, ho ! [*Charges the enemy.*
A foe to tyrants, and my country's friend ;
I am the son of Marcus Cato, ho ! [*Charges the enemy.*
Bru. And I am Brutus, Marcus Brutus, I ;
Brutus, my country's friend ; know me for Brutus
[*Exit* charging the enemy. Cato is overpowered, and falls.

Yonder—there. **Upward**—which means he is not mourning, he is not alive. **Slain**—killed. **Mighty**—powerful. **Own proper**—our own, own. (proper also means own; repetition is for emphasis. **Entrails**—bowels. **Breed**—produce. **Thy fellow**—your equal **Moe**—more. **Funerals**—funeral ceremonies. **Discomfort us**—discourages our troops. **Battles**—troops. **Try fortune**—try our luck. **Hold..........heads**—do not get discouraged ; do not lose heart. **Bastard**—mean fellow; ill-born.

Noise of battle. Re-enter Messala with Brutus, Strato, Volumnius, young Cato and Lucillius.

Bru. Where, Messala does the body of Cassius lie !

Mes. It is over there, and Titinius is mourning over it.

Bru. But Titinius is lying with his face upward.

Cato. He is also killed.

Bru. O, Julius Caesar ! you are still powerful. Your spirit is wandering about, and it makes our swords run into our own bowels.

[Low sounds of battle

Cato. Brave Titinius ! see he has placed the garland on the head of dead Cassius.

Bru. Can we find two living Romans as great as these two, who are lying dead ? You were last of the noble Romans. I bid you good bye. It is impossible that Rome should ever produce another Roman like you, Friend, I ought to shed more tears over the death of this man, than you see me shedding now. But, Cassius, I shall find time to do so. Come my friends, and send his body to Thasos, His funeral ceremonies should not be performed here in our camp, because it will fill our troops with grief, and make them disheartened. Come along Lucillius, and you Cato, we must move to the battle-field. Laboc and Flavius, Prepare our troops. It is now three o'clock ; before nightfall we shall try our luck in a second battle.

[*They go*

Scene IV—Another part of the field

Noise of battle. Enter fighting, soldiers of both armies; Brutus, young Cato, Lucillius and others

Bru. You, my countrymen, keep up your courage (*Do not get disheartened*).

Cato. Only some mean fellow would be disheartened. Who will follow me ? I will proclaim my name all over the battle field. All shall hear that I am the son of Marcus Cato, and like my father, I am the enemy of all cruel rulers, and a lover of my country.

Bru. And, I am Brutus, Marcus Brutus. I am a friend and lover of my country. Let every body know that I am Marcus Brutus

[He goes and Cato is overpowered. He falls

Luc. O young and noble Cato, art thou *down*?
Why, now thou diest as bravely as Titinius;
And *mayst be* honour'd, being Cato's son.

1 *Sold. Yield or* thou diest.

Luc. *Only I yield to die ;*
There is *so much* that thou will kill me *straight* ;
[*Offering money.*
Kill Brutus, and *be honour'd in his death.*

1 *Sold.* We must not. A noble prisoner !

2 *Sold.* Room, ho ; Tell Antony, Brutus is ta'en.

1 *Sold.* I'll tell the news. Here comes the general.

Enter Antony

Brutus is ta'en, Brutus is ta'en, my lord.

Ant. Where is he ?

Luc. Safe. Antony ; Brutus is safe enough :
I dare assure thee that no enemy
Shall ever take alive the noble Brutus :
The gods defend him from so great a shame !
When you do find him, *or* alive or dead,
He will be found like Brutus, like himself.

Ant. This is no Brutus, friends ; but I assure you,
A prize no less in worth. Keep this man safe;
Give him all kindness ; I had rather have,
Such men my friends, than enemies. Go on,
And see whether Brutus be alive, or dead;
And bring us word unto Octavius' tent,
How everything *is chanced.* [*Exeunt*

Scene V—Another part of the field

Enter Brutus, Dardanius, Clitus, Strato,
and Volumnius.

Bru. Come, poor *remains* of friends, rest on this rock.

Cli. Statilius show'd the torch light ; but, my lord,
He came not back : he is *or* ta'en or *slain.*

Bru. Sit thee down Clitus ; slaying is *the word* ;
It is a deed *in fashion.* Hark thee, Clitus. [*Whispers.*

Down—dead. **Mayst be**—may be. **Yield**—surrender. **Or**—otherwise **Only..........die**—I surrender only to be killed. **So much**—this much money. **Straight**—at once. **Be..........death**—win the honour of killing Brutus. **Or**— either. **A prize ....worth**—in worth a man equal to Brutus. **Is chanced**— has happened **Remains**—those who are still living. **Or**—either. **Slain**—killed. **The word**—the right word. **In fashion**—common; in vogue.

Luc. O, noble young Cato, have you also fallen dead ? You have died as bravely as Titinius. Being Cato's son, you will be honoured and remembered with respect.

1 *Sold.* Surrender, or I wilt kill you.

Luc. I surrender only to be killed. [*Or I will surrender only when I am dead*] Here I will offer you so much money, (*offers money*) if you kill me at once. I am Brutus (*Lucilius pretends to be Brutus*). Win the great honour of killing Brutus (*the most feared eneny of your generals*).

1 *Sold.* We must not kill Brutus. He is a noble man and is to be taken prisoner.

2 *Sold.* Make room, there. Tell Antony that Brutus has been taken prisoner.

1 *Sold.* I will give him this news. See, here comes the general Antony.

Enter Antony

My lord, Brutus has been taken prisoner.

Ant. Where is he ?

Luc. Brutus is safe, Antony ; he is quite safe. I assure you that no enemy of Brutus will ever capture him alive. May gods protect him from such dishonour. Whenever he is found, either dead or living, you will always find him free and noble as he is.

Ant. This is not Brutus, my friends, but I assure you that he is also an equally valuable prize. Keep this man safe ; be good and courteous to him. I would like such noble men to be my friends and not my enemies. Now go and find out whether Brutus is alive or dead. Bring us information in Octavius' tent how everything has happened. [They go

Scene V—Another part of the field

Enter Brutus, Dardanius, Clitus, Strato and Volumnius

Bru. Come, my poor friends, now you are the only ones left of my numerous friends. Come and sit on this rock for some rest

Clitus. Statilius gave the signal by waving a torch; but, my lord, he has not returned. He has been either taken prisoner or killed.

Bru. Sit down, Clitus ; killed is the right word. He has surely been killed. Now killing has become a very common thing (*it has become a fashion*), listen to me, Clitus. [*Whispers*

Cli. What, I my lord ? No, not for all the world :
Bru. *Peace* then ! no words.
Cli. I'll rather kill myself. [*Whispers*
Bru. Hark thee, Dardanius
Dar. Shall I do such a *deed* ?
Cli. O Dardanius !
Dar. O Clitus !
Cli. What ill request did Brutus make to thee ?
Dar. To kill him ; Clitus. Look, he *meditates*.

Cli. Now is that noble *vessel* full of grief.
That it runs over even at his eyes.

Bru. *Come higher*, good Volumnius, *list* a word.
Vol. What says my lord ?
Bru. Why this, Volumnius :
The ghost of Caesar hath appear'd to me
Two several *times* by night ; at Sardis once,
And, this last night, here in Philippi fields :
I know my *hour* is come.
Vol. Not so, my lord.
Bru. Nay, I am sure it is. Volumnius,
Thou seest the world, Volumnius, *how it goes* ;
Our enemies have *beat us to the pit* : [*Low alarums*
It is more worthy to leap in ourselves
Than *tarry* till they push us. Good Volumnius
Thou know'st that we two went to school together :
Even for that our love of old, I *prithee*,
Hold thou my sword-hilts, whilst I run on it.
Vol. That's not an *office* for a friend, my lord.
[*Alarum still.*
Cli. Fly, fly, my lord ; there is no tarrying here.

Peace—silence. **Deed**—an evil deed. **Meditates**—thinks. **Vessel**—man. **Come higher**—come here. **List**—listen. **Times**—on two different occasions. **Hour**—time to die. **How it goes**—how things are going. **Beat us**—driven us. **To the pit**—to the grave. **Tarry**—wait. **Prithee**—pray you ; request you. **Office**—duty ; function.

Clit. What do you say ? Shall I do such a thing ? No, my lord ? I would not do it even if I were to get this whole world for doing it [*I would not do it at any cost*]

Bru. Silence, then. Don't speak anything about it.

Clit. I will rather kill myself than do what you ask me to do.

Bru. Listen to me, Dardanius. [Whispers]

Dard. Do you think that I can ever do such a thing ?

Clit. O Dardanius !

Dar. O, Clitus !

Clit. What evil request did Brutus make to you ?

Dar. He asked me to kill him, Clitus. See he is lost in deep thought.

Clit. Now noble Brutus is so much full of grief that his eyes are full of tears [*his grief is flowing down his eyes in the form of tears*].

Bru. Come here, good Volumnius, listen to me.

Vol. What do you want to say, my lord ?

Bru. Well, this is what I have to say. Volumnius. I have seen Caesar's ghost on two different occasions, and each time it was in the night. First, I saw it at Sardis, and second time at Philippi, and it was only last night. I know that the end of my life (*the hour of my death*) is near.

Vol. No. my lord, do not say so.

Bru. No. I am sure it is so, Volumnius. You can see how our affairs are going on. Our enemies have defeated us, and they have driven us to the edge of our graves. [*We have been driven into the pit, just as wild animals are driven and trapped into the pits.*]

[Low noise of battle]

It is better for us to jump into the grave ourselves than to wait for our enemy to push us into it. [*It is better to kill ourselves than to get killed by the enemy, which means death as well as humiliation.*] Volumnius, my good friend, you very well remember that we two were school-fellows. In the name of that old friendship of ours, I request you to hold the handle of my sword, so that I may run on it, and kill myself.

[The noise of battle continues]

Vol. That is hardly the duty of a friend, my lord.

Clit. Run away, my lord. It is no time to stay here.

Bru. Farewell to you ; and you ; and you, Volumnius.
Strato, thou hast been all this while asleep;
Farewell to thee too, Strato. Countrymen,
My heart *doth joy*, that yet in all my life
I found no man *but he was* true to me.
I shall have glory by this *losing day*,
More than Octavius and Mark Antony
By this *vile conquest* shall attain unto.
So, fare you well at once ; for Brutus' tongue
Hath almost ended his life's history.
Night hangs upon mine eyes ; *my bones would rest*,
That have but labour'd to attain this hour.

[Alarum. Cry within, "*Fly, fly, fly* !"

Cli. Fly, my lord, fly, !

Bru. *Hence* ! I will follow

[*Exeunt* Clitus, Dardanius and Volumnius.

I prithee, Strato, stay thou *by* thy lord.
Thou art a fellow *of a good-respect* ;
Thy life hath had some *smatch* of honour in it ;
Hold then my sword, and turn away thy face,
While I do run upon it. Wilt thou, Strato ?

Stra. Give me your hand first. Fare you well, my lord,

Bru. Farewell, good Strato. [Runs on his sword]
Caesar, now *be still* :
I kill'd not thee *with half so good a will*. [*Dies*

Alarum. Retreat, Enter Octavius, Antony,
Messala, Lucilius and their Army.

Oct. What man is that ?

Mes. My master's man. Strato, where is thy master ?

Stra. Free from the *bondage* you are in, Messala;
The conquerors can but *make a fire of him*;
For Brutus only *overcame* himself,
And no man else hath honour by his death.

Lucil. So Brutus should be found. I thank thee, Brutus.
That thou hast proved Lucilius' saying true.

Doth joy—feels happy. **But he was**—who was not, **Losing day**—this day of my defeat. **Vile conquest**—mean, evil victory. **Night**—time of rest; death **My..........rest**—I will die and my bones would rest in the grave **Hence**—away ; you go away. **By**—near. **Of a good respect**—of good reputation. **Smatch**—smack; taste; touch. **Be still** —be at peace ; be calm [for you are avenged]. **With..........will**—with half so firm a determination [I did not kill you so willingly as I kill my-self, now). **Bondage**—chains of captivity ; state of being a prisoner. **Make..........him**—can only burn his body [but cannot capture him alive]. **Overcame**—conquered.

Bru. Farewell to you, to you and to you Volumnius Strato, you have been asleep all this time. Farewell to you also. My Country men, I am happy to think that during whole of my life, I have not found a man who was not loyal to me. This day's defeat will bring me greater honour than the honour which Octavius and Antony will get from their evil victory. So, I bid you good bye at once. I have already announced the end of my life (*my tongue has already spoken the last word about my life*). Now, darkness of death hangs over my head : my bones (*body*) that worked hard only to reach this end (*death*) now require eternal rest in death.

[Noise, cry within, fly, fly, fly.

Cli. O, my lord, run away at once.

Bru. You go away from here. I will follow you.

[Clitus, Dardanius and Volumnius go

Strato, I, pray, you stay back with me. You are a man with a good reputation. Your life has had a touch and taste of honour in it. Hold this sword of mine, and turn your face away while I run on this sword and kill myself.

Strato. Let me first shake your hand. I bid you farewell, my Lord.

Bru. Good Strato, I bid you farewell. [Runs on his sword

Caesar, now your spirit may rest in peace. I did not kill you as willingly as I have killed my self.

[Noise of battle. Sounds of retreat]

Enter Octavius, Antony. Messala, Lucilius and the army

Oct. Who is that man?

Mes. He is my master Brutus' servant. Strato, where is your master ?

Strato. He is now free from those chains of captivity in which you are bound, Messala. His enemies, who are victorious now, can only burn his body (*but cannot capture him alive*), Brutus conquered and killed himself ; no one else can claim the honour of conquering or killing Brutus.

Lucil. That was the proper end of a man like Brutus. I am thankful to you Brutus, that you have proved my words true (*He had said that Brutus will always remain a noble and free man*).

Oct. All that served Brutus. I will *entertain them*
Fellow, *wilt*, thou *bestow* thy time with me ?
Stra. Ay ; if Messala will *prefer* me to you.
Oct. Do so, good Messala.
Mes. How died my master, Strato ?
Stra. I held the sword, and he did run on it
Mes. Octavius then take him to follow thee,
That did the *latest service*, to my master.
Ant. This was the noblest Roman of them all :
All the conspirators, *save* only he,
Did that they did in envy of great Caesar ;
He only, *in a general honest thought*
And *common good to all, made one of them*,
His life was gentle, and the *elements*
So mix'd in him that Nature might stand up
And say to all the world, '*This was a man* !")
Oct. According to his *virtue* let us *use him*. [Execunt.
With all respect and *rites of burial*,
Within my tent his *bones* tonight shall lie,
Most like a soldier order'd honourably.
So call the *field* to rest; and *let's away*
To *part* the glories of this happy day.

Entertain them—-take into my service. **Wilt**— will. **Bestow**—spend. **Prefer**—recommend. **Latest service**—last act of kindness and faithfulness [killing Brutus in an honourable way]. **Save**—except. **In a general honest thought**—thinking of the common people; with the good of all Romans at his heart. **Common good to all**—for the common good of all Romans. **Made one of them**—became one of the conspirators. **Elements**—humours. **So mixed** ...... **him**—so perfectly blended and balanced in his nature. **This ...... man**—this was a perfect man. **Virtue**—noble character. **Use him**—treat him, **Rites of burial**—funeral ceremonies. **Bones**—dead body. **Field**—army; troops. **Let's. away**—let us go away. **Part**—share.

Oct. I will take into my service all those who were, till now, in the service of Brutus. My man, will you spend your time in my service ?

Stra. Yes, if Messala recommends me to you.

Oct. Do recommend him, good Messala

Mes. How did Brutus, my master, die, Strato ?

Stra. I held the sword, and he ran on it.

Mes. Octavius, you can take in your service this fellow who performed the last act of faithful service to my master (*Brutus*).

Ant. He was the noblest Roman of them all. All the conspirators except Brutus murdered Caesar because of jealousy and ill-will. But Brutus became one of the conspirators only for the common good of all Romans. All noble qualities and humours were so perfectly blended and balanced in his nature that Nature could stand proudly to proclaim that he was a perfect man.

Oct. We will treat him with all honour due to his noble character and will perform all funeral rites and ceremonies. To-night his dead body will rest in my tent with all honour and formality due to a brave warrior. Give the troops the signal for rest, and let us leave this place to share the glories of this day of glorious victory.

JULIUS CAESAR

QUESTIONS ON—

1. CHARACTERS
2. SCENES, INCIDENTS AND SITUATIONS

1. CHARACTERS

A word to the students : You have read the play. You have seen Brutus, Cassius. Julius Caesar, Antony, Calpurnia. Portia and a host of other characters. They have their virtues and weaknesses. For some, you have love and respect, for others, hatred. You have heard, all that they have said to one another and all that they have done to one another. Now it should not be difficult for you to make a fairly correct estimate of their personalities and characters.

Let us see how we can form an estimate of the character in a play.

1. The first thing that helps us in making an estimate of a character is all that he does and says. If he says good and intelligent things and does what he says, we can say that he is a good person.

2. The second thing that helps us is what other characters say about him. Here we should be careful. If a character is jealous of another character, he cannot see any goodness in that character. For example, Cassius is jealous of Caesar, so all that he says about Caesar is not wholly true. But Brutus is honest and he has no grudge against Caesar. So what he says about Caesar may be believed.

3. We should see what a character says and does in a particular situation. What are his professions and what are his real motives.

4. Soliloquy (स्वगत भाषण) gives us a glimpse into the head and mind and the real motives of a character. Cassius' soliloquy shows he has a grudge against Caesar. Antony's few words to himself, when the mob takes away the body of Caesar, show that he is an opportunist. He loves the living Caesar but he hands over the dead Caesar' to the mob. He is happy that the mischief is afoot. He does not bother about Rome and the Romans.

Great scholars and commentators have drawn the character-sketches of the characters in 'Julius Caesar'. We must read them later on. But, first we should make our own estimate of these characters. It is not important what others say about them. What is important is what we think of them.

I. CHARACTER OF JULIUS CAESAR

His power and popularity

We see, Caesar is the most powerful and popular Roman of his times. He is the hero of the common people. They worship him almost as a god. The common people are out in the streets to see their hero pass in a victory procession through the streets of Rome. When Brutus tells the angry mob that they killed Caesar because Caesar was ambitious, they cry "let Brutus be Caesar". It means that Caesar is so popular with the masses that his name has become a by-word for a man who is great and indispensable. He is loved not only by the masses but also by noble and honest men like Brutus. Brutus calls him the foremost man of this world. Caesar is feared and respected by his followers. When he speaks, Casca says.

"*Peace ho ! Caesar speaks*"

Antony is all love and admiration for Caesar. He says, "when Caesar says 'do this' it is done". In the Senate House we see how all the grey-haired senators look up to him for favour. Casca fawns almost like a dog. Cassius goes down on his knees and requests Caesar to recall Metellus Cimber's brother from his exile. All this proves that Caesar is undoubtedly the most popular and powerful Roman of his time. He is so popular and powerful that even after his death, his name and his spirit take a terrible revenge on his murderers. Antony exploits Caesar's name to rouse the anger of the mob against the conspirators.

His Intelligence and fearlessness

Caesar has a quick understanding of the characters of the people around him. He makes a correct estimate of the character of Cassius when he says

Such men as he be never at heart's ease
Whiles they behold a greater than themselves
And therefore they are dangerous

The editor of "Arden Shakespeare", says that a man who can judge his fellow men with this penetration, should rightly stand at the head of his nation". We see that Caesar has all intelligence and understanding to be the beloved leader of his people. He is brave and fearless. In his funeral speech Antony speaks of Caesar's great victories, and the wealth and trophies that he brought to Rome. Caesar's words sincerely express his fearlessness :

'*Cowards die many times before their death.*
The valiant taste of death but once.

His firmness

Caesar is a man of strong will and firm determination. The terrible storm of the night, the warning of the soothsayer and the requests of his wife fail to change his mind. When his servant brings the warning of the augurers, Caesar remains firm on his decision to go to the Senate House. He decides not to go only when his wife falls on her knees and requests him to stay at home. Though it looks that some fear was there in Caesar's mind, because when Decius gives a better interpretation to Calpurnia's dream, Caesar at once decides to go. But he remains firm in case of Cimber's brother's exile. All appeals fail to move him.

He is not ambitious but kind and generous

Brutus fears Caesar's ambition. But in the play we do not find anything which can prove Caesar to be ambitious. Brutus himself says—to speak truth of Caesar,

I have not known when his affections sway'd

More than his reason.

It means that Caesar is a just and reasonable man. He is very gentle and polite to the conspirators when they come to take him to the Senate House. He offers them wine and shakes hands with them like a good friend. What Antony says about Caesar may be wrong. But what Caesar's 'will' under his seal says cannot be belied. His 'will' gives a lot of his personal property to the people. An ambitious and power hungry man will never love his people so much and so sincerely. Again, if Caesar were ambitious he could gladly accept the Crown that was offered to him thrice. Artemidorus gives Caesar a piece of paper. He asks Caesar to read it because it concerns him most. At this Caesar says "What touches us ourself shall be last served". It also proves that Caesar is more concerned about the needs of others than about his own self.

His weakness

No man is a picture of perfection. Every man has his virtues and weaknesses. Caesar is no exception to this rule. Many people find Shakespeare's Julius Caesar as a bundle of weaknesses.

He is boastful and haughty

Caesar is a brave and fearless man, but he boasts of his bravery so often and in such a tone that he appears to be a haughty and boastful man. First he describes Cassius as a dangerous man, and then at once, he tells Antony that he is telling him what should be feared, not what he fears. He cannot fear anything because he is Caesar after all. This haughtiness and arrogance becomes more offending when he says that he and danger are "two lions littered in one day, and I the elder and more terrible." Caesar's arrogance becomes intolerable and inexcusable in the Senate-House. He compares himself to the Pole Star and says that there is only one man who is firm in this world. And that man is he himself. Then he uses foul language. He calls Cassius a dog and says if Cassius behaves like a dog Caesar will kick him, as a dog should be kicked. Caesar often uses his name. Instead of saying. 'I am listening'. He says "Speak, Caesar listens." This also shows that he considers himself nothing less than a king.

His physical weakness

Shakespeare's Caesar suffers from some bodily weaknesses. He is deaf in one ear. He suffers from falling sickness. Casca tells us how he fainted, fell and foamed at the mouth when the mob cheered him. Cassius tells Brutus how once he defeated Caesar in a swimming competition and also how he saved Caesar from being drowned in the flooded Tiber. He also tells Brutus how under a fit of fever in Spain he trembled, and like a sick girl, cried for water. But Cassius is jealous of Caesar. All that he says about Caesar should be taken with a grain of salt.

Superstitious

Caesar seems to have one more weakness, he is superstitious. When he is about to leave for the Senate-House, he sends his servant to the augurers to tell them to offer a sacrifice. He wants to know what will happen to him on that day. But this belief in augurers was a universal belief in Caesar's time. We should not call him superstitious. When his wife talks about the evil omens, he says that they are there for all. Why should he alone be afraid of them? Again, when the servant tells him that the sacrificed animal has no heart, Caesar gives it a different interpretation. He says that it means that Caesar, will be a man without a heart if he does not go to the Senate-House. The warnings of soothsayer does not move him. But he does have some fear lurking in his heart, because he agrees to stay not because of his wife. If it were so, why does he again decide to go after Decius', better interpretation of the dream? His wife is still there !

His vacillating mind and love of flattery

We feel that at times Caesar behaves like a fickle minded man. First he sends his servant to the augurers to know what they say about his day's mission. Then he pays no heed to their warning ; he does not agree to stay at home. But when his wife falls on her knees, he changes his mind and agrees to stay. But when Decius Brutus gives a different interpretation to it, Caesar laughs at his wife's foolish fears and again changes his decision. He decides to go. Decius tells us how Caesar loves to be flattered. Some critics say that Caesar falls a victim to Decius' subtle flattery. But flattery is the weakness of most of the great men.

His attitude towards his wife

One more weakness of Caesar is his indifference to his wife. In this respect he is a typical soldier. He can love his wife, pet her, fondle and humour her, but he does not have any regard and respect for her individuality. In this matter Brutus is a nobler and better husband. Brutus loves his wife and respects her. He is ready to share all his secrets with his wife. Caesar considers his wife only a woman not to be consulted on and trusted with important matters. First he agrees to stay at home to 'humour her', the next moment he calls her fears 'foolish fears' and goes out.

In conclusion we can say that inspite of a few weaknesses of his, Julius Caesar is the most powerful, most popular, deeply loved, greatly admired and highly respected Roman of his time. He is a brave general, a beloved leader, a kind, just and able administrator. His murder makes him even more powerful. It is his name and his spirit which win in the end. Brutus calls him the foremost man of this world. At last both Brutus and Cassius surrender to the spirit of Caesar.

Seeing Cassius dead, Brutus says : —

> " *O Julius Caesar, thou art mighty yet* !
> *Thy spirit walks abroad, and turns our swords*
> *In our own proper entails.*

When Brutus kills himself, his last words are

> *Caesar be now still;*
> *I kill'd not thee with half so good a will.*

Great Caesar fell a victim to the jealousy of men smaller than he. Brutus loved and admired him truly, but his honesty was blind to the realities. He killed Caesar not for what he really was but for what he might have become

QUESTIONS

Q. 1. Write a character sketch of Julius Caesar.

Ans. Please see the character of Julius Caesar above.

Q. 2. Discuss the character of Caesar under the following headings :—

(*a*) **Attitude towards his wife.** (*b*) **Popularity in Rome.** (*c*) **Boastfulness, and** (*d*) **Superstitious nature.**

Ans. (*a*) No man is a perfect being. Caesar too is a man after all. He has his weaknesses. His attitude towards his wife is the attitude of a typical man of action. For him his wife is a pretty thing to be fondled, petted and humoured. We see him only twice in the company of his wife. Both the times we feel that he does not have that respect and regard for the individuality of his wife that Brutus has for his wife, Portia. In Act I Scene (*ii*) he calls his wife with no word of respect or endearment. It is just 'Calpurnia'. Calpurnia cannot hear him because of noise. The great general again calls Calpurnia, when she says. "Here my lord". He just orders her "stand you directly in Antonio's way." This really is no way to talk to a wife in the presence of so many people. After that Calpurnia is out of his mind. Again when they return from the race of Lupercalia. Calpurnia is there, but there is no talk of her or with her. After this, we see Calpurnia and Caesar together at home. Calpurnia has had a bad dream. She is terrified by the strange happenings of the stormy night. She requests Caesar not to go to the Senate-House. Caesar just tries to laugh away her fears. He boasts of his fearlessness, but shows no consideration for the genuine feelings and fears of his wife. When his wife falls on her knees, the great general melts. But he says "*For thy humour I will stay at home*". He is still staying not for love, but only to satisfy a whim of his wife. For him she is just incapable of understanding great things. And, then comes Decius, who gives a different interpretation to her dream. And the great general is again his real self. Now he forgets his wife's humour. He says:

"*How foolish do your fears seem now, Calpurnia,*
I am ashamed I did yield to them
Give me my robe, for I will go.

This is no way of behaving with a loving wife. He treats her more as a pet maid servant than a beloved and honourable wife.

(*b*) Caesar is undoubtedly the most popular man in Rome. He is the darling of the common people. Gaily dressed crowds are out in the streets to see their beloved hero pass in a victory procession through the streets of Rome. They will scatter flowers in his path. Except a few disgruntled men like Cassius, Casca Flavius, Marullus and company, Caesar is loved and respected by all the distinguished Romans. Brutus loves and admires him greatly. He calls him the 'foremost man of this world'. Antony almost worships him. Octavius' servant stands stunned to see Caesar's dead body. He bursts into tears. These are tears of genuine grief over the death of a beloved hero. Caesar is so popular that even after his death his name is a by-word for greatness and honour. The angry mob understands nothing of Brutus' logic, but they respect Brutus and they cry. 'Let Brutus be Caesar'. For them Caesar was so great that they would honour Brutus by making him Caesar. Antony very clearly exploits this wide popularity of Caesar and rouses the mob's fury against the conspirators.

(*c*) The greatest defect in Caesar is his haughtiness and boastfulness. He is a fearless fighter, a great general, but he too often speaks of his fearlessness and firmness in a very haughty tone and boastful language. When he talks to Antony about Cassius, he says that Cassius is a dangerous man, but also adds that he is not afraid of him. He boasts: —

"*I rather tell thee what is to be feared*
Than what I fear ; for always I am Caesar"

When the servant brings a warning from the augurers, Caesar boasts even more offensively. He says that he is more dangerous than danger :—

"*We* (*Caesar and danger*) *are two lions littered in one day*

And I the elder and more terrible.

In the Senate, just before his death, Caesar becomes very haughty and boastful. He compares himself to the Pole-Star. He says that he is the only man who is constant, firm and fixed like the Pole Star. He becomes abusive even, and calls Cassius a dog and threatens to kick him. Caesar is really very haughty.

(*d*) In a way Caesar seems to be superstitious. He sends a servant to the augurers. He believes in augurers and foretellers. Though he says that he will stay at home to humour his wife, yet we feel that in the heart of his hearts he has some fear. Because as soon as Decius Brutus gives a better interpretation of the dream, Caesar at once stands to go. It means his wife's humour was not the only consideration that was detaining him. But, let us not forget that offering of sacrifices and consulting augurers was a universal practice in ancient Rome. We may call it superstition but for Caesar's contemporaries it was no superstition ; Caesar is not superstitious, because he does not pay any heed to the warning given by the soothsayer and the augurers. If he were superstitious, he would himself decide not to go to the Senate House. His wife's crying in the night and her terrible dream did not fill him with any superstitious fear.

Q. 3. *The murder of Caesar was not only a crime but also a blunder.* **"Discuss this statement."**

Ans. The murder of Caesar was a crime because any murder by one man or a group of men is a crime in the eyes of law. Murder in a declared war alone, is not a crime. Caesar was the man holding the highest position in the administration of Rome. He was one of the most important law makers and administrators. In fact, he was a virtual dictator. His word was law. So his murder was a crime, because it was against the law of Rome.

The murder of Caesar however, was the greatest blunder which harmed Rome and the Romans. It resulted in a terrible civil war which took the toll of some of the best Romans. On both sides there were Romans. The Romans shed the blood of their own brethren. It was a great loss to Rome in man and money. God alone knows, how many soldiers of Octavius and Antony, were killed. And how many soldiers of Cassius and Brutus were killed. It was really what Antony had prophesied. It was a civil strife that encumbered (*harassed*) the whole of Italy.

Caesar's murder was a blunder, because Rome of Caesar's time required a strong and competent commander like Caesar. The masses, the common people of Rome could not understand, and much less appreciate the value of honour, freedom and self rule. They could worship and follow a hero like Caesar. Only a few disgruntled officials like Flavius and Marullus, and a few persons who were jealous of Caesar's growing power were after Caesar's blood. Their personal grudge against Caesar made them blind to the political realities of Rome of that age. Cassius was shrewd enough to win honest but impractical Brutus to his side. But in his jealousy even shrewd Cassius failed to see that Rome and Romans required a strong man like Caesar. They killed Caesar but they could not kill the spirit of Caesar. Brutus, the impractical idealist thought that by killing Caesar they could kill Caesar's spirit. He was not against Caesar but against Caesar's ambition. He was as one critic puts it, 'honest but blind'. Caesar's murder was really a blunder committed by blind men. Brutus was blind because of his impractical idealism and others were blind because of their jealousy or, ill will against Caesar.

They killed Caesar, but brought in power Antony, a far more ambitious, cruel and crooked man than Caesar. Caesar was kind, generous, polite, competent and practical. Antony is only practical, otherwise he is a self-centred opportunist who can use even his closest friend as a tool. The other two with whom Antony shares the power are Lepidus and Octavius Caesar. They are no match to Caesar in wisdom, power and popularity.

Brutus, the idealist, is lost in the world of his books and philosophic thoughts. He frankly admits in a soliloquy that he has found Caesar reasonable and good. He joins the conspiracy only because he feared that Caesar might, some day, become a dictator, and a danger to Rome's freedom. This false logic of Brutus led him to the blunder of murdering Caesar. All others like Cassius and Casca blundered in the blindness caused by their ill will or jealousy.

II. CHARACTER OF MARCUS BRUTUS

Character of Marcus Brutus is far more complex than the characters of Julius Caesar, Caius Cassius and Mark Antony. According to the editor of Arden Shakespeare, Brutus is the dramatic hero of "Julius Caesar". The play "Julius Caesar" tells us the story of the revenge and victory of Caesar, but it is a tragedy of the fall of noble Brutus.

His honesty, integrity and respect

Out of all the characters in Julius Caesar, Brutus is a man of the greatest honesty and integrity. He is respected and honoured by all. In Casca's words, he sits high in all the people's hearts. There is no one who has even a word to say against Brutus. This integrity and moral force of his character makes him the leader of the conspiracy which took birth in the mind of Cassius. Though he is impractical and less experienced than

Cassius in the practical and political affairs yet he overrules everyone. His judgement and decision prevails, though quite often it is wrong. Even Antony, his deadliest enemy pays him the most glowing tribute, and says :—

> *"His life was gentle ; and the elements*
> *So mixed in him that nature might stand up*
> *And say to all the world "This was a man"*

His patriotism

Brutus is a patriot to the back bone. He loves his country more than anything else. He loves Rome, the Romans and their freedom and honour. He says to Cassius : —

> *What is that you would impart to me?*
> *If it be aught toward the general good*
> *Set honour in one eye and death in the other*
> *And I will look on both indifferently."*

To Brutus death for the good of his country and countrymen is the highest honour. Cassius, the shrewd conspirator plays upon this patriotic feeling of Brutus. He knows that Brutus hates tyranny. He some-how convinces Brutus that Caesar is likely to become a tyrant. Brutus loves and admires Caesar. He is right in saying that he killed Caesar not because he loved Caesar less, but because he loved Rome more.

His gentleness and consideration for others who depend on him

Brutus is a stoic who looks on pleasures and pain indifferently. He has infinite capacity to bear personal loss or sorrow. When he quarrels with Cassius for quite some time, he gives no hint of the greatest loss he has suffered in the suicide of his wife Portia. But this stoic's heart is full of the milk of human kindness. He is all tenderness, consideration and love for those who depend on him. He calls his guards to come in and sleep on the cushions, because he knows that they must have been very much tired and sleepy. He gives to Lucillius, his slave, the love of a father. The most moving and lovable side of Brutus is revealed in his relationship with his wife. He is a tender, loving, and dearly loved husband. He has a great regard and respect for the individuality of his wife.

His nobleness

Noble is one adjective which every one uses for Brutus, for every one he is noble. In his funeral speech, Antony calls him noble only ironically. But even Antony knows that Brutus is a noble man. In his last tribute Antony calls him the noblest Roman of them all. And it is a tribute paid in all sincerity. Brutus' nobleness coupled with his tenderness and love of his country makes him a man "with himself at war". Love of his people makes him fear Caesar's power. Love of Caesar makes him weep for Caesar even while he is stabbing him.

His power of inspiring loyalty

In the whole play, Brutus is one man who has no one disloyal to him. A sick old man, named Ligarius is ready to do the impossible if noble Brutus but orders him. In the last scene of the play, one by one, Brutus requests his friends to hold his sword so that he may run on it. But they all shrink back in horror. Brutus is right when be says.

"*My heart doth joy that yet in all my life*
I found no man but he was true to me,

His defects : Impractical

But Brutus, the noble-minded idealist, too, has his weaknesses. Brutus is a thinker, an idealist who is at home only in the world of books and ideas. As a man of action he fails. He has no understanding of human nature and human motives. For him every one is as noble as he himself is. He cannot see Cassius' jealousy. He misreads Antony and considers him only a limb of Caesar. He commits a blunder when he rejects Cassius' proposal to kill Antony along with Caesar. His next blunder is that he allows Antony to address the mob. There also he overrules Cassius' practical proposal. In this matter Brutus is a foil to Cassius who is more practical, and has a better understanding of people with whom he is dealing.

His sense of moral superiority, and his arrogance

Caesar's power and bravery makes him arrogant. Brutus' sense of moral superiority makes him blind as well as arrogant. He overrules all practical proposals just because he feels that he alone knows what is morally right. His arrogance is seen in the quarrel scene. In a very haughty and arrogant tone he says to Cassius.

"*There is no terror, Cassius, in your threats*
For I am arm'd so strong in honesty.

It is this moral arrogance of Brutus which makes him unreasonable, inconsiderate and even unjust to his fellow conspirators. He rejects Metellus Cimber's proposal to include Cicero also. He says, O, name him not !

For he will never follow anything
That other men begin.

Ironically, these words apply to Brutus as well. He also does not follow anything suggested by other men.

Conclusion

The Tragic Hero. Inspite of all his impracticality and moral arrogance. Brutus is a great character in Julius Caesar. Brutus is honourable, respectable and also lovable. He is really the most lovable character. We feel the horror of Caesar's murder, but we don't feel any pity or love for Caesar. We are not moved to tears by the suicides of Cassius and Titinius.

But we are moved almost to tears near the end of the quarrel scene when we see the deep wound that Portia's tragic end has given him. With this pain in his heart, he naturally became harsh to Cassius. But we cannot help loving him when we see that he forgives Cassius. Reconciled with Cassius, he tries to drown his sorrow in wine, and later, in music. With these shocks and wounds, Brutus is tender and loving to his guards and his slave. We feel pity for his fall and death, because we love him. We feel horror because, for a slight flaw of his character, such a noble and great man meets a tragic end. This pity and horror which Brutus' end fills in our heart make him the tragic hero of the play Julius Caesar.

QUESTIONS

Q. 4. Give in your own words the character sketch of Brutus.

Ans. For answer see "character of Marcus Brutus" above.

Q. 5. Write a note on the good and bad points of Brutus. What is your impression about his character ?

Ans.

Good points of Brutus—

Brutus' nobleness and honesty. Brutus is noble and honest.

He hates dishonesty and cruelty. He quarrels with Cassius because the latter exacted bribe from the people. Noble Brutus rejects Cassius' proposal to kill Antony along with Caesar, because he does not want unnecessary bloodshed. Only Caesar should be killed, because, according to Brutus, Caesar alone is a danger to Rome.

Brutus is a great Patriot. Brutus loves his country and his countrymen more than anything else. Death, for his country would be an honour for him. He joins the conspirators and kills his beloved friend only for the common good of his people. He has no personnel grudge against Caesar.

Brutus is a kind and loving man. Brutus has great power to endure personal loss and pain. But to others he is kind and tender. He loves his wife dearly. He gives to his slave the love of a father. He is kind and considerate even to his guards. When they are tired, he calls them in to sleep on the cushions in his tent.

He is loved and respected by all. Brutus is honoured and loved by all. Even Antony, his deadliest enemy, calls him "the noblest Roman of them all."

His bad points :—

Impractical. Brutus is an idealist. He is at home in the world of books, thoughts and theories. But he is an impractical man fated to fail in the field of action. He has no understanding of human nature and character. He is blind to the ill-will which his fellow conspirators bear against Caesar. Shrewd Cassius leads him by the nose, in the beginning at least. He misreads

Antony' character. His nobleness makes him the leader of the conspiracy. No one opposes him. But as leader he commits blunders after blunders and along with his followers meets a tragic end.

Arrogant as a leader. Brutus is all love, tenderness and kindness as a man. But he is quite arrogant, inconsiderate and even unjust as a leader. He always overrides the practical proposals of his followers. As a leader he thinks that he alone knows what is right. He knows no defect in Caesar yet he decides to join his killers for the good of Rome. But once involved in a bloody business, he arrogantly rejects the proposal of killing Antony along with Caesar. He gives a pompous moral lecture about killing the spirit and not tearing the body of Caesar to pieces.

But for all his impracticality and arrogance and ignorance, Brutus is the noblest Roman of them all. He fails only as a leader of a bloody conspiracy. But to the end he remains a noble minded man, honest, loving and lovable. His nobleness is his greatest weakness. He thinks that every one is as reasonable, honest and patriotic as he himself. I admire Brutus for his nobleness and integrity. I love him for his kindness. It is a pity that he has fallen among wrong men. He takes in hand a job for which he is totally unfit emotionally, intellectually and temperamentally. I feel that Brutus joins the conspirators because a very shrewd and cunning man like Cassius works upon his noble nature, in a very subtle way.

III. CHARACTER OF CASSIUS

A practical politician and man of action

Cassius is a thoroughly practical politician and man of action. He has a sharp and shrewd mind which can quickly read the characters of people with whom he deals. He knows their virtues and weaknesses. He knows Brutus's love of honour and freedom. In Scene (*i*) of Act II we see how cleverly Cassius plays upon Brutus's love of honour, and his patriotism. He knows Casca's hatred for Caesar and his importance for the success of the conspiracy. Noble minded Brutus considers Antony only a limb of Caesar. But the far-sighted Cassius knows that Antony will be the greatest threat to the cause of the conspirators. He gives the right advice of killing Antony along with Caesar. Again, after Caesar's murder he warns Brutus not to allow Antony to address the mob. But Brutus overrules it. The conspirators pay very dearly for this mistake of Brutus. Whenever there is a debate between Brutus and Cassius we see that Cassius is always right in his understanding of the situation and suggesting the way to tackle it. Brutus is always wrong. Cassius' suggestion to wait for the enemy at Sardis was also sound and practical.

Unprincipled

Men of action are often unscrupulous. Their one aim is to achieve their aim. They do not bother about means. They can adopt any and every means to achieve their end. Cassius is also such a man. His one aim is to kill Caesar who has become almost a dictator in Rome. Cassius is hatching a conspiracy against Caesar. He wants the support of some prominent and respectable men like Brutus. He must win people to his side by hook or by crook. He flatters Brutus in a subtle way, reminds him of his great ancestor who considered the rule of a king in Rome as the rule of an everlasting Devil. Thus, he poisons the mind of Brutus and flatters him by appealing to his sense of honour and love of freedom. He is not satisfied with this. He gives Cinna some forged letters and asks him to throw them into Brutus' room. So, for Cassius, flattery, forgery and deceit are all justified as means to achieve his end. In the quarrel scene, we see he defends Pella who had exacted bribe. He says that such things should be overlooked in a time of crises. He himself is guilty of selling higher posts for money.

Jealous of Caesar

Brutus loves Caesar and admires him. But like Flavius and Marullus, Cassius is jealous of Caesar. He himself says "Caesar bears me hard". It means he also bears Caesar hard. He has some personal grudge against Caesar. His ill will against Caesar becomes clear when he describes Caesar as a 'man of feeble temper' who in a fit of fever cried 'as a sick girl'. It is sheer jealousy which makes Cassius blind to the real greatness and worth of Caesar.

His republicanism

Cassius has a personal grudge against Caesar no doubt. But his hatred of tyranny and love of republicanism is genuine. He hatched a conspiracy against Caesar not only because he hates Caesar, but also because Caesar has become a virtual dictator. There is a genuine ring in his outburst when he says :

'*Now is it Rome indeed, and room enough*
When there is in it but one only man.

His devotion and submission to Brutus

Cassius is deeply devoted to Brutus. It seems that Brutus' nobleness forces him to surrender himself to Brutus. He knows that Brutus is wrong. Yet he yields and lets Brutus have his way. Most probably moral inferiority of Cassius deprives him of the courage to oppose Brutus with firmness. His love for Brutus, however is genuine. In the quarrel scene we see that Cassius keeps a wonderful control over himself. When he hears of Portia's death his grief is genuine and his sympathy for Brutus shows that he is not just a calculating crook with no human goodness. Cassius has his other good points also. He is a brave fighter, a good commander and a man who has loyal followers. Titinius calls him the Sun of Rome, and kills himself and falls near Cassius' dead body. Brutus pays a glowing tribute to him. He says that Rome will never more have a great man like Cassius.

Caesar's estimate of Cassius' character

In Act I, Scene (*i*) Caesar gives quite a correct estimate of Cassius' character. Cassius is a lean and thin half-starved looking man. He is given to too much reading and brooding. He is a minute observer of men, manners and motives. According to Caesar, men like Cassius are dangerous, because :—

Such men as he be never at heart's ease
Whiles they behold a greater than themselves.

Caesar's estimate of Cassius is fairly accurate. He is a schemer, a plotter, and a man who cannot surrender to any tyrant. But Cassius is not only jealous of Caesar, he also hates Caesar, because he has become a dictator, a tyrant.

QUESTIONS

Q. 6. Write a note on the good and bad points of Caius Cassius. What is your impression of his character ?

Answer.

Good points of Cassius. Cassius is a shrewd man with a sharp mind. He is politically and practically a far-sighted man. He has good understanding of human nature and human character. Cassius understands Brutus, Antony and others well. He knows how to deal with them. He is more practical than Brutus.

Cassius is a sincere and devoted friend. He is sincere and faithful to the cause of republicanism. He may not be honest, but he honours honesty in Brutus and surrenders to it. His love of Brutus and devotion to him is genuine. Even in the quarrel scene he keeps himself under control. Brutus is harsh to him, but Cassius is still restrained. It is Cassius who takes first step towards reconciliation.

Cassius has loyal friends and followers. It proves that he has something good and great in him. Titinius, his loyal friend, calls him the Sun of Rome. Noble Brutus pays him the most glowing tribute when he says :—

"It is impossible that ever Rome
Should breed thy fellow"

Bad points. Cassius is jealous of Caesar. He uses his intelligence and understanding in scheming and plotting, and hatching a conspiracy against Caesar. He has no principles. He wants to achieve his end. He does not bother about the means. He flatters Brutus and gets forged letters thrown into his room. He flatters Casca also. His only aim is to rouse their hatred for Caesar, and win them over to his side.

Cassius has no sense of honour. He is greedy. He sells higher posts for money. He appoints incompetent people on higher posts. He defends Pella who exacted bribes from the Sardinians.

Impression. Cassius has many bad points. But he has some saving graces also. He is not an opportunist like Antony who can use a friend as an ass. Cassius does commit a crime in hatching a conspiracy against Caesar. He does it out of jealousy. But it is not jealousy alone. He hates tyranny. And a tyrant can be got rid of only if he is murdered. We feel if Cassius were the leader of the conspiracy, he could be a match to Antony. If republicans were victorious, all the faults of Cassius would have become his virtues. Brutus' nobleness does the greatest harm to Cassius and his cause. Cassius cannot contradict Brutus, and Brutus cannot win a victory. So, Cassius, we feel is also, like Brutus, a victim of circumstances.

IV. CHARACTER OF ANTONY

A pleasure-seeking young man

Caesar himself says of Antony that he loves plays, music and sports. He says that Antony revels and indulges in merry-making late in the nights. Cassius also, calls him a "masker and reveller".

Clever and resourceful

But as soon as Caesar is murdered, Antony, the pleasure seeker, becomes a resourceful man of action. He meets the murderers of Caesar with their own weapons and takes a terrible revenge on them. At first he runs home in panic. But soon he sends his servant to seek 'Brutus' permission to meet them. Brutus gives the permission, Antony comes and he still does not hide his love for Caesar. As he enters, he first pays his tribute to Caesar. He is very clever. He does this only to impress noble Brutus with his sincerity to Caesar. He is sincere. But here he expresses this sincerity knowingly, with a purpose. Then in a very subtle way he requests them to kill him if they so desire. He knows that noble Brutus would not allow them to do any harm to him. Then he very cleverly flatters Brutus, and says that he will be with them, but they should give him some satisfactory explanation for Caesar's murder. When he has fully studied the mood of the conspirators, he requests Brutus to allow him to take Caesar's body to the market place, and to make a funeral speech from the stage. Cassius warns Brutus. But Antony gets what he wants.

A great orator

Antony's practical wisdom, his deep understanding of mob-mind, his power of playing upon the hearts and minds of the people are revealed in his funeral speech. He does not talk of freedom and honour, which masses do not understand. He just proves that. Caesar was not ambitious. First, he does not say anything against the conspirators. He calls Brutus noble, but proves that noble Brutus is wrong in calling Caesar ambitious. He gives concrete examples to prove that Caesar was not ambitious. Then he mentions the will of Caesar and says that he will not read it. This he does only to make the people more anxious to hear the will read. In short, Antony uses every trick to rouse the mob against the conspirators. He sobs, weeps, and then chides them for being ungrateful to Caesar. Then he gets down and shows the holes made in Caesar's cloak by the daggers of his murderers. And when the mob is moved to tears, he uncovers the dead body of Caesar. Antony proves more than a match to Brutus' nobleness and Cassius' practicality. The mob runs mad for the blood of the conspirators. Then Antony becomes the master of the situation. With the help of Octavius and Lepidus, he organises a strong army and gives a crushing defeat to the conspirators.

Cruel and unprincipled

Antony is really a very cruel and unprincipled self seeker. He uses the name of Caesar only to quench his thirst for power by rousing the mob against the conspirators. He loved Caesar when he was alive. Dead Caesar, his name, his popularity are now, for Antony, only a means to attain power. Even Caesar's dead body is used by him as a means to achieve his end. He lets the angry mob carry it. Himself he says :—

"*Now let it work, mischief thou art afoot,*

Take thou what course thou wilt"

He has roused a storm, and he will fish in troubled waters. He has no thought of Rome, Romans or even Caesar. He crushes the conspirators not to avenge Caesar, but to fortify his own position. In the proscription scene he barters the life of his nephew for the life of Lepidus' brother. He insults Caesar's spirit when he tampers (हेरा-फेरी) with Caesar's will. To say that he did it with the concurrence of his colleagues is not to defend it. Colleagues or no colleagues, a man who professed such love for Caesar should never have agreed to such a plan. Not only this, Antony is a treacherous man, When Lepidus is away, he tells Octavius that they should use Lepidus only as a tool, rather an ass.

His love of Caesar

Antony has genuine love for Caesar. His out-bursts during his funeral oration, do tell of his love for Caesar. He is shocked at Caesar's murder.

He is sincere when he curses the murderers of Caesar. But when he is in power he has no thought of Caesar. Even on the plains on Philippi it was Octavius Caesar, and not Antony, who talked of avenging Caesar. Antony only refers to their fawning before Caesar, and that too, as a biting retort.

We cannot make a correct estimate of Antony's character, because in the play we do not see him developing fully, as we see Brutus and Cassius. We know nothing about his relations with his soldiers, servants, fellows and friends. We know him only as a lover and admirer of Caesar, and as a public agitator.

V. CHARACTER OF CASCA

Timid treacherous and double-faced

Casca is a minor character. Cassius includes him among the conspirators because of his hatred for Caesar. He is a double faced man. When he is in the presence of Caesar, he is officious and flattering. But at Caesar's back he ridicules him. When he is with Caesar and Caesar says something, Casca at once shouts "Bid every noise still". He is almost a slave here. But when he describes the scene of offering of the Crown to Caesar, he ridicules Caesar. He is blunt and coarse, as well as inconsistent. First he pleads for Cicero to be included in the conspiracy, but when Brutus rejects the proposal, he says, 'Indeed he is not fit.'

Timid, but a boaster

Though Casca is a boaster, yet he is afraid of the stormy night and its strange happenings. First he is terror-stricken. The next moment he says that he will join the conspiracy and face any danger.

Brutus tells about Casca that he was quick mettle when he was a school going boy. But now he has grown stupid. Cassius says that he is still quick in carrying out any honourable plan. His bluntness is only a pose which makes his remarks more interesting.

Jealous of Caesar

Antony rightly calls him 'envious Casca'. Because it is he who first stabs Caesar in the back.

His contempt of the mob

Casca hates the common people. When he describes the scene of the feast of Lupercalia, he talks of the cracked hands, sweaty caps, and foul smelling breath of these dirty people. He says that choked with that bad breath, Caesar fainted. Casca himself did not open his lips lest the bad air should enter his lungs.

In short, Casca has no strength of character, and no independent opinion, He is jealous of Caesar, but has no courage to face him.

VI. CHARACTER OF CICERO

Though Cicero speaks only in the third scene and that, too, for a short while, yet we get a vivid picture of his personality. First we see him with his eyes red with anger. He returns with Caesar's train. Brutus says that Cicero:

"Locks with such ferret eyes
As we have seen him in the capitol
Being crossed in conference by some Senators".

We see that Cicero is a serious minded thinker. He is irritated and disgusted with the foolery he witnessed at the celebration of Lupercalia. Casca tells us that when Caesar begged the forgiveness of the mob, Cicero made some remark in Greek. Most probably it was some sarcastic remark aimed at Caesar. He is a greyhaired wise man who is respected for his wisdom and good judgement. That is why Metellus Cimber suggests that he should also be won over to their side.

Cicero is a philosopher and meets the terrors of the stormy night with a philosophic calm. Like a philosopher he says that people interpret things in their own way. They often fail to know the real meaning or significance of the things and so wrongly interpret them in their own way.

After this we do not see Cicero. We only hear that he was killed by the order of the Triumvirs.

VII. CHARACTER OF DECIUS BRUTUS

Self important

Decius Brutus is very proud of his power of trapping others through flattery and diplomacy. When Cassius says that Caesar may not come to the Senate House, Decius Brutus says that he will bring Caesar by flattering him very cleverly. He says—

Let me work
For I can give his humour the true bent
And I will bring him to the capitol

A clever man

He gives a different interpretation to Calpurnia's dream and proves that it is a good dream. Then he tells Caesar that some one may taunt him if he does not go to the Senate House. And then very cleverly he adds that he has said all this because he loves Caesar. Thus Decius Brutus is a flatterer who takes an undue advantage of Caesar's love for him.

VIII. CHARACTER OF LEPIDUS

Lepidus is one of the Triumvirs. Antony and Octavius Caesar are the other two. Octavius says that Lepidus is a 'tried and valiant soldier'. But we see that he is no more than an errand boy for Antony. He carries Antony's messages. Antony considers him only an ass whom they will set free as soon as his work is over. Lepidus has no will or opinion of his own. He is satisfied with the honour of being a Triumvir. He is, in Antony's opinion, as light unmeritable man fit to be used only as a tool. He agrees to kill his brother if Antony's nephew is also killed along with him. Really he is not a man but only a tool.

IX. CHARACTER OF OCTAVIUS CAESAR

A foil to Antony

Octavius Caesar's character presents a sharp contrast to the character of Antony. Octavius Caesar is calm, cold and firm, whereas Antony is fiery, impulsive and unstable.

Cold, authoritative and cunning

Though Antony is older and far more experienced than young Octavius, yet in the proscription scene Octavius speaks in the tone of a man with highest authority. As soon as Lepidus agrees to get his brother killed, Octavius does not wait, he says

"*Prick him down, Antony*"

In the battle-field of Pillippi also, he shows some impatience with words. He asks the leaders on the other side (*Brutus and Cassius*) to stop wasting words and start exchanging blows. He draws out his sword and declares that it will go back into its sheath only when all the thirty three wounds of Caesar have been avenged. He will either avenge Caesar's murder or die at the hands of Caesar's murderers. At last when he sees that the enemy is not yet in a mood to fight, he challenges them to come to the field and fight right now or whenever they are willing to fight.

His authoritative, almost imperious attitude is seen when Antony asks him to take his forces to the left. He tells him that he will keep to the right. When Antony says:

Why do you cross me in the exigent ?

Octavius Caesar's curt reply is "I do not cross you, but I will do so". Octavius Caesar is the living symbol of dead Caesar's spirit.

X. CHARACTER OF PORTIA

Portia appears on the stage only in two scenes and that too, not for very long time. Yet her character and personality stands before us quite vividly.

An ideal wife

Portia is a truly noble wife of a truly noble husband. She is legitimately proud of being the daughter of a noble father and wife of a noble husband. She is all love and devotion to her husband. She notices the strange behaviour of her husband. She sees that he is disturbed by some secret thoughts. But for some time she keeps quiet. She lets her husband to be free and alone. She has full faith in her husband. She knows that he will share his secret with her at the time he thinks proper. But when the conspirators with their faces covered come and hold some secret conference with her husband, her self-control gives way. Her woman's heart has its dark doubts and fears. When the conspirators leave, she at once comes to her husband. She requests him to tell her his secret that is troubling him.

Conscious of her right and duty as a wife

Portia is tender and loving, but she knows that as a wife, she has every right to share her husband's secrets, his pleasures and pains. First she kneels down and makes an appeal to him in the name of her love, her beauty, his vows of love, and the vow of marriage which joined them and made them one. When Brutus asks her not to kneel, she speaks in a moving and forceful language and with the confidence of a woman who knows her rights. She asks Brutus if she is his mistress or his keep who must be with him only for some time, or his wife, his better half who should share everything with him.

Her endurance and self control

Portia herself says that she is a woman, but at the same time, she is the daughter of a noble father and wife of a noble husband. From her stoic father she has inherited endurance and self control. She gave a wound to her thigh only to give a proof of her endurance. She assures her husband that she will never give out his secrets.

But a woman after all

For all her extraordinary endurance and stoic self-control. Portia is tender-hearted woman and devoted wife. As the time of the terrible deed draws nearer, her control gives way. She comes out and asks her servant just to go to the capitol and come back. She is so much disturbed and nervous under the strain of her anxiety about her husband's fate that she doesn't know what she is saying to her servant. She is so much excited that she hears a noise coming from the side of the capitol. It is all the doing of her excited imagination. She feels that she is too weak to bear the strain of keeping that secret. She fears that in her anxiety, she may blurt out the secret. She says :

How weak a thing
The heart of a woman is.

Portia is essentially a woman. Yet she keeps her word to her husband. Even in the end when she gets information that her husband is fighting a losing battle on the plains of Philippi, the strain of anxiety and the fear of the impending tragedy is too heavy for her to bear. But she keeps her word ; she kills herself by swallowing burning coals.

In short we find in Portia a perfect blending of all the qualities of a perfect woman. About her also, Nature can stand and proudly say. "This is a woman".

XI. CHARACTER OF CALPURNIA

Meek, submissive and a shadow of her husband

Calpurnia has no individuality of her own. She is just a shadow of her great lord, Caesar. First we see her with Caesar who is going to celebrate the festival of Lupercalia. Her husband calls her, and she says "Here my lord". He gives her an order, and she obeys, but says nothing. She has nothing of Portia's sense of honour and the consciousness of her rights as a wife. Next we see her with Caesar at his home. Caesar is ready to go to the Senate House. Calpurnia is worried about her husband. She has had a bad dream in the night. The strange happenings and the storm of the previous night and the evil omens have filled her with fear. She fears that there is some danger to her husband's life. Like a typical submissive wife Calpurnia requests Caesar not to go out. But Caesar simply laughs away her fears. For him they are foolish fears of a woman. Calpurnia falls on her knees and begs her husband not to go out. Like any other ordinary wife, she has only requests, tears and entreaties. She cannot assert herself as Portia does. It is only once that she uses words with some force. It is when she says to Caesar :

"*Your wisdom is consumed in confidence*"

But it is the outburst of a wife who otherwise feels helpless.

Superstitious

Calpurnia is superstitious, like any other ordinary woman of her age. Portia does not make any reference to the terrors or omens of the stormy night. But Calpurnia takes these omens as the warning given by gods. She believes that comets in the sky announce the death of kings and great men only.

Pitiable creature

She is a devoted but pitiable wife. She has no interest in the public life of her husband. She does not want to share his secrets. She does not ask any questions. She loves and wants to be loved. That is all for her.

QUESTIONS

Q. 7. How do Calpurnia and Portia strike you in the play *'Julius Caesar'* ?

Or

Compare and contrast the characters of Calpurnia and Portia quoting lines from the text where-ever possible?

Ans. Both, Calpurnia and Portia are deeply devoted wives to their husbands. Calpurnia is married to the most powerful and popular man in Rome. Portia is also married to a man who is highly respected in Rome.

Portia strikes us as a perfect woman and an ideal wife. Unlike Calpurnia she is legitimately proud of her noble father and noble husband. She has an individuality of her own. She is not a shadow of her husband, but a life-partner in the right sense of the word. She is conscious of her right as a wife and she asserts it forcefully. She knows that she is a woman, but not an ordinary woman. She has some of the strength and endurance of her father as well as her great husband. She gave a wound in her thigh just to prove that she can bear the pain of a wound like a brave fighter. She says to her husband :

I have made strong proof of my constancy
Giving myself a voluntary wound.
Here in the thigh can I bear that with patience
And not my husband's respect ?

She plainly tells her husband that she is his wife and not a keep or mistress. She must share her husband's pleasures and pains and his secrets as well. Portia is really a perfect woman. In her, the graces of the body, the force of character, the sharpness of intellect, and the tenderness of heart—all are beautifully and perfectly blended,

Calpurnia, on the other hand, is just a foil to Portia. She has no intellect, no force of character and no individuality of her own. She is just a shadow of her great husband. She is meek and submissive. Only once we see her being bold when she says to Caesar:

Alas my lord
Your wisdom is consumed in confidence
Do not go forth today, Call it my fear
That keeps you in the house, and not your own.

Her husband stays only for her "humour". As soon as Decius enters, she is forgotten. And at last her husband calls her fears "foolish" and goes to the Senate House. She is a loving and devoted wife, no doubt. But that is all, she is nothing more, She does not assert her right as a wife. She does not want to share her husband's secrets. She takes no interest in her great husband's public life. She has nothing of that manly courage and boldness which we see in Portia. We admire Portia, but we can at best, only pity Calpurnia. Calpurnia gets from her husband what she deserves. He loves her, pets her, humours her, but still he considers her only a woman not to be taken seriously in regard to important matters.

Portia gets from her husband all that she deserves—love, respect, admiration and devotion. We see Portia as a woman breaking under the weight of her husband's secret, and her anxiety about him and his mission. But this essential womanly tenderness is the most lovable trait of Portia, Her committing suicide too, is an honourable act even though done out of despair.

In conclusion we can say that Portia strikes us as a perfect woman, where-as, Calpurnia appears to be only a shadow of her great husband. We have love and admiration for Portia, Calpurnia deserves only our pity and sympathy.

XII. MINOR CHARACTERS

1. Cinna, the poet

Cinna appears only once and he falls a victim to the fury of the mob excited by Antony. They tear this poor poet simply because his name is Cinna, and it is the name of a conspirator also. Cinna impresses us as a witty and intelligent man. The way he answers the mob shows his wit. Several of them put him several questions and everyone wants an answer immediately. Cinna answers them all at one and at the same time. His death at the hands of the mob proves that a mob is really a mindless multitude.

2. The Tribunes

Flavius and Marullus, the two Tribunes appear only in the first scene. Then we hear about them that they have been dismissed under the orders of Caesar for disrobing the statues of Caesar.

Both these Tribunes are jealous of Caesar's growing power. They fear that Caesar is becoming all powerful in Rome. They think that honours heaped on Caesar are like his wings. He will rise high with these wings. So they decide to remove all decorations, from Caesar' statues. They rebuke the gaily dressed people who are out in the streets. They tell the mob that Caesar has won no great victory. He is returning only after killing the sons of Pompey who was once their hero.

Flavius is older. He is somewhat sympathetic to the people. He advises them as an elderly man. He does not rebuke them as Marullus does. Marullus is younger in age. He is very harsh and abusive. He seems to have nothing but contempt for the common mob. He calls them 'knaves' 'saucy fellows' 'blocks and stones' and etc.

The Tribunes give us the first hint that some kind of hostility towards Caesar is brewing in Rome. Some officials and members of upper classes are jealous of Caesar's growing power. This hostility towards Caesar results in the conspiracy against Caesar and his murder.

3. Popilius Laena

Popilius Laena is a Senator and one of the conspirators. In the Senate-House he first wishes Cassius success in his enterprise. Then he goes to Caesar and whispers something to Caesar. This fills Cassius with some doubt. He thinks that their secret is out. Popilius Laena's whispering to Caesar brings out Cassius' lack of confidence. He is so much disturbed that he says that he will commit suicide if their secret is out. Brutus, on other hand is confident and firm. He does not lose his balance of mind. He looks at Caesar who is smiling. He assures Cassius that Laena has not said anything about their conspiracy. For, hearing such a thing Caesar could not have smiled.

4. Cinna the conspirator

Cinna, is one of the conspirators. He plays an important part in the conspiracy against Caesar. Cassius trusts him. He sends Cinna with the forged letters to be thrown into Brutus' room. It means that Cassius has full faith in Cinna. Again it is Cinna who suggests that Brutus should also be won over to their side. Though Cassius has already done his work of winning Brutus, yet Cinna's independent suggestion shows his intelligence as well as importance among the conspirators.

It is Cinna who first shouts 'Liberty, Freedom, Tyranny is dead.' It shows his hatred for tyranny and love for freedom.

5. Metellus Cimber

He is one of the conspirators. He is with the conspirators because he has a personal grudge against Caesar. Caesar has banished (*exiled*) his brother from Rome. He remains faithful to the last. He starts the work of the conspirators in the Senate House. He is the first man to request Caesar to recall his brother from his exile. After that Cassius and Brutus appeal to Caesar. Caesar remains unmoved. Then Casca stabs Caesar in the neck. Thus we see that Metellus Cimber is also quite active among the conspirators.

6. Trebonius

He is also a conspirator. He is an important man among the conspirators. Because Artemidorus tries to warn Caesar against him. Cassius praises him for his action.

7 Publius

He is an old Senator. He does not play any important part in the conspiracy. He gets panicky when Caesar is murdered. Brutus has to assure him that no harm is going to be done to him.

8. Titinius

He is a friend of Cassius. He fights on the side of the republicans led by Brutus and Cassius. Titinius is deeply devoted to Cassius. For him Cassius is the Sun of Rome. When he sees Cassius' dead body, he says that the Sun of Rome has set with Cassius's death. His grief is so deep that he cannot bear it. He kills himself.

9. Messala

Is also a friend of Cassius. He also fights on the side of the republicans. He is not very much devoted to Cassius. When the conspirators have been defeated, he gladly joins the forces of Octavius Caesar.

10. Lucillius

Lucillius is a friend of Brutus. He considers Brutus a man of great honour. He is so much devoted to Brutus that in order to give Brutus a chance to escape, he poses to be Brutus before the soldiers of Antony. Faithful friends like Lucillius prove that Brutus was truly a noble man who inspired such faith and devotion in his friends.

11. Volumnius

Volumnius is an old friend of Brutus. He is also a devoted and faithful friend of Brutus. Brutus asks him to hold his sword, so that he may run on it and kill himself. But Volumnius shrinks back in horror of such an act. He cannot see Brutus dying.

12. Young Cato

Young Cato is also a devoted friend of Brutus. He fights on the side of the conspirators. He is a brave soldier and a noble man.

13. Lucius

Lucius is a young boy. He is very much devoted to his master. He is ever ready and glad to serve his master. Even when he is sleepy, he plays on his harp to please his master. Lucius brings out the tender side of Brutus' character. Brutus gives this young slave of his, the love and care of a father. When he is overpowered with sleep and dozes over his harp, Brutus himself takes away his harp. He lets him sleep with the love and affection of a father—rather, that of a mother.

14 Strato

Strato is also a devoted and faithful servant of Brutus. He is so much devoted and obedient that he cannot say 'no' to Brutus. When all other friends of Brutus refuse to hold a sword to let Brutus run on it, Strato obeys his master. He holds his sword and Brutus runs on it and kills himself. Strato is proud of his master. When Messala asks him about his master (*Brutus*), Strato says with legitimate pride :—

Free from bondage you are in, Messala

15. Pindarus

Pindarus is a slave of Cassius. He is loyal to his master. He obeys his master's order and stabs him to death. His master sets him free before he stabs him. But Pindarus says that he would not have his freedom if he could act according to his own will.

QUESTIONS

Q. 8. Write a note on the character of the mob, and the part played by it in *'Julius Caesar'*.

Or

What idea do you form of the common people of Rome from the play *'Julius Caesar ?'*

Ans. The mob (*the crowd of common people)* plays a very important role in 'Julius Caesar'. Besides Octavius and Antony, the mob is the third character which seals the fate of the conspirators and drives them to their doom.

Rough and crude. Common people in the Rome of Julius Caesar are like common people of everywhere and in every age. They are poor, ignorant, dirty and without any culture, good taste or refinement. First we see the mob in the first scene. They are wearing their best clothes. But Casca talks of their sweaty caps, their cracked hands and their foul-smelling breath, their shouting and throwing of caps in the air.

Fickle minded. The mob is vacillating and fickle-minded. Even the most reasonable man in a crowd loses his sense of judgement and sense of proportion. The crowd of common people in Julius Caesar is also fickle-minded. They are out in the streets to give a grand reception to Caesar. But when they are rebuked by the Tribunes, they go home like chidden dogs. They don't utter even a word of protest. So far Caesar was their hero. But when Marullus reminds them of Pompey, Caesar becomes the murderer of the sons of their former hero, Pompey. This fickle mindedness is seen in the scene in which Brutus and Antony make their funeral speeches. When Brutus speaks they are easily convinced that Caesar was ambitious and a tyrant. They cry 'Live Brutus Live'. One of them says 'Let him be Caesar' Another one says 'This Caesar was a tyrant'. The fact is that they have understood not a word of Brutus' philosophical speech. Yet they are all for Brutus, because he is before them on the stage. But when Antony, who understands the mob better, comes and makes an emotional speech, the common people are roused to such a fury that they are mad for the blood of the conspirators. Now Antony is noble, and Brutus is a murderer. Such is the fickle mindedness of the mob.

Cruel and senseless. The crowd of common people in Julius Caesar is very cruel also. When Antony has roused their passions and fury, they cry "Revenge ! About—Seek ! Burn—fire-kill. "They are after the blood of the conspirators. The senseless cruelty of the mob comes out with all its horror and nakedness in the scene in which they murder poor Cinna, the poet. First they put silly questions to him. When he tells his name, they take him for Cinna the conspirator. When he further explains that he is Cinna, the poet, and not Cinna the conspirator, then one of them says, 'kill him for his bad verses'. What is important for them is killing. None of them have even read his verses. Yet they must kill him on one pretext or the other.

Ignorant of the Political affairs. The common people everywhere remain indifferent to and ignorant of the political affairs. They remain busy earning their livelihood and enjoying themselves by snatches. They want some strong man to rule over them. They are hero worshippers. For them freedom, honour and self-respect are empty words. Brutus tells that they killed Caesar because Caesar was ambitious ; he had made Romans poor slaves. But the mob understands not a word of it. Brutus before them is their hero. So, they cry "let Brutus be Caesar."

Mob, a great force. But the common people are a great force. The man who knows the mob, and who can humour it, flatter it and excite it against his enemies, becomes the most powerful man. Caesar is powerful because he knows the mob. He can flatter them, he can convince them that he is all for them. Casca tells us how Caesar begged their pardon after coming to his senses. How he opened his doublet for them to stab him if he had displeased them. After Caesar, Antony is the man who has his fingers on the pulse of the mob. He knows that the mob is all emotion and passion. The common people can love, hate, be angry and may kill. But logic or reason, they don't understand. Antony rouses their love for Caesar; he makes an appeal to their hearts. He moves them to tears and finally rouses them to a mad fury. Brutus fails because he does not know the mob and cannot deal with it. Antony becomes the master of the situation, because he wins the sympathy of the mob and turns their fury on to the conspirators.

Q. 9. Discuss what you know of the common people of Rome, under the following heads,

(*a*) **Hero worship** (*b*) **Cruelty** (*c*) **Inability to understand political matters.**

Ans. (*a*) For Shakespeare, mob is really a mindless multitude. In Julius Caesar Shakespeare has painted the common people as irrational and blind hero-worshippers. Liberty has no meaning for them. They want a strong man—a hero to lead them. When Caesar is in power, he is their hero. They admire him and worship him. They cheer and applause Caesar. When a crown is offered to Caesar they grow mad with joy and excitement. They throw up their caps and rend the skies with their applause. And when Caesar is dead. Brutus becomes their hero. They fail to understand the logic of Brutus. They just shout 'let Brutus be Caesar'. They just want a hero,—a hero like Caesar whom they may follow blindly and worship like a god. Again, when Antony makes a moving speech, they forget all about Brutus and his justification of Caesar's murder. Now Caesar again becomes their hero. They run wild with anger. They rush to kill the conspirators who have murdered their beloved hero. They set the houses of the conspirators on fire. Antony knows this hero-worship of the common people of Rome. Very cunningly he wins their hearts and becomes their hero. With the help of these blind hero-worshippers, Antony gives a crushing defeat to the conspirators.

(*b*) This mindless mob is very cruel also. Once their passions are roused, they become wild and ferocious. Antony rouses the passions of the common people. They rush about mad with rage. They are out to catch, burn and kill all the conspirators. They meet Cinna, the poet. Their thirst for blood is so great that they tear the innocent poet to pieces. They tear him to pieces just because his name is Cinna, and a conspirator's name was also Cinna'.

(*c*) These common people have no understanding of the political matters. They know that Brutus is a noble and honest man. But they cannot understand why Brutus was also one of the killers of Caesar. Brutus says that he killed Caesar only because Caesar was ambitious. Caesar was becoming a threat to the freedom of Roman citizens. He had become a virtual dictator. But all these arguments fall flat on the deaf ears of these people. They just shout "Let Brutus be Caesar." They are quite incapable of understanding the political matters. They just cannot know what danger the powerful Caesar was to the Republic of Rome. When Antony rouses their emotions and passions, they become his worshippers. They need a hero. They understand and appreciate power. Political problems are too difficult and dull to rouse their interest.

COMPARISON OF CHARACTERS

Q. 10. *"Caesar dead is more powerful than Caesar alive"*. **Explain and illustrate.**

Or

Write a note on Caesar before and after his death.

Ans. Caesar alive is the most powerful and popular man in Rome of his time. We see that Caesar is a hero, almost a demi-god for the Roman masses. They love him and worship him. He is feared, loved and admired by the distinguished Romans who are close to him. Noble Brutus calls him the foremost man of the world. Antony admires him and is deeply devoted to him.

Yet living Caesar, we meet in Shakespeare's play, is a great man whose powers are now declining. He suffers from falling sickness. He is deaf in one ear. He is often haughty, bragging and boastful. He has grown superstitious also. He consults augurers. He believes that if Antony, while running the race on the eve of the feast of Lupercalia; touches his wife, she can be cured of her barrenness. Decius Brutus tells him that senators are going to offer him a Crown, and they may change their mind if he does not go to the Senate House. This makes Caesar decide to go. It shows that Caesar does have a hidden desire to wear the Crown. Before the mob he may have refused only to win their sympathy. But the greatest weakness of living Caesar is that a deep discontent is brewing among many people who are otherwise quite close to him. Officials like Flavius and Marullus, men like Cassius, Metellus Cimber, Casca and Cinna are jealous of his growing power. If Caesar had lived for a longer time this hostility and discontent would have spread among a larger number of people. And instead of a conspiracy there would have been an open revolt against Caesar. By hatching a conspiracy with a handful of their supporters Cassius and Brutus committed a blunder. Brutus wants to kill Caesar's spirit (*Caesarism*) in order to make Rome a republic. But by killing Caesar he only kills his body ; Caesar's spirit, *i.e.*, Caesarism, grows stronger.

After Caesar's death, Caesar's spirit rises younger and stronger. Young Antony and still younger Octavius Caesar keep the spirit of Caesar alive. They give a death blow to the conspirators and their cause of republicanism. Antony exploits Caesar's name and his popularity, to the maximum. He makes the wounds of dead Caesar rouse the Roman mob to a mad fury. He makes them remember Caesar, his greatness and his generosity. He makes them weep for Caesar and take a terrible revenge on the conspirators. In the very beginning he makes a prophecy that Caesar's spirit with Ate, the goddess of revenge will create havoc in the whole of

Rome. His prophecy comes true. Caesar's spirit becomes more powerful than living Caesar.

Ghost of Caesar haunts Brutus. Spirit of Caesar haunts his murderers in the battle camps. Caesar's ghost appears before Brutus first at Sardis and then at Philippi. Brutus himself confesses that Caesar is mighty even after his death. Over the dead body of Cassius, Brutus says.

O Julius Caesar thou art mighty yet
Thy spirit walks abroad, and turns our swords
in our own proper entrails

When Brutus kills himself, again he says,

"......... *Caesar, now be still*
I killed not thee with half so good a will."

Thus we see that Caesarism which the republicans want to kill grows stronger after Caesar's murder. It is right to say that Caesar dead is more powerful than Caesar alive.

Q. 11. Discuss the statement *"Cassius might have been a better politician than Brutus, Brutus was a better man".*

Or

Compare and contrast the characters of Brutus and Cassius.

Ans. Brutus is a conspirator not by choice. Brutus finds no fault in Caesar. He has no grudge against him, yet he joins the conspiracy. He does so not of his own choice, but under the effect of Cassius' clever working upon his noble nature and honest mind. A noble minded man who can neither think ill nor can speak ill of others should not undertake an enterprise which requires cruelty, unscrupulousness, deceit, lying and treachery. Brutus commits this mistake. Because of his nobleness he becomes the leader of the conspirators. But as a leader he commits blunders and pays for it with his life and the lives of his followers.

Brutus, a dreamer and idealist has no practical sense. He considers every one as noble minded as he himself is. He is blind to the weaknesses and evil intentions of his colleagues. He does not know that Cassius and others hate Caesar more than they love Rome. They all have personal grudge against Caesar. He does not know Cassius' real motive; that is why he falls an easy prey to his persuasion. He misreads Antony and considers him only a limb of Caesar. His noble mind hates unnecessary violence and bloodshed. So he rejects Cassius' practical proposal of killing Antony along with Caesar.

Cassius is a better politician. Cassius is gifted with all those qualities which a practical man of action must have. He is shrewd and cunning. He reads people's characters very quickly. He has quick insight into the hidden motives behind the moves of the enemies. He has a better grasp of the practical problems. His one aim is to achieve his end. He has no scruples about the means. He can use flattery, deceit, lying and forgery and bribery to achieve his aim. Every time Cassius' suggestions and proposals are more practical. He rightly suggests that Antony must be killed along with Caesar. Again he rightly warns Brutus not to allow Antony to address the mob, On the plains of Sardis he rightly proposes that their forces should wait there for the enemy forces. Because in coming there, the enemy forces will suffer some losses, consume some of their food and get tired. This proposal is also rejected by Brutus.

But Cassius is not a better man than Brutus. Compared with Brutus, Cassius appears a deceitful, clever and cunning person, who has no qualities which a good man must have. He is jealous of Caesar. He finds no good in Caesar. He flatters Brutus and poisons his mind against Caesar. He tells lies about Caesar's crying like a sick girl. He defends Pella who exacts bribes from the Sardinians.

Brutus is a political blunderer but a noble man. It is his honesty and nobleness that makes him a poor politician. He lives and admires Caesar. His motive in killing Caesar is a noble motive. All others are butchers of Caesar, Brutus alone is a sacrificer who sacrifices Caesar on the altar of his country's freedom. Brutus is kind and generous. He is kind even to his slaves and servants. Brutus is honest ; he quarrels with Cassius because Cassius exacted bribes and sold higher posts for money. He says that he would rather cut his heart into pieces and use them as coins than snatch money from the hands of the poor peasants. Brutus is so noble that he does not want unnecessary bloodshed. That is why he rejects Cassius' proposal of killing Antony also. As a husband Brutus is loving and devoted. He treats his wife with due regard and respects her for her individuality. In fact Brutus is a better man than Cassius. He is a perfect man. Even Antony his enemy also says, "He was the noblest Roman of them all." Brutus is a poor politician only because he is a better man.

Brutus and Cassius both love freedom. Both of them have great hatred for tyranny. Both have love and respect for each other. But that is all where they are similar. Otherwise Cassius serves as a foil to Brutus. His shrewdness and practical sense proves Brutus a poor politician. But his cruelty, his complete disregard of morality, his cold, calculating and callous approach to political problems which are human problems also prove Brutus a better and nobler man than he (*Cassius*).

Q. 12. Give the good and bad points of Caesar's character. What is your impression of his character ?

Ans.

Good Points :—

Power and popularity : Caesar is undoubtedly the most popular and powerful man. In the Rome of his times, he was loved and worshipped by the masses. Honest men like Brutus love and admire Caesar's goodness and greatness. Brutus more than once says that he has nothing against Caesar. He calls Caesar, 'the foremost man' of the world. All this shows that Caesar is a truly great man. Some people like Marullus Flavius, Cassius and Casca and Co. are jealous of him. But their jealousy is one more proof of Caesar's greatness.

Generous. Caesar is not ambitious, as Brutus wrongly thinks him to be. If he were ambitious he could gladly accept the crown that was offered to him thrice. His will under his seal is another proof of Caesar's generosity and his love of his countrymen. He leaves so much for his people.

Kind and unsuspecting. Caesar is a great and powerful man, yet he is free from suspicions and doubts. The conspirators who are after his blood, come to take him to the Senate House. Caesar receives them and offers them wine. Brutus, the honest man, feels the irony of the situation, but great Caesar has no suspicion. He is betrayed by those, whom he trusts most.

Bad Points :—

Physically declining. But this great general is now aging. He is deaf in one ear. He suffers from falling sickness.

Superstitious. He is somewhat superstitious also. Before going to the Senate House he sends his servant to the augurers. His wife asks him not to go, because evil omens of the night and her bad dream are a warning of some danger to his life. First Caesar boasts that he is more dangerous than danger itself. But it looks as if he were full of fear at heart, because be decides to stay. He says that he is staying for his wife's fear. But it is wrong. Because as soon as Decius Brutus gives a more agreeable interpretation to the dream, Caesar calls his wife's fears "foolish fears' and decides to go.

Haughty and boastful. Haughtiness and boastfulness of Caesar are his worst points. No one doubts Caesar's bravery and courage, but his repeated reference to his fearlessness shows his haughtiness and boastfulness :

> "*Danger knows full well*
> *That Caesar and he are two loins litter'd in one day*
> *And I the elder and more terrible*

It is an empty boast fit only for a youngster trying to impress his companions. From a great and mature man's mouth, these words are really offensive. In the Senate House, his haughtiness becomes all the more offensive. He boasts that in the whole world he is the only man who is firm and constant like the Pole Star. He comes down to an extent of abusing. He calls Cassius a dog and threatens to kick him, as a dog is kicked.

Love of flattery. One more, though minor, bad point of Caesar's character is his love of flattery. Decius Brutus flatters him by saying that his wife's dream indicates that Rome will receive new life and vitality from great Caesar, clever Decius works upon Caesar's serse of pride and persuades him to go to the Senate House.

Our impression of his character. Caesar is mortal after all; no mortal can claim to be an embodiment of perfection. He has his weaknesses. But all his weaknesses are common infirmities of men who are great and successful. Consulting augurers was a common practice in ancient Rome. This cannot be called a superstition. Caesar is haughty, but this is no excuse for the criminal murder of a great man. We feel that Caesar is a great man. The play does not give us much chance of seeing him doing great things. Much of him we know through reports of others. What Casca, and Cassius say of him is to be taken with a grain of salt. For, they both have personal grudge against him. Caesar certainly is not a 'sick girl' crying for water from the sick bed, as Cassius reports about him. We can believe Brutus for he is an honest man though a poor judge of man. Yet what he says of Caesar is true. Caesar certainly appears to be the foremost man if not of the world, at least of the Roman world of his time. Caesar has been betrayed and cruelly stabbed in the back by those whom he loved and trusted most. His love and regard for noble Brutus gives him the death blow, Mortally hit by Brutus' ingratitude, mighty Caesar falls with Brutus' name on his tongue.

Q. 13. Give the good and bad points of Antony's character. What is your impression of his character ?

Ans.

Good Points :—

Gamesome and pleasure seeking. We meet Antony as a healthy young man who hangs round Caesar and is ever ready to do what his great friend and hero asks him to do. Such people are open, frank, trusting and trust-worthy. Caesar also says this when he describes Cassius and compares him (*Antony*) with Cassius.

Devoted to Caesar. Out of all the people around Caesar, Antony is one who is sincerely and deeply devoted to Caesar. He is ever ready to obey Caesar. When Caesar asks him to touch Calpurnia, during the race, he says :

"*I shall remember,*
When Caesar says 'do this' it is performed

His grief over Caesar's death is genuine. He hurls curses upon the murderers of Caesar. He rouses the mob's fury against the conspirators and takes a terrible revenge for Caesar's murder.

Intelligent and a practical man of action. After Caesar's death there comes a sudden change in this pleasure-seeking youngman. He becomes a shrewd man of action, Very carefully and cautiously he returns to the Senate House. He deals with Brutus, Cassius and others in a very clever way. Inspite of Cassius' warning, Brutus allows him to take Caesar's dead body to the market place and make a funeral speech.

A great speaker. Antony is really a very good public speaker. He knows the art of handling the mob and holding its attention. He knows that reason and logic cut no ice with the crowds. Common people are all passions and emotions, and no reason. Antony's speech is really a master-piece of public speaking. With his theatrical gestures and moving words he rouses the mob against the conspirators.

Bad Points :—

Cold, cruel and calculating. After Caesar's murder, Antony undergoes a great change. He becomes cruel, cold and calculating. He flatters Brutus, and shakes hands with all the conspirators. He gives them an assurance that he will be with them if they give a satisfactory explanation for Caesar's murder. But all these are the calculated moves of a clever man who knows the situation and the people he has to deal with. He rouses the mob, and lets them go with Caesar's body. Very coldly he says :

"Mischief thou art afoot"
Take thou what course thou will,

This man is not worried about Rome and Romans. He has raised a storm which will blow off many an innocent man like Cinna, the poet. Cruel Antony will now fish in troubled waters. He will now be a Triumvir, one of the three highest Administrators.

Self centred ; ambitious and insincere. Antony certainly is a self-seeking and ambitious man. It is wrong to say that he does all this only to avenge Caesar's death. For such people, it is always out of sight out of mind. He loved Caesar when he was alive. But dead Caesar for him is only a property, like Lepidus. He uses Caesar's body, his wounds, his name, his popularity only to realize his dream of stepping into Caesar's shoes. In the proscription scene we see how cruel he is, and how insincere also. He agrees to kill his nephew if Lepidus is ready to kill his own brother. What a barter ! What a human bargain ! It was too cruel, even if it were a pose of impartiality. He sends Lepidus to bring Caesar's will. What for ? Because now he will tamper with sacred will and reduce the amount that Caesar had left for his people. Is it a tribute to Caesar ? Octavius and Antony both are ambitious. Antony is mean also. At Lepidus's back he calls him an ass and compares him to his horse. Some learned people may defend Antony but to us be looks like an unredeemed (बचाने के अयोग्य) monster of insincerity, cruelty and selfishness.

Our impression. In giving the good and bad points we have already given our impression. Still, if only to repeat, we find in Antony only one saving grace. He is deeply devoted to living Caesar. We do admire his intelligence and tact. We do stand wonder struck at his wonderful eloquence and oratory. But for all this, the lasting impression that he leaves upon our mind is that of a cruel, cold, calculating man who can do anything in order to achieve what he wants to achieve.

Q. 14. Compare and contrast the characters of Antony and Cassius.

Both practical politicians. Antony and Cassius are similar in many ways. Both are practical politicians. Both have good understanding of human nature and human motives. Cassius knows Antony as well as Antony knows Cassius. Cassius knows how the mind of a mob works. That is why he warns Brutus against permitting Antony to address the mob. Antony also knows what mob is. He handles the mob in a very intelligent way and turns their fury against the conspirators.

Both unprincipled. As practical men of action both Antony and Cassius are unprincipled. Their eyes are fixed on their end (*aim*). They can use any and every means to achieve it. They can flatter, lie, cheat, deceive and even kill those who stand in their way. Antony flatters the common crowd, sighs, sobs and weeps before them, just to rouse them against his enemies. Cassius also flatters Brutus and Casca to win them over to his side. He tells a few lies about Caesar only to poison Brutus' mind against Caesar. He sends forged letters to be thrown into Brutus' room. He suggests that Antony should also be killed along with Caesar. Antony in his turn, is equally cruel and unprincipled. Cassius exacts bribes, Antony tampers with Caesar's sacred will, just for money. He uses Lepidus only as an ass. He is ready to kill his nephew only if Lepidus kills his brother.

Both lack firmness. A man with a weak character generally has a weak will. This is true of both Antony and Cassius. Cassius always gives a right suggestion. But he is overruled by Brutus, who has a strong character and strong will. Cassius always gives way to Brutus. Antony too gives way to Octavius Caesar who has a stronger will. Antony is older and more experienced, but whenever there is a difference of opinion he yields to Octavius Caesar.

Both are impulsive and emotional. Brutus the leader of conspirators is a balanced man governed by his reason. But Cassius is emotional. His jealousy has made him blind to everything else. While quarrelling with Brutus, he himself admits that he has inherited an irritable temper from his mother. In the quarrel scene Brutus is harsher and more arrogant, but Cassius is more impulsive and emotional. He blows hot and cold in the same breath. First he says he may kill Brutus, and then he draws his sword and asks Brutus to tear out his heart. He often talks of committing suicide Antony is even more emotional. His love of Caesar and hatred for the conspirators are his only motives in taking a terrible revenge on the conspirators. He has no other thought. He does not think of Caesarism or Republicanism. He thinks only of Caesar whom he loved, and the conspirators who killed Caesar.

Both are deeply devoted to their leaders. Antony is deeply devoted to Caesar. Cassius also has real love and admiration for Brutus. He willingly bows down before Brutus. He does not become as harsh as Brutus when they quarrel in Brutus' tent. Antony admires Caesar and obeys him. He says :

"*When Caesar says 'do this', it is performed.'*

Contrast :

Cassius has some ideal. Antony has only a personal aim. But, in some way Antony and Cassius are different from each other. Antony has only one saving grace that is his love of Caesar. But Cassius has some touch of humanness in him. He is not selfish alone. His love of freedom and republicanism is genuine. He is fighting for a noble cause. His jealousy for Caesar is not the only cause of his hatching a conspiracy against Caesar. Antony, on the other hand, has no such impersonal motive.

Cassius is human ; Antony, inhuman and cruel. Cassius' love of Brutus is deep and moving. When he offers his bare breast for Brutus to stab, he is genuinely sad and shocked at his dear friend's harshness to him. When he hears the news of Portia's tragic death, he is almost in tears. He sincerely feels that he has been cruel in quarrelling with Brutus at a time when his heart was torn with such grief. We see nothing, of this love and attachment in Antony. Cassius has a brave friend who cannot bear the loss of his dear friend. For Titinius, Cassius is the Sun of Rome. Titinius kills himself when he sees his dear friend lying dead. Brutus pays the highest compliment to Cassius when he says that Rome will never more have a great man like Cassius. But Antony does not have any such near and dear friend attached to him. It seems as if after Caesar he has no one to love him, and no one to be loved by him. No love seems to have been lost between him and Octavius. Who knows if both of these ambitious adventurers were secretly treating each other as 'property' or mere-tools ! Antony surprises us with his ability and shrewdness. But for Cassius, we have some sympathy as well as love. He was not so bad a man after all. He remained true to the cause of conspiracy till his very end.

2. INCIDENTS, SCENES AND SITUATIONS

Q. 1. Write a short note on : *if Cassius were the leader of the conspirators.*

Or

Write a note on Cassius as a conspirator.

Ans. A shrewd man and a good judge of human nature and character. Cassius has all the qualities and qualifications which a politician, a man of action and schemer should have. He is sharp, shrewd, cunning and a very good judge of human nature and human motives. Brutus, his leader, misreads and misjudges every one around him. But Cassius has a deep insight into the hearts and minds of the people that he deals with. He knows how dangerous Antony can be. So he advises Brutus to kill Antony along with Caesar. He knows Brutus' patriotism and his love of freedom and honour. So he works upon his mind and wins him over to his side. If Cassius were the leader of the conspirators, the cause of republicanism would win a victory over Caesarism.

Unprincipled. As a man of action Cassius has his eyes on the aim or end. He can adopt any means to achieve his end. He is not like Brutus, who will not use any irregular or under-hand means. Cassius believes in killing all those who can be a danger to his cause. He can raise money through bribes and other irregular ways, because he knows that all is fair in love and war.

More experienced and better judge of situations and practical moves. As a conspirator Cassius is a better judge of a situation. He knows that after Caesar's murder the masses are in a state of shock and panic and excitement. They can be easily incited to do anything. That is why Cassius warns Brutus against Antony allowing him to address the mob. Really, if Cassius were the leader of the conspiracy Antony would not be alive to rouse the fury of the mob against them. Octavius Caesar was away. By the time he came to Rome, the conspirators could easily be the masters of the situation. Again, his suggestion that they should wait for the enemy at Sardis is correct. Here again Brutus has his way and the cause of conspiracy is doomed.

We can say that Cassius was a better politician. As the leader of the conspirators he would have been successful.

Q. 2. What do the two Tribunes say to common people crowding the streets ?

What estimate do you make of the character of these two Tribunes (*Marullus and Flavius*) ?

Or

Describe in your own words, scene first Act I of Julius Caesar'. What do you learn from this scene ? About the common people and the two Tribunes.

Ans. Marullus and Flavius, the two Tribunes find gaily dressed people crowding the streets. They ask them why they are making the working day a holiday. One of the people in the crowd says that they are going to welcome Caesar and rejoice in his victory.

At this Marullus, the younger Tribune, rebukes them. He asked them what great victory Caesar has won. He brings no prisoners tied to his chariot. He has not won any new territory. He has not brought any wealth to enrich treasury of Rome. Marullus calls them ungrateful wretches who have forgotten Pompey the great. He reminds them that many times when Pompey used to return after his great conquests, these very people used to rush out with their babies in arms. They used to climb on roofs, walls towers and chimney tops. There, they used to wait patiently for Pompey, their hero, to pass through the streets of Rome in a victory procession. But today, they have gathered to welcome Caesar, to scatter flowers in the path of Caesar who is returning to Rome after killing great Pompey's sons. Marullus tells them that gods will curse them for their ungratefulness towards Pompey. They should go home and fall on their knees and pray to gods to avert this misfortune.

Flavius, the elder Tribune who is gentler in his words calls them gentlemen and asks them to go home and weep and repent of their sin of ungratefulness.

The people move away like chidden dogs. Then Flavius says that they should go about the streets and remove the decorations from Caesar's statues. These honours, heaped on Caesar are making him the most powerful man in Rome.

We find that both these Tribunes are jealous of Caesar's growing power. They want that this rise of Caesar should be halted. We also note that Flavius the older of the two is softer to these commoners. He calls them idle creatures once. Then he calls them 'gentlemen'. Marullus the younger one is more abusive and harsher, 'Knaves' 'saucy fellows' are the abusive words which Marullus uses for them. We further note that Marullus is a bit superstitious and timid. When Flavius asks him to remove all the decorations from Caesar's statues, he says that it may be wrong to do so on the day of the feast of Lupercalia.

As far as the common people are concerned, we learn that they are fickle-minded and thoughtless. Once they worshipped Pompey. Now they worship Caesar. But when they are rebuked they go away like chidden dogs. No one of them puts even a word of protest. They are very much like dumb driven creatures who must be ruled and driven with a strong hand.

Q. 3. Show how Cassius succeeds in poisoning the mind of Brutus against Caesar in Act I Scene (*ii*).

Ans Cassius is a very shrewd and cunning man. He is jealous of Caesar. He wants to hatch a conspiracy against Caesar. He wants the support of distinguished and honourable men like Marcus Brutus. He proceeds very carefully and cautiously. Caesar and his train leave the stage. They have gone to take part in the celebrations of the feast of Lupercalia. Brutus and Cassius stay back.

First, Cassius complains against Brutus' indifference towards him. He says that now Brutus is not as warm and friendly to him as he used to be. Now he treats him harshly. Brutus, then, tells him that these days he is troubled by some problems of his own, His mind is torn between conflicting thoughts. He, sometimes forgets to show love and politeness to his friends only because of this mental conflict. He has nothing against his friends. He assures Cassius that he considers him (*Cassius*) one of his best friends.

Once assured of Brutus's friendship, Cassius takes one more step. He says that he is sorry that he misunderstood Brutus. Because of misunderstanding he kept away from Brutus many important things. Then Cassius tells Brutus that he (*Brutus*) is a great man, but he cannot see his own greatness, as his eye cannot see itself. Thus Cassius now tries to touch Brutus' sense of honour and self-respect. Brutus asks him into what danger he is trying to drag him, and why he is asking him to see in himself what he does not have. Very cleverly, Cassius passes on to assure Brutus that he (*Cassius*) is not a man who gives his love to any one and every one. At this point they hear a noise of shoutings. Brutus says that he fears that people have chosen Caesar their king. Now Cassius is assured. He gets a hint that Brutus also does not want that Caesar should become an all powerful king and destroy the freedom of Rome.

Brutus says that he loves Caesar, but he will not like him to be the king of Rome. Then he tells Cassius that for the common good of his people he will even die and feel honoured. Now cunning Cassius says that he does not know what Brutus and others think of these times. But, as far as he is concerned, he would rather die than live as a slave of Caesar who is just a mortal man like them. First, he calls Caesar their equal, but then he proceeds on to prove that Caesar is a man of weak temper. He has no strength and endurance. He tells how once he defeated Caesar in swimming competition in the flooded Tiber and how he saved him from being drowned. He also tells him how, once in Spain, Caesar was under a fit of fever, and how, like a sick girl he cried for water. Then, he says that the eye of this weak man today makes the Romans tremble. Cassius, who once defeated Caesar, is a petty man. He must bow down, if Caesar only nods at him. Cassius concludes his long dialogue, saying :

> '*Ye gods it doth amaze me*
> *A man of such feeble temper should*
> *So get the start of the majestic world*
> *And bear the palm alone.*

The real aim of Cassius is not to prove Caesar's weakness but to prove how powerful he has become now. He calls Caesar a colossus under whose huge legs the Romans peep about, and look for their graves. For, under Caesar they must live as slaves, or die and be buried as dishonourable men. Surely, Cassius is rousing Brutus's love of freedom. He is directly hinting that mighty Caesar has made all the Romans his petty slaves. Then Cassius goes on to say that Caesar has become so powerful only because Romans have lost their sense of honour and love of freedom. He says that Brutus' name is as sweet sounding as Caesar's, yet Caesar's name is on every body's tongue. Cassius is now trying to rouse Brutus' jealousy. He says that in every age there were many great and honourable men in Rome. But now there is only one great man in Rome. And that one man is Caesar. All others are mere slaves.

In the end cunning Cassius rouses Brutus' family pride. He reminds him of Junius Brutus who fought against the last king of Rome. Junius Brutus was, Marcus Brutus' ancestor.

Thus we see that Cassius has filled Brutus' mind with dark doubts about Caesar. Brutus is not yet fully won over. But the poison is now in, and it has started working, because Brutus says !

> *Brutus had rather be a villager*
> *Than to repute himself a son of Rome*
> *Under these hard conditions as this time*
> *Is like to lay upon us.*

Now Brutus also confesses that he is not satisfied with the conditions prevailing in Rome.

Then Cassius uses Casca. Casca returns with Caesar's team. He tells them how three times Antony offered Caesar a crown; how every time he refused it. The people shouted every time the crown was refused. Casca also throws a hint that though Caesar refused the crown, yet in his heart of hearts he had a desire to wear it. Thus Cassius' fears are now confirmed by Casca's words. Brutus' mind is now all the more poisoned. He takes leave of Casca and Cassius. But now the poison poured by Cassius is at work.

Q. 4. Describe the circumstances leading to Caesar's death.

Do you think Caesar's pride was reasonable for his death ?

Ans. Caesar's growing power and popularity and jealousy and discontent among some people close to Caesar. Caesar returns to Rome after defeating and killing Pompey's sons. Now he has no one to challenge his authority in Rome. But deep discontent is brewing among some people who are close to Caesar. They feel inferior in the presence of this great general and mighty conqueror. They are both afraid and jealous of Caesar. Marullus, Flavius. Casca Cassius and many others are such people. They are jealous of Caesar. There are men like Metellus Cimber who have been personally hit by Caesar's orders. They bear personal grudge against Caesar.

Fear of Caesar's becoming a king. The common people in Rome want a strong man like Caesar who can rule over them. They want Caesar to be their king. The Senators also decide to offer Caesar a crown. This thing shocks the freedom loving and honourable Romans like Brutus. Brutus is one of the murderers of Caesar simply because he fears Caesar. He fears that as a king Caesar will become a danger to the freedom and honour of Rome and the Romans.

Presence of a clever and cunning organizer like Cassius. Brutus has nothing against Caesar. But clever Cassius so poisons his mind that he also joins the conspiracy. Cassius finds out all others who bear a grudge against Caesar. He brings them together and makes an elaborate plan to murder Caesar in the Senate House.

Caesar's own weaknesses. The murderers should still have an excuse to murder Caesar. How should they behave in the Senate House ? They decide to go as petitioners. Cassius knows that Caesar is haughty as well as obstinate. He is certain that Caesar will not grant their request, rather he will be haughty and threatening. That will give them an excuse to stab him under provocation. This is exactly what happens in the Senate House. Metellus Cimber requests Caesar to call his brother back from his exile. Brutus and Cassius plead for Cimber's brother, Caesar remains adamant. Very boastfully he compares himself to the Pole Star. He comes down to an extent of abusing. He calls Cassius a dog and threatens to kick him, as he would kick a dog. This haughtiness of Caesar becomes the immediate cause of Caesar's murder.

It is true that Caesar's pride is one of the causes of his murder. If Caesar had paid some heed to the warning of the soothsayer, his augurers, and his wife, he might have saved himself. But in fact, it is Caesar's growing power rather than his pride which is the real cause of his murder. The conspirators were jealous not of his pride but of his power. Cassius already had his fears that Caesar might not come to the Senate House. So even if Caesar had stayed back that day, the conspirators would have chosen some other day. So the real cause of Caesar's murder is his growing power and the fear of his becoming a king. Clever Cassius makes no reference to Caesar's pride. He harps on the one string—Caesar's power and his worthlessness.

Q. 5. How does Cassius manage to win over Brutus to his side against Caesar ?

What impression do you form of his character?

Ans. Cassius is a very shrewd and cunning man. He knows that Brutus loves and admires Caesar. But he knows this also that Brutus is a lover of freedom and honour of his country and people. So very cleverly Cassius proceeds to prove that Caesar has become the most powerful man in Rome. He has become a virtual dictator, and the people are going to make him king of Rome. First Cassius proves that Caesar is a weak and worthless man. He tells Brutus how, once, he defeated Caesar in a swimming contest and how he saved him from drowning in the flooded Tiber ; how once in a fit of fever, Caesar cried for water like a sick girl. Then he says that he wonders how this worthless man has become so powerful in Rome. Now he is the only great man in Rome. All others are his slaves.

Cassius then touches Brutus' family pride. He reminds him of Junius Brutus, the great ancestor of Marcus Brutus. He fought against the last king of Rome and drove him out of Rome.

Thus Cassius poisons Brutus' mind against Caesar. He puts in Brutus' mind dark doubts about Caesar. But Cassius is a practical man of action. He asks Brutus to detain Casca when he returns with Caesar's train. Casca tells them how Antony thrice offered a crown to Caesar and how every time Caesar refused to have it. The crowd shouted every time Caesar refused the crown. Casca also tells them how in his heart of hearts Caesar seemed to be unwilling to let the crown go. The clever Cassius gets Brutus' fears confirmed. He already knows Casca's hatred for Caesar. He knows that Casca will give a report that will corroborate what he has already told Brutus. Thus he pours poison in Brutus' mind.

But Cassius is a practical man. He will not leave anything half done. He makes a plan. He forges some letters in different hand writings. These letters will make an appeal to Brutus to see his greatness and do something to set the wrongs right. Brutus will think that those letters are from different Roman citizens. So cunning Cassius uses even forgery to win Brutus to his side. Cassius gives these letters to Cinna and asks him to put them at different places in Brutus' house.

In Act II Scene (*ii*) we see Brutus smarting under the effect of the poison poured into his mind by Cassius. He is torn between his love for Caesar and his love for Rome.

Brutus is alone in his garden, He is debating with himself. He says that now he finds nothing wrong in Caesar. But if he becomes a king, he may become a danger to the freedom of Rome and the Romans. So he should be killed before he becomes the king of Rome. Then, his servant gives him a letter forged by Cassius. Brutus reads it. And at last he says :

Rome I make thee promise

If the redress will follow. thou receivest

Thy full petition at the hand of Brutus.

Brutus has been won over. But Cassius must not leave it here. Along with other conspirators, he bursts upon Brutus at mid-night. He does not want to give Brutus time to cool down. He believes in striking when the iron is hot. They hold a meeting and almost unconsciously Brutus becomes the leader. It is Brutus who rejects the proposal of taking an oath, who rejects the proposal of winning Cicero to their side and who rejects the proposal of killing Antony along with Caesar. Thus cunning Cassius wins over Brutus and makes him the most important man among the conspirators.

We find that Cassius is a very shrewd, sharp and cunning man. He is a great plotter and schemer. He has a thorough understanding of the nature and character of the people around him. He knows Brutus and successfully wins him over to his side. He understands Antony, and rightly proposes that he should be killed along with Caesar. He knows the importance of the ritual of oath-taking. But the impractical Brutus is ignorant of these matters.

Cassius lacks moral courage. Cassius can flatter Brutus and deceive him through forged letters. But we find that Cassius has a weaker will and weaker character. That is why he always gives way to Brutus. He knows that Brutus is wrong. But he lacks moral courage to oppose Brutus.

Q. 6. What did Brutus tell the Roman people in explanation of the murder of Caesar ?

What was the effect of his speech on his listeners ?

Ans. Brutus is a thinker, a philosopher. He is ignorant of the working of the common people's minds. He thinks that all of them are as honest, rational, noble and patriotic as he. He does not know that a mob is all emotions and passions, no reason.

Brutus gets to the pulpit and tells the crowd of the people that he loved Caesar and admired his greatness. He was happy that Caesar was fortunate. Yet they killed Caesar because Caesar was ambitious.

Brutus makes an appeal to the sense of honour and love of freedom of his listeners. He says that they are all freedom-loving honourable Romans. No one of them will like to live as a slave.

By killing Caesar, he has done a wrong only to that man who has no love for his country and who has no love of freedom. He asks them if there is any such man. But, not understanding even a word of what Brutus said, they all cry "None, Brutus none". Brutus tells them that he loved Caesar, but he loves Rome more. He killed Caesar because Caesar was a danger to the freedom of Rome and the Romans. He tells them that he has done to Caesar what they all should do to him (*Brutus*) if he also becomes a danger to the freedom of Rome and the Romans.

Brutus' speech is an appeal to reason, to the sense of honour and love of freedom. There is nothing emotional or touching in it. It is all impersonal, and cold logic. Every word of it goes over the head of the mindless mob. They understand not at word of it. How can they understand that a man can love a person, can admire him, can weep over his death, and yet can kill him for a noble cause. 'Freedom' and 'Honour" are empty words for the common people. They fail to understand that Brutus was not so much against Caesar as against his spirit, his Caesarism, his desire to become a dictator or a king. They listen to Brutus not because they understand him, but because after Caesar they find a hero in Brutus. They want a strong man, a hero whom they can worship devotedly and follow blindly. This is the reason why one of them says "Let him-be Caesar". What an irony ! Idealist Brutus wanted to kill the spirit of Caesar and spare Caesar, if he could. But he has actually killed Caesar, and left Caesarism alive, rather stronger. The mob has no thought or independent opinion. One of them says "This Caesar was a tyrant". He is not saying what he feels or thinks. He is just repeating what Brutus has said. So we see that Brutus' speech has no great effect on his listeners. Only a powerfully emotional and exciting speech of Antony can affect them or move them deeply,

Q. 7. Reproduce briefly the funeral speech of Antony and discuss why he succeeded with the Roman people.

Or

What did Antony tell the common people about *Caesar in his* **funeral speech ?**

Ans. Antony is a very clever and shrewd man. He knows that a mob (*crowd*) does not understand logic. People can understand common examples. They can see with their eyes, they can feel with their hearts, but they cannot think with their head.

First Antony says that he has 'come to bury Caesar, not to praise him. The good deeds of a man are forgotten with his death, but his faults are remembered even after his death. He asks the people to forget Caesar's virtues and remember only his faults. Clever Antony knows that the very mention of Caesar's goodness will make people recollect (*remember*) it.

Then Antony goes on to prove that Caesar was not ambitious. Though Brutus is a noble and honest man, yet he is a liar if he calls Caesar ambitious. Caesar did all for Rome, nothing for himself. After his conquests, Caesar brought many prisoners of war, whose ransoms enriched the treasury of Rome. It was no ambition. Caesar wept for the suffering of the poor. An ambitious man cannot be so kind hearted. Caesar was thrice offered a crown on the feast of Lupercalia, but he refused to have it every time. If he were ambitious he would gladly wear the crown and become a king. Romans once loved Caesar, but now they do not mourn Caesar whose dead body is lying in dust.

Then very cleverly, he says that Caesar has left a will. If they hear it read, they will rise in mutiny against Caesar's murderers. But he adds that he will not read the will. Thus he excites their curiosity. Then jumping down the stage, he reaches the dead body of Caesar, and asks the crowd to make a ring round him. He points out the holes made in Caesar's cloak, by daggers of his murderers. He says that the wound given by Brutus was the cruelest and most fatal. For, Caesar loved Brutus and trusted him so much. Then he uncovers Caesar' body and shows his wounds. Finally he reads Caesar's will in which he had left some amount of money for each Roman citizen, and given his private walks and garden for public use. All this fills the crowd with fury and rage against Caesar's murderers. They rush on madly to catch and kill every one of them.

Antony succeeds with the Roman people because he knows what they really understand. He does not use cold logic, as Brutus did. He gives them concrete examples. He makes an appeal to their hearts, to their emotions and passions. He is a perfect actor. He uses every trick and gesture to move the common people. He sighs, sobs, pauses for breath, pretends to be overwhelmed with sorrow. He appeals to their senses. He shows the wounds of Caesar and makes them move the hearts of the people. He knows that common people measure goodness in terms of personal gains. He proves Caesar's goodness by telling them that in his will Caesar had left seventy five drachmas for every Roman citizen. Thus he makes them feel that the loss of Caesar is a personal loss to every-one of them. How much Caesar loved them, how much he had left for them, how much more he would leave if he were to live longer–all these things told by Antony roused the mob against the conspirators.

Antony's language, too, is poetic and moving. He moves the people through their ears also. The spate of moving words, the rise and fall of the pitch and tone of his voice–all these so overwhelm the people that they stand hypnotized (अर्धसुप्त अवस्था). Antony now makes them do what he wants them to do.

Q. 8. Discuss briefly why Brutus turned down the following suggestions of Cassius ?

(*a*) Killing Antony along with Caesar.

(*b*) Not marching to the plains of Philippi.

Ans. (*a*) Brutus is an impractical idealist. He lives in the world of his ideas and ideals. He does not know that in the field of action there is a logic called the logic of necessity. Cassius knows all this. He knows that after Caesar Antony will be the greatest challenge to them. So he should be killed along with Caesar. Brutus hates unnecessary bloodshed, and he misreads Antony's character. He thinks that Antony is no more than a limb of Caesar. In Brutus' opinion, once Caesar's head is off. Antony will be as harmless as Caesar's arm.

Brutus, the idealist argues that they are not against Caesar, they are against Caesar's spirit or *Caesarism.* They would spare Caesar if they could get hold of his spirit. But as they cannot kill Caesar's spirit without killing Caesar, they must kill him. But they must be sacrificers, not butchers. Killing Antony will be like cutting Caesar's body to pieces, which will look like an act of butchery. If they kill Caesar only and touch no one else, people will think that Caesar's killing was necessary. Otherwise they will think that they killed Caesar and Antony out of jealousy and ill will.

The result of the turning down of this proposal of Cassius was most disastrous. Antony became the living spirit of Caesar. He roused the Roman mob against the conspirators and drove them out of Rome. Then with the help of Octavius, he raised a strong army and gave them a crushing defeat on the plains of Philippi. This defeat resulted in the death of Brutus and Cassius.

(*b*) Cassius' proposal of not marching to the plains of Philippi was a sound proposal. In military matters Cassius was abler and more experienced than Brutus. He argued that in coming to them the enemy force will have to march a long way. In this long march they will suffer some losses. Their soldiers will be exhausted, whereas the soldiers of Cassius and Brutus will be fresh and ready to meet the enemy. But here also Brutus comes out with his bookish logic. He says that they are at the height of their power and if they wait, their power will decline. Moreover, the enemy is increasing their number every day. There is always a right opportunity of doing things. Those who take opportunity and act accordingly get success. Those who miss the opportunity, suffer forever, they never succeed.

The result of turning down of this proposal was also very bad. Cassius' and Brutus' forces suffer because of it. Antony also hopes that Cassius and Brutus will not bring their forces down the hills to meet them at Philippi because Antony, too, was an experienced general. The morale not only of the soldiers but even of Cassius is down. He also talks about ravens and crows hovering over them. There is little coordination between the forces of Cassius and Brutus. Cassius' forces suffer a defeat. They run away. In anger, Cassius kills his own flag bearer because he is running away from the field. Thus, we see that in turning down both the proposals of Cassius, Brutus committed a blunder for which he and his colleagues paid very dearly. They lost their cause as well as their lives.

Q. 9. Describe briefly how Antony took revenge on the conspirators for the murder of Caesar ?

Ans. Antony was in the Senate House when the conspirators stabbed Caesar to death. But as soon as Caesar fell, Antony ran for his life. After some time he sent his servant to the Senate House. The servant requested the conspirators to assure Antony that no harm would be done to him. He would not be touched if he came to meet them in the Senate House. Brutus gave this assurance.

Then Antony reached the Senate House. Very cleverly, he paid tribute to Caesar to impress upon Brutus that he was still honest, and sincere to Caesar. He called them hounds and murderers of Caesar. But he said it in such a way that they thought that he was overwhelmed with grief, and he had no control over his tongue. Then he shook hands with them and said that he wanted only a satisfactory explanation for Caesar's murder. He then requested Brutus to allow him to take Caesar's body to the market place, and make a funeral speech. Cassius warned Brutus, but Brutus allowed him to do that on the condition that first Brutus himself would address the people. Antony would address them from the same stage after Brutus.

Antony made a powerful speech. He proved that Caesar was not ambitious. He did everything for his country and for his people. He brought great wealth and honour to Rome. Antony proved that Caesar's murderers were cruel people who betrayed Caesar by stabbing him in the back. Antony showed the common people the holes in Caesar's cloak. He told them that the hole made by Brutus' degger was the cruelest and most fatal. Because Caesar loved and trusted Brutus so much the people were moved to tears. Then Antony uncovered Caesar's dead body and showed his wounds. At this people were mad with anger. Then Antony read out Caesar's will and told them that Caesar had left seventy five drachmas for each Roman ; he had left his private walks and gardens for free use by the people. Now the people were mad with rage. They ran with Caesar's body to catch and kill all the murderers and set fire to their houses. Thus, Antony turned the fury of the mob against the conspirators. Brutus and Cassius ran for their lives. Antony, then, was the master of the situation.

He, Octavius Caesar and Lepidus became the Triumvirs. They raised a strong army, and gave the conspirators a crushing defeat on the plains of Philippi. Cassius committed suicide Brutus also killed himself.

Thus Antony took a terrible revenge on the conspirators for Caesar's murder.

Q. 10. (*a*) **Reproduce the conversation which took place between Caesar and Calpurnia** *Act II Scene* (*i*) **regarding her request to him not to attend the meeting of the Senate.**

(*b*) **What light does it throw on their characters ?**

Ans. (*a*) Caesar is ready to go to the Senate House to attend an important meeting there. He sends his servant to the augurers to ask them to offer a sacrifice and tell him the result of it. Just then Calpurnia, his wife enters. She asks Caesar not to move out of his house today. Caesar very boastfully says that he will certainly go. Dangers disappear as soon as Caesar turns his face towards them.

Calpurnia then, recounts the strange things that happened in the last stormy night. A lioness gave birth to her young ones in the street. The graves opened and the dead bodies walked out of those graves. A bloody battle was going on in the sky. She says that she is full of great fear. At this Caesar says what gods have decided must happen. Man cannot avoid it. Moreover, Caesar, says that all these happenings and evil omens do not concern him alone, they are for all. Calpurnia again argues that when beggars die there are no comets seen in the sky. But sky itself foretells the death of princes and greatmen. Calpurnia suggests that evil omens of the night foretell some evil for her husband. His life is in danger. Caesar once again says boastfully that he is more terrible and dangerous than Danger itself.

Calpurnia loses her patience and says that Caesar's over-confidence has destroyed his wisdom. She then requests him to stay at home for her sake. If he has no fear, let him stay for her fear. At this Caesar agrees to stay just for her whim (*humour*). After this Decius comes and gives a more flattering interpretation to Calpurnia's dream. Then Caesar changes his mind. He calls Calpurnia's fears "foolish fears" and decides to go to the Senate-House.

This conversation between Caesar and his wife brings out some of their weaknesses. Calpurnia is a weak and superstitious woman. She is a devoted wife. She is anxious about the safety of her husband. But she has no individuality or force of character that we see in Brutus' wife, Portia. She is just a shadow of her husband. She can fall on her knees, and request with tears in her eyes, but she cannot assert herself. When Decius Brutus gives a different interpretation to her dream, her husband laughs at her foolish fears. He says that he is ashamed that he gave way to her fears. Poor Calpurnia says not a word in protest or contradiction.

This conversation brings out Caesar's boastfulness very clearly. Caesar is bold no doubt. But it is an empty boast to say that he and danger "are two lions littered in a day" and that he is the elder and more terrible of the two. We also see that Caesar's attitude towards his wife is not very good. He treats her only as a pretty plaything to be petted and humoured. He does not have that regard and respect for his wife, which Brutus has for Portia.

(*b*) Here we see Caesar's fickle-mindedness and love of flattery. First he says that he will stay for his wife's humour. But when Decius gives a flattering interpretation to Calpurnia's dream, Caesar at once changes his mind. This also proves that Caesar did have some fear of that dream. Even the bravest man can have his fear. But boastful Caesar does not confess it.

Q. 11. Why did Calpurnia ask Caesar not to go to the Senate meeting on the Ides of March ?

Or

How did Decius Brutus finally persuade Caesar to attend the meeting ?

Ans. Calpurnia feared some danger to her husband's life. The strange happenings of the previous stormy night appeared to her as evil omens that were pointing to some danger to her husband's life. Besides this, she had a dream in the night. She saw Caesar's statue throwing out blood through many openings, and some healthy Romans gathering round his statue and bathing their hands in that blood. It was a bad dream which also foreboded some evil that was to befall her husband. Her fears were further confirmed by the warning sent by the augurers. Because of these fears Calpurnia asked her husband not to go to the Senate-House that day.

Decius Brutus came to Caesar's house to take him to the Senate House. Decius was a clever man. He knew the art of flattery. He knew that Caesar was proud of his power and importance in Rome. Caesar first told him that he would not go to the meeting of the Senate, just because he had a will not to go there. Then he told him about the dream of Calpurnia. Clever Decius at once said that Calpurnia's dream had been wrongly interpreted. The dream was a good one. It indicated that Rome would receive fresh blood and fresh life from Caesar. Under Caesar's leadership Rome would prosper. And the great Romans would crowd round Caesar to get honours, titles and recognition from him. They would dip their handkerchiefs in his blood to keep them as relics (*memorial*). This flattering interpretation really flattered Caesar.

But Decius Brutus did not leave the matter there. He then touched Caesar's ambition. He told him that the Senators were going to offer him a crown that day. If he did not go there, they might change their mind. Decius further touched Caesar's pride. He told him that the Senators might laugh at him if they came to know why Caesar did not come to attend the meeting. Some one might even say that they should postpone the meeting till Caesar's wife met with some better dream. They might also say that Caesar was hiding at home because he was afraid. Caesar was really flattered and provoked with this. He told his wife that he was ashamed of himself, for, he had given way to her foolish fears. He decided to go to attend the meeting in the Senate House and asked for his cloak.

Q. 12. What was the main stand taken by Brutus in his funeral speech, justifying the murder of Caesar ?

How did Antony prove this to be utterly false and therefore dishonourable ?

Ans. The main stand that Brutus took to justify Caesar's murder was that Caesar was ambitious. Caesar wanted to become a dictator or a king. He was a danger to the freedom and honour of Rome and all the honourable Romans. He told the people that he loved Caesar; he admired his greatness; he rejoiced in his success, but he killed him because he was ambitious.

But Antony is a very clever and cunning man. He knows how the mind of a mob works. He does not use logic or reason with the common people. He gives concrete examples to prove that Caesar was not ambitious. He says that Caesar did all for Rome and nothing for himself. After every conquest of his, he brought honour and wealth for Rome and the Romans. He further tells them that Caesar often wept when he saw sufferings of the poor. An ambitious man cannot be so kind and tender-hearted. Then Antony refers to the event of Lupercalia where most of these very people were present. He says that he himself offered Caesar a crown, not once but thrice. Yet every time Caesar refused it. If Caesar were ambitious, he would gladly wear the crown and become a king of Rome. Antony's masterstroke, which proves noble Brutus to be a liar, comes when Antony reads out the will under Caesar's own seal. He reads that Caesar has left seventy five drachmas for each Roman. He has left his gardens and private walks for free public use. A man who can leave so much for his people can never be called ambitious.

Antony is a shrewd and clever man. He goes on calling Brutus a noble man, an honourable man and an honest man. But with each example his tone becomes more and more ironical and sarcastic. So much so, that in the end, 'honourable' simply means the opposite-dishonourable. Antony successfully and cunningly proves that though Brutus is known as an honourable man, yet, in fact, he is dishonourable and a liar.

Q. 13. Write a note on the differences dividing Brutus and Cassius on the eve of the Battle of Philippi.

How were these ultimately patched up ?

Or

What made Brutus and Cassius quarrel with each other on the eve of the battle of Philippi ?

What new things in their characters are revealed during the quarrel ?

Ans. The quarrel between Brutus and Cassius starts because Cassius tells Brutus that he has done a great wrong to him. This thing Cassius says outside the tent, in the presence of the soldiers.

On Brutus's suggestion both the friends go into Brutus' tent. There, Cassius says that Brutus condemned Lucius Pella, a lieutenant of Cassius, for taking bribes from the people of Sardis. Cassius had written a letter in defence of Lucius Pella, but Brutus paid no heed to that letter even. Brutus, the honest idealist says that it was wrong on Cassius' part to defend a corrupt man. Cassius, the practical man of action, rightly says that in times of crisis such lapses should be overlooked.

Now it is Brutus's turn to charge Cassius with exacting of bribes. Brutus says that Cassius himself is greedy. He has an itching palm. He sold higher posts for money. He appointed incompetent persons on important posts. This accusation shocks Cassius, and he loses his temper. Brutus, then, brings another charge against Cassius. He says that he had sent Cassius a message for some money because he had to pay his troops. But miserly Cassius denied this help to Brutus. Both the friends exchange threats and hot words. They curse and even call each other names. Cassius says that he did not deny him money. His messenger was a fool who gave Brutus a wrong information.

How the quarrel was patched up. The first step towards reconciliation is taken by Cassius. Deeply shocked and grieved at this serious charge, Cassius draws out his sword and offers his bare breast to Brutus. He asks Brutus to stab him and take out his precious heart. This moves Brutus. He says that he is as mild as a lamb. His anger is short-lived like the spark given by a flint when it is rubbed very hard. Cassius also confesses that he has inherited an evil temper from his mother. He requests Brutus to bear with him when he loses his temper. But real patching up of the quarrel takes place when Brutus tells Cassius that Portia, his dear wife killed herself by swallowing live (*burning*) coals. Cassius is deeply grieved at this shocking news. He admits that he has been very cruel with Brutus when he had so much of pain in his heart. Then both the friends sit down to drown their pain and grief in a cup of wine.

New things in their characters, revealed by this scene. This scene vividly brings out some traits in the characters of Brutus and Cassius. These traits were not revealed in previous scenes. Here we see that Brutus is not so calm and balanced as he has appeared so far. He is harsher than Cassius. It is true that his mind and heart is deeply disturbed. But a stoic like Brutus, should not lose his balance of mind so much as to curse a dear friend like Cassius. Brutus becomes cruel when he says :

"By the gods
You shall digest the venom of your spleen
"Though it split you ; for from this day forth
I'll use you for my mirth, yea for my laughter
When you are waspish

But, Cassius, reveals a better and lovable side of his personality. Cassius is not a cool, calculating and cruel plotter alone. He has also a tender heart. He is deeply devoted to Brutus. He shows wonderful self-control in the face of all the provocation from Brutus' side. His grief over Portia's death is genuine. It is Cassius who takes the first step towards reconciliation. Brutus is more arrogant. He is proud of his honesty, and honour. He says :—

"There is no terror Cassius in your threats
For I am arm'd so strong in my honesty,"

Cassius does not become so harsh, biting and bitter as Brutus does. He is humble rather. When he hears of Portia's death, Cassius exclaims :

'How 'scaped I killing, when I crossed you so'

Here is a dear friend deeply grieved at the greatest loss of his dear friend whom he loves and respects very deeply.

Q. 14. Write a note on relationship between Brutus and Portia.

Ans. It is only in Act II Scene (*i*) that we see Brutus and Portia together. But even within this short span we see them as loving and devoted husband and wife. Brutus and Portia make an ideal couple. Brutus is a noble Roman who comes of a noble family. Portia too is the daughter of Cato, one of the noblest Romans of his times.

Both deeply devoted to each other. Portia is deeply devoted to her husband. She observes her husband with all the care, concern and love of a deeply devoted wife. His face and his strange behaviour fills Portia with great anxiety. Brutus is also a loving and devoted husband. He loves his wife as dearly as the red drops of blood that visit his heart. He says.

You are my true and honourable wife

As dear to me as are the ruddy drops
That visit my sad heart.

Both of them have a great regard and respect for each other's personality and individuality. Portia is not an ordinary woman; she knows that she is wife of a noble husband and daughter of a noble father. She is not just a thing to be loved, petted and humoured by her husband. She is a life partner of her husband. She is his better half. She must share all his pleasures, pains, problems and secrets. She proudly says :-

"I grant, I am a woman but withal
A woman lord Brutus took to wife."

Portia knows her husband's nobleness, and she is legitimately proud of it. Brutus too has great regard and respect for the individuality of his noble wife. He does not brush aside the requests of his wife as Caesar does Calpurnia's requests. He has kept his secrets to himself only because he does not want to disturb the peace of his dear wife's mind. When she insists, he discloses everything to her. Later on, we see that she knows the secret, and is trying to keep it hidden in her heart, though it is almost breaking her heart. Brutus' respect for his wife's personality is clear when he says :—

"O, Ye gods
Render me worthy of this noble wife.

Thus we see that relation between Brutus and Portia is ideal and perfect in every way. There is a perfect marriage—a marriage of two bodies, two hearts, two minds and two souls. Really both are ideally cut out for such other. They, have all that a happy married couple needs—love, faith, devotion, understanding appreciation and a very good reputation.

Q. 15. How and why was Cinna, the poet murdered ?

Ans. Cinna, the poet had a dream the previous night. In his dream he feasted with Caesar. The dream filled his mind with some fear. He did not want to move-out because of this fear. But, some mysterious power drove him out of his home.

In Act III Scene (*iii*), we see this poet out in the street. A crowd of citizens reaches there. They are excited and mad with anger. They are after the blood of the conspirators.

Each one of them puts a question to him and wants an answer immediately. One asks his name, the second asks him where he is going, the third asks where he lives, and the fourth asks whether he is married or a bachelor. None of these fools lets him have a chance to answer the foregoing questions. Cinna seems to be a witty man. He answers all of them all at once. First he says that to answer them wisely he must say that he is a bachelor. At this a married fool among the crowd shouts at him. He asks him if he considers married people fools. Then Cinna tells them that he is going to attend Caesar's funeral. He is going there as a friend. At last he tells them his name. When he says that his name is Cinna, one of the citizens shout. "Tear him to pieces, he is a conspirator." The poor fellow pleads that he is not Cinna, the conspirator. He is Cinna, the poet. One of the citizens shouts to tear him to pieces for his bad poems. This fool must not have read any poem by Cinna. They are now mad with anger, they must kill the poor poet on one pretext (बहाना) or the other. The poor poet again says that he is not Cinna, the conspirator. At this another fool shouts that they should kill him just for his name. They should tear out his heart and then his name from it and then let him go away. So they drag him away.

This senseless murder of an innocent man is the example of the mindlessness of a crowd. The mob is really a mindless multitude of people. Once their passions are roused the people in a crowd become blind and inhuman. They lose their reason. They behave like wild animals. The crowd of Roman citizens had been roused by Antony. They were now blood thirsty. They must burn, kill and destroy whatever they can lay their hands upon.

Q. 16. Describe briefly the reasons for the failure of the conspiracy.

Ans. Caesar's murder, a political blunder and a crime. Rome of Caesar's time required a strong man like Caesar to rule over her people and maintain law and order. But men like Cassius. Casca, Flavius, Marullus and Cimber were blind to this fact. They were jealous of Caesar's growing power. They were more interested in killing Caesar than in saving the freedom and Republicanism of Rome Among the conspirators, Brutus was the only man who was against Caesarism. But his idealism and ignorance of practical political needs of the country, made him blind. He thought that by killing Caesar they would kill Caesarism. But actually they killed only Caesar, and made Caesarism even stronger. Brutus could not win the mob, because he could not impress the mob with his arguments. Common people do not understand abstract ideas like freedom and honour. They could not understand Brutus, when he said that he loved Caesar, but he killed Caesar because he loved Rome and the Romans more. They could not understand how one could kill a man whom he loved. Antony knew the pulse of the mob. He won over the mob by telling them what Caesar had given to them in his will and what more he would give them if he were to live longer. So the mob could understand love and worship and follow a strong man. He might either be a Caesar or an Antony.

Faulty leadership of the conspiracy. Another reason for the failure of the conspiracy was that its leadership slipped into the wrong hands of an impractical idealist. The idea of the conspiracy originated in the mind of Cassius. But because of his weak will, Cassius surrendered to Brutus' stronger will. Brutus was a thinker, an idealist who had no understanding of the problems and persons that he was dealing with. Every time Cassius made a right proposal Brutus always overruled it and had his own way. Cassius proposed that Antony should be killed along with Caesar. Brutus again overruled him. Antony became their deadliest enemy and drove them all to their doom. Again Cassius warned Brutus not to allow Antony to display Caesar's dead body and make a funeral speech before the common people. As usual Brutus overruled him and drove a fresh nail in the coffin of the conspiracy. Then, at Sardis, Cassius gave the right proposal. He said that they should wait for the enemy at Sardis. In crossing the distance from Philippi to Sardis, the enemy forces would suffer some losses and get exhausted. Their own soldiers, on the other hand, would be fresh and ready to meet the enemy. Here again, Brutus used his bookish knowledge and talked of the tide in "the affairs of man." He rejected Cassius' proposal. This was the last nail driven in the coffin of the conspirators and their conspiracy.

Antony's practicality and resourcefulness. A very important reason for the failure of the conspiracy was Antony's ability and resourcefulness in handling the mob and mastering the situation after Caesar's murder. He was very cunning and a clever man of action. Very cleverly he worked upon the noble mind of Brutus and get permission to address the mob. A man with lesser ability and tact would have failed to win the sympathy of the mob because Brutus' personality had already influenced them. But Antony moved very tactfully. And very cautiously he roused their love and sympathy for Caesar, and then, their fury against the conspirators

In shrewdness and practicality Brutus was no match to Antony. Rather, Antony was more than a match even to Cassius. Cassius still had some love, tenderness and goodness. But Antony was a cool, calculating and cruel schemer who would stop at nothing in order to achieve his end. With the help of Octavius, he raised a strong army. He had no scruples about shedding unnecessary blood. He killed all those who might pose a threat to him. He decided to kill his nephew and Lepidus' brother. Even under the leadership of Cassius, the conspirators might have got some success fighting against Antony. But under the leadership of a man like Brutus, they were doomed to be defeated and they were defeated.

Conspirators not of one mind. We have already seen that the conspirators had different motives. Cassius, Flavius and some others were motivated by jealousy. Metellus Cimber, by purely personal grudge because Caesar had banished his brother. Brutus was motivated by his love of Rome and the freedom and honour of Rome. So we see that in a way the conspirators lacked emotional and intellectual unity. They were rather at cross purposes, which made their efforts weak.

Q. 17. Narrate briefly the supernatural happenings in *"Julius Caesar"*. What use did Shakespeare make of them ?

Or

Describe the various portents and alarms in the play *Julius Caesar*. Also bring out their significance.

Ans. Belief in supernatural powers and happenings, very common in olden times. Belief in supernatural powers and happenings was very common in ancient Rome as well as in Shakespeare's own times. We cannot say whether Shakespeare himself believed in them or not. But as a dramatist he made a free use of the supernatural in his plays.

Supernatural in Julius Caesar. In Julius Caesar also we hear of many strange and supernatural happenings. The stormy night itself has something strange about it, because, Casca talks of 'tempest dropping fire'. He says that it looks as if a civil war were going on among the gods in heaven. He says that he saw a slave whose hand was giving out flames, but the slave was not feeling any pain of burning. He saw a lion in front of the capitol. The lion looked at him with anger, but it moved away without harming him. It was also a strange happening, because a wild lion would not walk through a busy street. He saw some women crowded together. They were terror stricken. They told him (*Casca*) that they had seen men enveloped in fire walking up and down the street. An owl was seen in the market place just at noon. It was also strange, because owl is a night bird. Casca thinks that these supernatural happenings and evil omens point out some evil that may befall Rome.

After this, we hear from Calpurnia. She also tells her husband that she has heard from some one about the strange and supernatural happenings. A lioness had given birth to her young one in the street. Graves opened and the ghosts of the persons, buried in them, walked into the streets. Soldiers clothed in fire were seen fighting among the clouds Blood rained from the sky upon the Capitol. Like Casca, Calpurnia, too, is superstitious. She is also full of great terror.

The appearance of the ghost is another supernatural happening. We see that even Cassius becomes superstitious as his morale goes down. He himself says that he has started believing in omens. He saw some ravens, crows and kites flying over the heads of his soldiers. He thought that it was a bad omen. May be, here, Shakespeare wants to suggest that when a man begins losing self-confidence, he grows superstitious.

The use made by Shakespeare :

Shakespeare makes a very artistic use of the supernatural. Nothing supernatural happens on the stage ; it is only reported by different characters. But as the characters describe it, it fills us with a sense of terror. It prepares our minds to receive the shock of the terrible tragedy of

Caesar's murder and also the tragic end of Cassius and Brutus. The supernatural forces playing a part in shaping human affairs give us a sense of fate and the supremacy of fate. We feel as if even the forces beyond the control of man were driving Caesar, Brutus and Cassius to their doom.

It creates the atmosphere. The stormy night with all the terrible and supernatural happenings is the right atmosphere for the hatching of a terrible and bloody conspiracy. The conspirators can safely move out on such a terrible night. The streets are deserted. No one is out to see or detect them, for the supernatural happenings and omens have filled them with terror. They stay at home.

Brings out some traits of different characters, Shakespeare makes another use of the supernatural. Different characters react to it in different ways. Casca is timid and superstitious. He is mortally afraid of these supernatural happenings. Cicero is a philosopher. He does not want to stay out because the weather is not good. But he is not disturbed by the supernatural happenings reported by Casca.

Calpurnia, too is very much afraid of them, but Caesar says that even if they point to his death he is not afraid, because 'brave men die but once'. Death must come when it wills. Cassius, on the other hand, is not afraid of it, but he makes use of the supernatural to his own advantage. He tells Casca that all these unnatural or supernatural things point out that something unnatural and terrible is going to happen to Rome. And then he says that there is a man in Rome who is as terrible as the happenings of the stormy night. In this way clever Cassius uses these terrors to rouse Casca's fear and jealousy.

Appearance of the ghost. Brutus, a stoic, does not believe in ghosts and omens. So, first he has doubts. But soon after he thinks that the ghost is only an illusion of his weak eyesight. But appearance of Caesar's ghosts plays another part. It proves that Caesar may be dead, but Caesar's spirit is still walking abroad. Caesarism is still alive and strong. Brutus had killed Caesar, though he wanted to kill Caesar's spirit.

We have already noted that as man loses confidence in himself, and grows conscious of his growing weakness, he becomes superstitious. Before the battle of Philippi, even Cassius becomes superstitious. He also fears that ravens, crows, and kites flying over them, indicate defeat and death for his soldiers.

Thus we see that Shakespeare uses supernatural for many purposes.

Q. 18. Discuss who the hero of the play is—*Caesar or Brutus.*

Or

Who is the hero of the play *'Julius Caesar'* ?

Ans. Play is named after the hero. Caesar is really one of the most important characters of the play 'Julius Caesar'. The play is named after him. It has been a practice with Shakespeare to name his plays after the heroes. Hamlet, Macbeth, King Lear, Othello are some of his plays named after their heroes.

Caesar dominates the play. Though Caesar dies and disappears in the middle of the act III scene (*i*). Yet Caesar's name, his spirit dominates the play throughout. It is Caesar against whom the conspiracy is hatched. It is Caesar who is loved by some, and hated by others. It is Caesar in whose name the common people are roused. It is Caesar whose murder is avenged by Antony and Octavius. Even Brutus admits before his death that 'Caesar is mighty yet'. Caesar's ghost appears twice, once at Sardis and again at Philippi. Thus we see that Caesar is the central figure. And so we may argue that he is the hero of "Julius Caesar." If we consider Julius Caesar a political play in which the real conflict is between republicanism and Caesarism (*or monarchy*), we can safely say that Caesar, the symbol of Caesarism, is the hero of the play. 'Julius Caesar'. But the editor of the Arden edition of Shakespeare's Julius Caesar rightly says that Caesar is the titular hero, but Brutus is the dramatic hero.

Julius Caesar in fact is a tragedy of character. The main conflict is not the political conflict between two forces, but a conflict in the mind of a noble man who suffers death and destruction because of a tragic flaw in his character.

Caesar fails to touch the grandeur and nobility that the hero of a tragedy should have. All Caesar's glory and grandeur is more a matter of report and history. But the Caesar we meet in the play is a bundle of weaknesses. We find him an aging man surrounded by flatterers or persons who keep a smiling face but nurse ill-will and jealousy for him. He is deaf in one ear. He is a patient of falling sickness. He is haughty and boastful. His murder is a crime no doubt, but it is not a tragedy. We feel that a proud man like him whose "wisdom is consumed in his confidence" gets what he asks for. Caesar's murder does not fill us with terror or pity, the emotions which the tragic end of a tragic hero should rouse in us.

Conflict in Caesar's mind. He is just a great ruler, feeling secure, quite confident, rather complacent.

Brutus is a noble man who wins our love and admiration. Brutus is an impractical idealist, but a noble and honest man. He is a patriot to the back bone. He loves his country so much that he can sacrifice anything for the good of his country. He is a sincere and loving friend of Caesar. There is a conflict in the mind of Brutus between his love for Caesar and his love for Rome. That is the real dramatic conflict in a noble mind. The real tragic flaw of his character is the very extreme of his nobleness and honesty. In his nobleness and idealism Brutus becomes blind to the reality that faces him. We get irritated every time when Brutus overrules practical proposals of Cassius. But we cannot help admiring the nobleness of his motive. Sparing Antony was a mistake. But it was a mistake from the point of view of the practical needs of the conspirators. Otherwise it was a noble man's instinctive reaction. It was hatred for unnecessary bloodshed. He misjudged Antony. This wrong judgement was also the result of his extremely noble nature. For very often we see only ourselves in others. Noble Brutus saw his own nobleness and honesty in others. He does betray Caesar, and does play a part when he first pleads for Cimber's brother. But this he does with real pain and with a sense of guilt in his heart. We know what he says when he sees unsuspecting Caesar shaking hands with them at his own house. Brutus says :—

> "*That every like is not the same*
> *O Caesar*
> *That heart of Brutus yearns to think upon.*"

Here is most painful prick of an honest man's conscience. He bears it because he honestly feels that he is going to serve the greater cause of his country. This inner conflict of Brutus is at its height in Act II Scene (*i*). Brutus is alone in his garden. He confesses to himself that he has nothing against Caesar, yet he fears that after becoming a king he will become a danger to Rome. He is at this time really torn between his love of Caesar and his love of Rome. We feel that he is really a faithful sacrificer of Caesar, others are his butchers.

Brutus has that human kindness and tenderness which wins our love, and fills us with pity over his death. Besides nobleness, honesty and purity of motives, Brutus has a heart full of the milk of human kindness. He himself can bear pain, but he cannot see the heaviness of sleep in the eyes of his slave and his guards. He is all love and tenderness for his wife. This human side of Caesar does not come out in the play. So we can say that it is Brutus who is the real hero of the play 'Julius Caesar'. The play, Julius Caesar' in fact, is the tragedy of noble Brutus, he was too noble to be a successful conspirator. It was an irony of fate that he was involved in a situation where his very virtue became his fatal flaw. It is Brutus alone who brings us to the verge of tears over his tragic end. Even when he decides to end his life, he is proud of his loyal friends. He says to his friends :

> *My heart doth joy that yet in all my life*
> *I found no man but he was true to me.*

It is the loss of this nobleness of Brutus that fills us with pity and horror. Horror at the thought that the laws of nature are so inexorable

(निष्ठुर) that they will not forgive any flaw or imbalance. Pity at the thought that so noble a man suffered so much ending in such a tragic death.

Q. 19. Describe the midnight meeting of the conspirators at Brutus' place. What light does it throw on different characters ?

Answers:

Brutus is restless when the conspirators burst upon him. Brutus is alone in his garden. Cassius along with other conspirators come in. Cassius introduces them to Brutus who shakes hands with them. They, then, hold a conference to decide what they should do and what steps they should take to carry out their plan of murdering Caesar.

Cassius' proposals overruled by Brutus. Cassius proposes that they should all take an oath of secrecy. Idealist Brutus rejects this proposal. He says that only weak and dishonest men take oaths. They are all honest Romans. Their noble motive and their word of honour is enough to keep them united and faithful to their cause.

After this, Metellus Cimber suggests that they should include Cicero among the conspirators. He is a wise old man respected for his wisdom. If he is with them, people will not condemn them for Caesar's murder. Brutus rejects this proposal also. He says that Cicero is a self opinionated man. He can never follow a thing started by another man.

Then Decius Brutus asks if they should kill some other men or not. At this Cassius says that they should kill Antony, who loves Caesar very much. It was a right proposal, Brutus rejects this proposal also. He says that Antony is only a limb of Caesar. After Caesar's death, he will be harmless and helpless. Moreover, if they kill Antony along with Caesar, their action will appear as cruel and bloody. People will think that they have killed, Caesar out of anger and ill-will. They should behave as sacrificers, not as butchers.

After this, Cassius expresses his doubt. He fears that Caesar may not come to the Senate House. Decius Brutus asks them to leave it to him. He says that Caesar loves flattery. He will go to Caesar's house, flatter him, and bring him to the Senate House. They agree to include Ligarius in this venture. Then they take leave of Brutus. Brutus bids them farewell and advises them to keep smiling faces to hide their bloody thoughts.

Characters :

This scene throws light on certain traits of certain characters :—

Brutus : Brutus is an idealist. He is an impractical man. He has no personal grudge against Caesar. He murders Caesar for the freedom of Rome and the Romans. He is honest and honourable; so he hates oath taking. But as an impractical man he rejects the right proposal put forward by practical Cassius. He completely misreads Antony's character.

Brutus has a stronger will than Cassius. This is why Cassius' weak will always surrenders to Brutus' stronger will.

Cassius : Cassius is shown as a practical man of action. He reads Antony's character, rightly. His proposal for oath-taking was also a right thing. Such a ritual becomes necessary in such plans and action. Cassius understands human nature better than Brutus.

Casca : Casca appears to be a fickle-minded fool. He has no opinion of his own. First he is in favour of winning Cicero to their side. But when Brutus rejects the proposal, Casca says "leave him, he is not fit".

Cicero : According to Metellus Cimber, Cicero is a wise old man respected for his wisdom and judgement. He should be won over. But Brutus considers him a self-opinionated man who cannot follow any other man.

Caesar : Caesar, according to Brutus is a great man. He should be killed because he may become a king and a danger to the freedom of Rome. But he should be sacrificed on the altar of the freedom of Rome. He should not be butchered in anger and out of ill-will.

Antony : According, to Cassius, Antony has great love for Caesar. He may prove a challenge to the conspirators. He should be killed along with Caesar. But, Brutus wrongly considers him a pleasure loving young man who is no more than a limb of Caesar. He will be harmless and helpless after Caesar's murder.

Q. 20. Describe the murder scene in Julius Caesar, and point out its dramatic significance.

Answer:

The Senate is sitting above. A crowd of people has gathered there. Artemidorus and a soothsayer are also among the people. Caesar enters ; he is followed by Brutus and other conspirators.

Caesar pays no heed to warnings. Artemidorus hands over a piece of paper to Caesar. In it he has to warn Caesar against some of the conspirators. He requests Caesar to read it first, because it concerns him most. But Caesar proudly waives it aside, saying that what concerns him shall be attended last of all. Caesar taunts the soothsayer also. He says that Ides (*15th*) of March has come. The soothsayer again warns him that it is not yet gone. But proud Caesar pays no heed to it.

Popilius Laena's behaviour disturbs Cassius. Popilius Laena wishes Cassius success in his plan. Then Laena goes to Caesar and whispers something into Caesar's ears. This makes Cassius suspicious. He tells Brutus that their secret is out. And says that he will kill himself if their secret is really out. Brutus, who is more confident, looks at Caesar and finding him smiling, he assures Cassius that everything is all right.

Metellus Cimber makes appeal to Caesar. When Caesar is in his seat, Metellus Cimber falls on his knees and requests Caesar to recall his banished brother from his exile. Caesar very proudly asks him not to bend low. These bowings and bendings may flatter an ordinary man. Caesar is not such a weak man. He will not change his mind. Cimber then asks some one else to appeal to Caesar. Then, Brutus and Cassius plead for Cimber. But Caesar is adamant. He compares himself to the Pole Star, and says that he will not change. He rebukes Cassius and asks him not to behave like a dog crawling at his feet. He threatens to kick him as he would kick a dog. At this Casca says "Speak hands for me" and stabs Caesar in the back. Then the other conspirators stab him. When he sees Brutus stabbing him. Caesar is mortally shocked—he stammered Brutus' name; and saying "Et tu Bute" (*you, too, Brutus*). Caesar falls dead.

As soon as Caesar falls dead, there is panic. People run helter skelter in search of refuge. Antony also runs home. Brutus asks the people not to feel scared.

Cassius warns, but Brutus allows Antony to address the mob : The conspirators bathe their hands in Caesar's blood. They cry "Liberty, freedom, tyranny is dead". Antony's servant comes and tells Brutus that if they assure that no harm will be done to him, Antony, his master will like to meet them. Brutus gives the assurance. Antony comes. He pays his tributes to Caesar. Very cleverly he calls the conspirators hunters and he is still sincere to Caesar. He, then, shakes hands with the conspirators one by one. He says that he wants only a satisfactory explanation for Caesar's murder. He has one request more to make. They should allow him to take Caesar's body to the market place, and make a funeral speech before the people. Cassius warns Brutus that Antony should not be allowed to take Caesar's dead body to the market place. But noble Brutus allows Antony to do so. The conspirators leave Antony alone with Caesar's dead body. Antony hurls curses on the conspirators and says that Caesar's spirit will take a terrible revenge on them.

Dramatic significance. This scene is the climax of the play. Here the cause of the conspiracy is at the height of its strength and victory. After this the conspirators and their cause rush head way down. The next scene is the turning point. Antony turns the table on the conspirators.

This scene is the most powerful scene from the dramatic point of view. There is suspense, conflict and swift movement and action. The powerful dialogues, ending into Caesar's murder and utter confusion are exciting, almost nerve racking. Here is a powerful play of human feelings passions, bitterness, betrayal, flattery, dark doubts and fears. And finally, Antony's passions for a bloody and terrible revenge on the conspirators, fill us with horror and almost take our breath.

The scene brings out some traits of different characters. We see Cassius' fickleness and imbalance, when he doubts about Laena and thinks of suicide. But he is practical as ever. He rightly warns Brutus not to allow Antony to address the mob. But he is weak-willed.

Brutus is, as ever, an impractical idealist, strong willed and confident, but a wrong judge of men and situations. He is wrong in overruling Cassius' suggestion.

Antony comes in a new colour. This pleasure-seeking young man, suddenly becomes a shrewd, tactful and resourceful man of action. He proves more than a match to Cassius in his shrewdness and practicality.

Q. 21. Reproduce in your own words Casca's report of the incidents on the eve of the feast of Lupercalia.

What light does it throw on the characters of Caesar and Casca ?

Or

Describe in your own words the scene of the offering of the crown to Caesar.

What light does it throw on the characters of Caesar and Casca and of the Roman mob ?

Answer :

Brutus and Cassius ask Casca about the events of Lupercalia. Casca returns with Caesar's train. He was present at the celebration of the festival of Lupercalia. He saw all that happened there. Brutus and Cassius are standing by the road-side. They are busy talking about the state of affairs in Rome. Brutus detains Casca, because they want to know what happened there on the occasion of the celebrations. They also want to know why people shouted there three times.

Casca reports about offering of a crown to Caesar. In his own rude and sarcastic manner. Casca tells them that Antony offered Caesar a crown. But Caesar refused to accept the crown. It was offered to him three times. And every time it was refused by Caesar. The crowd of dirty people shouted every time Caesar refused the crown. When the crown was refused for the first time, the crowd shouted and cheered Caesar. Though Caesar refused it, yet it looked, as if he were willing to accept and wear it. The crown was offered to him again. And again Caesar refused it. He pushed it aside with his hand. But, Casca says; that it looked as if Caesar's fingers were unwilling to let the crown go. Then the crown was offered for the third time. This time the people were just mad with joy. They threw their sweat-soaked caps up in the air. They shouted loudly, and filled the atmosphere with their foul smelling breath.

Caesar choked with the air polluted by the bad breath of the people. When Caesar inhaled the air poisoned by the bad breath of the dirty crowd, he was choked. He fainted, fell and foamed at the mouth.

Caesar comes to his senses, and flatters people by offering his breast for them to stab if it pleases them. Brutus, here, remarks that Caesar suffers from falling sickness. At this clever Cassius says that not Caesar, but they themselves suffer from falling sickness. They have all fallen under Caesar's tyranny. Then, Casca tells them what happened when Caesar came to his senses. Caesar stood up and begged pardon of the crowd if he had said something wrong to them. He bared his breast and asked them to stab him if they liked. Casca, here remarks that he would have really stabbed Caesar if he had been one in the crowd. People in the crowd were all fools. Some two or three girls standing near Casca expressed sympathy for Caesar. But Casca says that they were foolish girls. Even if Caesar had murdered their mothers, they would have forgiven him even then.

Attitude of Cicero. Cassius asks Casca how Cicero, the great orator, reacted to this foolery. Casca says that Cicero made some remarks in Greek, which he (*Casca*) could not understand. But people who understood him smiled. It means, Cicero made some sarcastic remarks at this silly behaviour of Caesar and the mob.

Character of Casca revealed in this scene. We note that Casca is a rude and rough man. He has nothing but contempt for the common people. He considers them dusty and foolish Casca seems to be jealous of Caesar. Because he describes the whole scene as if it were mere foolery, and Caesar behaved most foolishly and ridiculously.

Caesar's character as revealed in this scene. If Casca's report is true, we find that Caesar is a hypocrite. In his heart he longs for the crown, but outwardly he refuses it to show that he has no ambition to become a king. Caesar wants cheap popularity. He tries to flatter the foolish people, just to win their sympathy and support. Caesar is a weak and diseased person. He suffers from falling sickness.

Casca points out the Roman mob in very dark colours. We find the common people of Rome are poor, foolish, dirty and ignorant. They do not understand Caesar and his real ambition. They are just blind hero-worshippers. They have no culture and refinement. They shout and throw their caps in the air like fools.

Q. 22. Describe the storm scene and write a short note on its dramatic significance.

Ans. It is a stormy night. There are terrible flashes of lightning followed by loud thunders. Casca is terrified. He comes with a drawn sword and meets Cicero by chance. He tells Cicero that he has seen terrible storms and tempests, but never before had he seen such a terrible storm. The sky is raining fire. Casca thinks that a civil war has broken out among gods in heaven, or gods are angry with human beings and they are sending death and destruction for all mankind.

Cicero asks him if he has seen anything more wonderful. Casca, then, says that he saw a common slave lifting up his hand. His hand was all flames, yet he was not feeling the pain of burning. He saw a lion near the capitol. He saw a hundred women crowded together who told him that they had seen men enveloped in fire walking up and down the streets. Cicero, however, is not afraid of all these happenings. He takes them in a calm way.

Cassius uses Casca's fear to his own advantage. Cicero goes away. Cassius comes and meets Casca. Cassius tells Casca that all these strange and unnatural happenings point out that something wrong and terrible is going to happen to Rome. He further tells him that there is one man in Rome, who is as dangerous and terrible as this stormy night. He moves about like a lion, Casca takes the hint. He knows that Cassius is talking about Caesar. Then clever Cassius says that he has done a wrong thing. He has opened his heart to Casca, who may be a willing slave to Caesar. This remark touches Casca's pride. He gives Cassius his hand, asks him to organise a party, and assures him that he will support him fully.

Cassius gives some forged letters to Cinna. At this moment Cinna also reaches there. He informs Cassius that all the conspirators are waiting for him at a place. Cassius gives Cinna some forged letters and asks him to place those letters at different places in Brutus' house. Cinna and Casca ask Cassius to win Brutus over to their side. Because Brutus is a noble man respected by all. If he supports them, the people will approve of their act of murdering Caesar.

Dramatic significance. This scene with its flashes and thunders, and its strange unnatural happenings, creates a proper atmosphere for the bloody murder of Caesar. It prepares the mind of the readers (*or spectators*) to witness the terrible crime of Caesar's murder. It looks as if all the forces, natural and supernatural, were pointing at the terrible political storm that was to overtake Rome after Caesar's murder.

This scene marks an important stage in the development of the plot (*conspiracy*) against Caesar. Cassius has won Casca and Cinna, Brutus is also nearly half won. Cassius has taken one more step to win over Brutus completely. The forged letters will win him over fully.

The scene brings out some traits of the different characters. We see Casca as a timid and superstitious man. His is mighty afraid of all these strange happenings. Cassius, on the other hand, is a clever man. He is not afraid of these happenings. He uses Casca's fears to his own advantage.

Cicero is a thinker. He is also not disturbed by the terrors of the stormy night. He takes them to be a natural phenomena.

Q. 23. Describe the scene between Brutus and Portia on the morning of Caesar's murder.

What light does it throw on the characters of Brutus and Portia?

Ans. The conspirators hold a meeting at Brutus' house. They take certain decisions and then, take leave of Brutus. It is at this point that Portia, Brutus' wife, comes in.

Portia worried about her husband's restlessness. It is past mid-night. Brutus has been left alone by the conspirators. He is alone in his garden. Portia, his wife comes to him. She finds her husband restless. She feels that something is wrong with him. Brutus tells her that the damp air of the early morning will be injurious for her health. So she should go in and take rest in her bed. But Portia answers that it will be equally injurious for his health too. She further tells Brutus that it was wrong on his part to leave his bed. She sees him brooding and sighing in the night. He scratches his head, and stamps the ground with his foot. He asks her to leave him alone. And she does that. She thinks that it is some kind of a passing mood. But soon after she feels that there is something seriously wrong with her husband. He must tell her the cause of his trouble.

Brutus tries to evade the issue by saying that he is just ill. Portia, then, says that he is not ill. He has some secret thought hanging heavy on his mind. Her doubts and fears were roused by the visit of some six or seven persons who had just left her husband. Portia kneels and begs her husband to tell her his secret. She says that she is a woman, yet she is not an ordinary woman. She is the daughter of a noble father and wife of a noble husband. She has great power of enduring pain. She once gave a wound in her thigh just to prove her power of enduring pain. She assures Brutus that she will not disclose his secret. She also says that as his wife she has a right to share his pleasures, pains and his secrets as well.

Brutus prays to gods to make him worthy of such a noble wife. But there is a knocking at the gate. Brutus asks her to go in. He assures her that soon he will share his secret with her.

This scene throws a flood of light on the characters of Brutus and Portia. We see that Brutus and Portia make an ideal couple. They are ideally married. Each seems to have been cut out for the other.

Portia is a deeply devoted wife. Even the slightest trouble of her husband makes her worried and anxious. But, Portia is not a traditional wife. She is really a life-partner. She is conscious of her rights as a wife. She wants to share all her husband's pains, pleasures and secrets as well.

She knows and admires the greatness of her husband. She is rightly proud of being the daughter of a noble father and wife of a noble husband.

Brutus too, is worthy of such a noble wife. He loves his wife and has a great regard for her individuality. He does not treat his wife slightingly, as Caesar does. Really the marriage of Brutus and Portia is an ideal marriage. It is a marriage of two bodies, two hearts, two minds and two souls.

Q. 24. How does Antony deal with the conspirators immediately after the murder of Caesar ?

How does he get Brutus' permission to address the mob ?

Ans. Antony is a very cunning and clever man. He knows how to deal with his enemies with their own weapons. When the conspirators stab Caesar to death, Antony is panicky. He runs home. But he loves Caesar. He wants to take a terrible revenge on the conspirators for Caesar's murder.

Antony sends his servant. Antony instructs his servant and sends him to the Senate-House. Antony knows that Brutus is a noble man. Brutus is not jealous and cunning like Cassius. So Antony sends his servant to fall at Brutus' feet and request him to allow Antony to meet him. Antony wants that Brutus should assure him that no harm will be done to him. Noble minded Brutus gives this assurance.

Antony comes and pays tributes to Caesar. Antony comes. First he pays tributes to Caesar. He says that all Caesar's glory, all his victories have been reduced to a handful of dust, that, is his dead body. Cunning Antony does this only to impress noble Brutus with his sincerity to Caesar. Antony knows that Brutus will admire this faithfulness and sincerity of his. After this, Antony speaks to the conspirators. He calls them gentlemen. He says that he does not know what more they intend to do ; who else is yet to be killed after Caesar. If they want to kill him, they should kill him right here and now. Because the time of Caesar's death will be the best time for his death. He would like to be killed with those very swords with which Caesar has been killed, and by those very noble men, who have killed Caesar.

This is all a calculated move of clever Antony. He knows that Brutus will not allow any one to touch Antony. Brutus tells him that they mean no harm to him. They are ready to welcome him as a friend. Cassius also tells him that he will have an important position among the administrators of Rome. He will be consulted in matters of giving important posts, titles and honours to the people.

Antony shakes hands with the conspirators. Very cleverly Antony flatters Brutus and his followers. He says that they are all wisemen. Then he shakes hands with them one by one. And then, like a master actor, he poses to be over-whelmed with grief. He says that Caesar's soul will be grieved to see that his dear friend Antony is shaking hands with his murderers. He calls Caesar a brave hart (*deer*) and the conspirators, the bloody hounds who killed that brave hart. Thus, clever Antony hits the conspirators quite hard. But he does it in such a way that they do not feel offended.

When Cassius checks him, he says that even Caesar's enemy will say this much about him, as he has said. Then Cassius asks him what sort of an agreement he wants to have with them. Here also Antony gives an evasive (कुटिल) answer. He says that he shakes hands with them, because he wants to be friendly to them. But, they should give him reasons why they killed Caesar. Brutus assures him that they will fully satisfy him in that regard. After this Antony requests Brutus to allow him to take Caesar's dead body to the market place, and make a speech before the people. Cassius warns Brutus. But Brutus pays no heed to his warning. He allows Antony to make a funeral speech. But he lays one condition that first he himself will address the people, and then, Antony will address them from the same stage. They all leave Antony alone with Caesar's body.

Left alone Antony pours out all his hatred for the conspirators. He hurls curses on them.

Q. 25. Briefly describe the forum scene.

What light does it throw on the characters of Brutus, Antony and the Roman mob ?

Ans. A huge crowd of people has gathered in the forum. They want to know why Caesar has been killed. They shout "Let us be satisfied"

Brutus speaks. Brutus gets on the stage. He tells the people that he loved Caesar as much as any body else loved him. But he killed Caesar only because Caesar was ambitious. He wanted to become a king. As a king he would have become a danger to the Freedom of Rome. Caesar has been killed for the freedom and honour of Rome and the Romans. Brutus killed Caesar because his love for Rome was greater than his love for Caesar.

The mob wants Brutus to be Caesar. The people are impressed with Brutus' personality. But they have understood not a word of his logical speech. They say that Brutus should be made Caesar. What an irony ! Brutus says that Caesar was killed because he was ambitious, he was killed for his ambitious spirit *i.e.*, for Caesarism, and the people say that Brutus should take Caesar's place !

Then, Antony gets on the stage to speak. Antony is a clever man. He knows the mob. He knows that the common people do not understand reason and logic. They are emotional and passionate. They can be roused and excited, but they cannot be convinced with logic and arguments. Antony makes a powerfully moving speech. He gives examples to prove that Caesar was not ambitious. Caesar did all for Rome, nothing for himself. He wept when he saw the sufferings of the poor. Such a kind hearted man can never be ambitious.

Antony shows the mob the wounds of Caesar, and reads out his will. Antony is a master actor. He gets down the stage and shows the people the holes in Caesar's cloak, made by the daggers of the conspirators. This sight moves the mob to tears. Then Antony uncovers the body of Caesar and shows them the wounds on Caesar's body. When the mob is very much excited and enraged Antony reads out the will of Caesar. He reads that in his will Caesar has left seventy five drachmas for each Roman citizen. He has left many of his gardens for free public use. Now the people are just mad with anger. They carry Caesar's body. They run to catch all the conspirators and kill them. They are out to burn, kill and destroy.

This Scene shows that Brutus is an idealist. Brutus has little understanding of men and their motives. He does not know Antony. Cassius warns him not to permit Antony to speak before the mob. But Brutus does not pay any heed to this warning. Brutus does not know the working of the mind of a mob. His speech is cold and logical. He tries to convince the people with his arguments. So he fails miserably.

Antony is a clever and practical man. He can flatter the conspirators, and get from Brutus the permission to address the mob. He knows the mind of the mob. He makes an emotional speech. He touches their heart, because he knows that a mob has no head to think. Antony proceeds very carefully. First he proves Brutus a liar. He rouses people's love and sympathy for Caesar. Then he moves them to pity. After that he fills them with a mad fury against the conspirators. When the mob is in mutiny, Antony is happy. He has roused the evil passions of the people. Now he will see the mob violence take its own course.

Mob. Roman mob, like any other mob, is a mindless multitude. These people in the crowd have no ideas and opinions of their own. They can see, feel, hear, weep, shout, love and kill, but they cannot think and understand anything. When Brutus speaks, he is their hero. They want him to be Caesar. Caesar becomes a tyrant for them. When Antony speaks to them, they forget Brutus. Now Antony is their hero. When he reminds them of Caesar's greatness and generosity, they become mad for the blood of the conspirators. So we see that the mob is fickleminded, ignorant and hero worshipping. The common people can be blind followers of a great hero. To them 'freedom' and honour mean very little.

Q. 26. Describe the Proscription Scene [*Act IV scene (i)*]. What light does it throw on the characters of Antony, Octavius Caesar and Lepidus.

Ans. The Triumvirs (*Octavius Caesar, Antony and Lepidus*) are in a room in Antony's house. They are preparing a list of those people who are dangerous, and so should be killed.

Lepidus' brother and Antony's nephew are to be killed. Octavius tells Lepidus that his brother should also be killed. Lepidus agrees to it on the condition that Antony's nephew is also killed along with his (*Lepidus'*) brother. Antony give his consent.

Lepidus is sent to bring Caesar's will. Then Antony tells Lepidus to fetch Caesar's will. They have decided to reduce the amount of money and some property that Caesar had left for the people of Rome. Lepidus leaves the room.

Antony considers Lepidus only an ass, a beast of burden. When Lepidus is gone, Antony talks about him. He tells Octavius that they should use Lepidus only as an ass. He is a worthless man. He is not fit to be their equal. He has no ideas, no opinions and no taste of his own. He imitates others. He fills his mind with borrowed and second-hand thoughts. For the present, he is sharing the burden of doing certain unpleasant things. But his titles and honours are being borne by him just as an ass bears gold. As soon as they reach their goal, they will take away all his titles and honours. They will leave him like an unloaded ass to graze in the common pastures. The two friends, then drop talking about Lepidus. They discuss important matters. Antony says that Brutus and Cassius have raised a strong army. So, they should also prepare themselves fully to meet the enemy.

Characters :—

Antony. This scene brings out the darker side of Antony. He is a dishonest and insincere friend. He indulges in back-biting. He calls his colleague an ass and says that he should be used only as a tool. He betrays Caesar also. He agrees to tamper with the sacred will of his dearest friend. Antony is very selfish and cruel also. He can barter his nephew for Lepidus' brother.

Octavius. Octavius Caesar is a man of few words. His attitude is that of a man in authority. He is very clever also. When Lepidus agrees to kill his brother, Octavius does not wait for him to complete his sentence. In an authoritative tone he says "Prick him down, Antony."

Lepidus is really a poor and pitiable, fellow. He is no more than an errand boy to Antony. Antony sends him to bring Caesar's will. He is really fit to be used only as a tool. Antony says that Lepidus is a tried and "valiant soldier", but we do not see his courage or bravery.

Q. 27. Describe the Parley between the leaders of the two opposing armies on the eve of the Battle of Philippi. What light does it throw on their characters ?

Ans. Forces of Antony and Octavius stand ready to fight. Octavius and Antony are on the fields of Philippi. Their forces are waiting for their orders. Octavius says that Antony has been wrong in supposing that the enemy would not come down the hills to face them. Antony says that he knows the enemy forces and their intentions. They are really afraid of them, but they are marching down with a show of bravery and military splendour.

A messenger informs them that the enemy forces are marching with all their military splendour.

Brutus, Cassius and their forces reach there. With their forces, Cassius and Brutus also reach there. Now the two forces stand facing each other. Brutus and Cassius move to hold a parley with the leaders of the enemy forces.

An exchange of bitter taunts, hot words and challenges. Brutus asks them if they want to exchange words before exchanging blows. Octavius who is impatient, says that he does not love words as Brutus and Cassius do. Brutus retorts that good words are still better than bad blows. He taunts Octavius that he (*Octavius*) is not a very good soldier or warrior. Antony, here makes a biting remark. He tells Brutus that he is a hypocrite; he can speak sweet words with his tongue and give treacherous blows with his hands. This is what he did to Caesar. With his tongue he cheered Caesar and with his hands he stabbed him. Cassius taunts Antony that his tongue has stolen all the honey of the bees. Antony retorts that his 'words are not only bitter but biting also. He tells them that they betrayed Caesar. They grinned like monkeys before Caesar ; they crawled like dogs at his feet, but they killed him treacherously.

Octavius loses his patience. Octavius does not like this exchange of words. He wants actual fighting to start. He draws out his sword and says that he will either avenge Caesar's death or die at the hands of his murderers. Brutus here arrogantly remarks that dying at Brutus' hand would be a good fortune for Octavius. Octavius calls him a traitor. Cassius calls Octavius "a peevish school boy," and Antony, a 'masker and reveller.' Octavius grows impatient; he challenges them to come to the battlefield and fight.

Characters :

Antony. We see that Antony can be very bitter and biting, Brutus and Cassius cannot answer him properly.

Octavius Caesar. Octavius Caesar is impatient to fight and avenge Caesar's death. He does not like wasting words in vain.

Cassius and Brutus now seem to be suffering from a guilty conscience. They wince (तिलमिलाना) under the verbal lashes of Antony. They have no real answer to make. Cassius tries to be harsh but fails. Brutus shows his arrogance when he says that death at his hands would be a good fortune for Octavius Caesar.

Q. 28. Describe the feelings of Cassius on the eve of the Battle of Philippi. What changes do you notice in him ?

Ans. Cassius is now in a depressed and demoralized state of mind. His thoughts are gloomy. The taunts of Antony have struck him home. The enemy forces have moved away. Cassius says that he is now going to act against his will. He tells Messala that once he had no belief in portents and omens. But now he believes in these omens and portents which foretell coming events. He tells him how while they were marching from Sardis, two huge eagles came down and sat on the foremost flag of their army. They were fed by their soldiers. But now those eagles have disappeared. Only ravens, crows and kites are hovering over their heads. They indicate that their armies will be defeated and destroyed.

Then Cassius asks Brutus what he will do if they are defeated. Brutus says that he will not commit suicide like Cato, his father-in-law. But he will not let himself be carried to Rome as a prisoner. Cassius would rather kill himself than be a prisoner. The two friends part with heavy hearts and a faint hope of victory.

Here we see Cassius a changed man. All his intellect and intelligence has been crushed by a sense of guilt and prospects of a defeat. All his confidence is gone now. He is now waiting for his doom. Mentally he has surrendered to the spirit of Caesar.

Q. 29. Describe the events leading to the suicide of Cassius. What light does this incident throw on his character ?

Ans. Cassius is defeated. Forces of Brutus gain some advantage over the forces of Octavius. They feel certain of their victory, and so take to looting and plunder. Cassius does not get any help or support from Brutus' side. There is panic in his ranks. His soldiers are running away from the battle field. Cassius is defeated. He himself kills one of his flag-bearers, who was running away from the field.

Cassius sends Titinius. Cassius sees some troops in the distance. He sends Titinius to find out if those troops are friends or enemies. Titinius leaves Cassius with Pindarus. Cassius is very much disturbed and impatient. He just cannot wait for Titinius. He asks Pindarus to climb higher up the hill on which they are standing, and see Titinius riding. Pindarus should tell him all that he sees in the distant battle-field.

Pindarus gives a wrong report. Pindarus sees some soldiers on horse-backs rushing towards Titinius. Some of them get down their horses. Titinius also gets down. The soldiers surround him and shout. These are the victorious soldiers of Brutus. They, in fact cheer Titinius. But poor Pindarus misunderstands the whole incident. He tells his master that Titinius has been surrounded and taken prisoner by enemy soldiers.

Cassius cannot bear the shock and so he kills himself. When Pindarus comes down. Cassius sets this slave free (*Pindarus was Cassius' slave*). Then he gives Pindarus his sword, and asks him to run it into his body. Pindarus a faithful slave cannot but obey his master. Cassius covers his face, and Pindarus runs the sword into his master's heart. Cassius dies with these words.

"Caesar, thou art revenged.
Even with the sword that kill'd thee."

This incident shows that Cassius does not have that balance and patience which we find in Brutus. He is imbalanced and suspicious. He cannot wait to make certain whether Pindarus' report is correct or not. He is so impulsive that without even a moment's thought he kills himself. In the murder scene also, we see him losing all balance and self control, when he sees Popilius Laena whispering something into Caesar's ear. But, otherwise, Cassius is a true Roman. He dies a free man. He prefers death to dishonour and slavery. He does deserve the tribute that Brutus pays to him.

Q. 30. Describe the death of Brutus. What light does this incident throw on various characters ?

Ans. Brutus with a few friends in a corner of the fields of Philippi. Cassius and Titinius are dead. Forces of Brutus and Cassius have been routed. We see Brutus with a few friends who are still living. Brutus has now made up his mind to commit suicide. Brutus asks Clitus to kill him. But Clitus shrinks back in horror Brutus requests all of them, one by one but they all refuse to kill their noble friend. Voluminius says "That is not an office for a friend my Lord." Brutus is proud of these faithful and loyal friends. He says :—

"My heart doth joy that yet in all my life
I found no man but he was true to me."

There is an alarum. Clitus asks Brutus to run to some safer place. Brutus tells them to go and says that he will follow. They all leave Brutus with Strato, his servant. Brutus asks Strato to hold his sword. Strato does that, and Brutus runs on it and falls dead.

His last words are :

"Caesar now the still :
I killed not thee with half so good a will".

Like Cassius, Brutus also surrenders to the all powerful spirit of Caesar.

This incident shows us the loyalty of Brutus' friends. They all love him and are faithful to him. We find nobleness and grandeur of Brutus' character even at the last moment of his life, He is proud of his loyal friends, and meets death with a perfect calm .

Q. 31. Write a note on the character of Caesar basing primarily on the references made to him by the various characters in the drama.

Or

Write a note on Caesar in the eyes of the other characters in the play *"Julius Caesar."*

Ans. Caesar himself does not appear for long. Julius Caesar himself appears only in three scenes. First we see him heading the procession which goes to the place where feast of Lupercalia is held. Then we see him with Calpurnia, his wife, at his home. And lastly we see him in the Senate-house where he is murdered by the conspirators. Caesar's character does not develop before our eyes as fully as Cassius' and Brutus' characters do. We come to know of Caesar through other characters. Some are prejudiced against him, some are jealous of him and some, like Antony, are deeply devoted to him.

Caesar in the eyes of the mob. Caesar is almost a god in the eyes of the common people of Rome. They come in the streets to welcome Caesar, their hero. They scatter flowers in his path. They are mad with joy when they see Caesar refusing the crown. Caesar is for them a living symbol of all honour, power and glory. When Caesar is dead, they must make Brutus a Caesar. For they cannot follow and worship anyone who is not Caesar. When Antony reawakens their love for Caesar, they weep for Caesar and run madly after the blood of Caesar's murderers. Caesar is the most powerful and popular hero of the common people of Rome.

Caesar in the eyes of Casca. For Casca, Caesar is a fearful man. He flatters him and kneels before him. But, otherwise he considers Caesar a silly fellow who is weak in the body. In Casca's opinion. Caesar seeks cheap popularity and flatters the crowd of dirty fools. In his eyes, Caesar is ambitious and power hungry. Though he refuses the crown outwardly, yet in the heart of his hearts he longs for it.

Caesar in the eyes of Decius Brutus. Decius Brutus is also jealous of Caesar. He considers Caesar a man who can be won through flattery. According to him Caesar loves to be flattered. He can be flattered into doing anything. He says

"*When I tell him, he hates flatterers,*

He says, he does : being then most flattered.

Decius gives a flattering interpretation to Calpurnia's dream, and also tells Caesar that the senators are going to offer him a crown. Thus he makes Caesar change his decision of staying at home.

Caesar in the eyes of Calpurnia. In the eyes of his wife, Caesar is a great man, a prince whom gods are warning through omens. He is a great man to be worshipped and loved and obeyed. But, she thinks him to be overconfident. She says "My lord your wisdom is consumed in confidence". Caesar pays no heed to her warning as well as to the warning given by his augurers.

Caesar in the eyes of Antony. For Antony, Caesar is a beloved friend, a great-general, a beloved leader of his people and a kind and generous man. In his funeral speech he speaks of the great victories won by Caesar. He tells the people that after his victories Caesar brought great wealth to Rome and the Roman people. He reads out Caesar's 'will.' He tells the mob that Caesar has left seventy five Drachmas for each Roman citizen, and many of his gardens for free public use. All this proves that for Antony Caesar is a great lover and real servant of his people. He is not at all ambitious.

Caesar in the eyes of Cassius. Cassius is jealous of Caesar. He is blind to all greatness and goodness of Caesar. He finds Caesar a weak and worthless man, who has become all powerful just by chance. He has become a wolf because Romans have become weak and mild like lambs. Caesar has become a giant, only because the Romans have lost their love of freedom and honour. Cassius thinks that this worthless man has become a dictator, a tyrant. He has made all Romans his petty slaves. He must be killed to save the honour and freedom of Rome.

Caesar in the eyes of Brutus. Brutus loves Caesar. For him Caesar is a great man. He is good and reasonable. He himself says "I have not known when his affections swayed more than his reasons". He calls him "the foremost man of the world. But he fears that Caesar's ambition will make him a danger to the freedom of Rome and the Romans. He considers him like a serpent's egg which may one day become a dangerous snake. Brutus fears that Caesar will become a king. When he becomes a king, he will become a cruel tyrant. So he should be killed before he becomes a king.

We see that Cassius and Casca look on Caesar through coloured glasses. We cannot believe all that they say against Caesar. Caesar has something great in him. He is a very powerful and the most popular man of Rome. He must have some worth and merit in him which makes him so great.

Q. 32. Describe the appearance of Caesar's ghost.

Ans. Brutus's state of mind when the ghost appears. Brutus has had a bitter quarrel with his closest friend and colleague Cassius. His heart is heavy with the deep grief and pain caused by the tragic death of his wife. He has taken a cup or two of wine to drown the pain of his heart. He is sleepy and tired. It is night. His servant Lucius, and his guards are fast asleep. All round there is deep silence. A dim candle is flickering in Brutus' tent. Brutus' eye sight, too, is slightly weak. So, the atmosphere is favourable for the appearance of the ghost of Caesar. It may be the figment of Brutus' own mind, a kind of hallucination (*illusion,* मतिभ्रम). Ghosts and supernatural beings are generally seen only in such an atmosphere of loneliness, silence and haziness (धुंधला प्रकाश).

Brutus challenges the ghost. Brutus first thinks that it is only an illusion of his weak eyes. He asks the ghost if it is really a ghost. A sudden fear overpowers Brutus. His hair stand on end. Brutus again asks who he is. The ghost says, "Thy evil spirit, Brutus". Brutus further asks him why he has come. The ghost says that it has come to tell Brutus that it will meet him again in the plains of Philippi. The ghost disappears. Brutus wakes his guards and his servant. He asks them if they have seen something. They say that they have not seen anything.

Brutus again sees this ghost in the field of Philippi. But this time the appearance of the ghost is reported by Brutus. The ghost does not appear on the stage. In the first meeting the ghost was on the stage,

There is a controversy about this ghost of Caesar. Some people think that the ghost is a real one. Some say that it is only a product of Brutus' disturbed mind and excited imagination. This controversy is futile. Caesar's ghost is seen only by Brutus. And it plays an important part. It shows that Caesar's spirit is still wandering about to take a terrible revenge on his enemies. Shakespeare has presented the ghost in such a way that we can take it as a real ghost or as only a figment of Brutus' fevered fancy.

Q. 33. How has destiny or sense of fate been revealed in the play *"Julius Caesar"* **?**

Or

"The play Julius Caesar is pervaded by the notion of irresistible destiny". **Discuss.**

Ans. Fate seems to play an important role in the play.

Caesar suffers death because he is proud and pays no heed to the warnings given to him. Brutus is drawn into the conspiracy because he loves Rome and the freedom of Rome, and because a clever man like Cassius convinces him that ambitious Caesar is a danger to the freedom of Rome. Antony succeeds because he is a practical man. Brutus fails because he is impractical. Thus we see that in 'Julius Caesar' characters suffer or succeed because of their own strength or weakness. But, still we feel that some superhuman force is at work. It looks as if the major characters were driven to their doom by some invisible but irresistible force. In the beginning, fate seems to be favouring Cassius and his cause of conspiracy. He gets supporters easily. He wins Casca and Brutus. Caesar, too does not pay heed to any warning. It looks as if fate draws Caesar to his doom. His wife warns him, the augurers warn him, the soothsayer warns him, and Artemidorus hands him a written warning, yet Caesar pays no heed to anyone of these.

In the second phase the fate seems to have changed sides. After Caesar's murder destiny is against the conspirators. The leadership is now in the hands of Brutus, who is least fit to lead a conspiracy. Brutus commits the most fatal blunder. Inspite of Cassius' warning he allows Antony to address the mob. Antony becomes an instrument of fate. He rouses the fury of the mob against the conspirators. Now the tables are turned on the conspirators.

Brutus, Cassius, Caesar—all are puppets in the hands of this blind goddess of fate. At one point Cassius says :

"The fault dear Brutus, is not in our stars

But in ourselves that we are underlings.

But this very Cassius grows superstitious and fatalistic near his end. He sees ravens, crows and kites as the warnings of fate announcing death and destruction of his troops. Fate plays the dirtiest trick on Cassius when Pindarus misunderstands, Titinius' welcome by Brutus' soldiers. He gives Cassius a wrong report. This fatal mistake made by chance leads to Cassius' suicide.

Portia and Cinna. Portia falls a victim to an unfounded fear when she swallows burning coals. Poor Cinna suffers for no fault of his. He admits' that :

"*I have no will to wander forth*

Yet something leads me forth."

This something is that irresistible fate which sends Brutus to his doom. Once Brutus said that he considers cowardly to commit suicide. But fate forces him to commit suicide against all his principles.

Supernatural element is the force of fate. The stormy night with all the strange and supernatural happenings *e.g.*, Calpurnia's dream, the result of the sacrifice offered by the augurers, Cinna's dream in which he feasted with Caesar, and the appearance of Caesar's ghost—all these things prove that some force beyond the control of man is at work.

EXERCISE FOR PRACTICE

1. Describe in your own words what Marullus says to the crowd of common people, in (Act I Scene I) ? What light do these words throw on his character ?
2. How does Cassius convince Brutus of Caesar's ambition ?

   Or

   Describe in your own words the meeting of Brutus and Cassius. What do they say to each other ?

   What light does this first meeting throw on their characters ?
3. How does Cassius use the supernatural happenings and Casca's fear of them to his own advantage ?

   Or

   In Act I, Scene (*iii*) Cassius meets Casca. Cicero has just left them. Write in your own words what passes between Cassius and Casca. How does Cassius win Casca over to his side ?
4. What do the conspirators decide in their meeting at Brutus' house ? What light does it throw on their respective characters ?
5. Reproduce in your own words the dialogue that Portia has with her husband ?

   What estimate do you make of Portia's character ?
6. Compare and contrast Julius Caesar and Brutus as husbands ?
7. How did Antony prove to the mob of Roman citizens that Caesar was not ambitious ?

   How did he rouse their fury against the conspirators ? What did the angry mob do ?
8. What do you think of Brutus as a public speaker ?

   Or

   Discuss Brutus' character under the following headings. (*a*) His honesty. (*b*) His idealism and his impractical mind. (*c*) His moral arrogance and (*d*) His tenderness.
9. What mistakes did Brutus commit ? How did those mistakes harm the cause of conspiracy ?

   Or

   Which was Brutus', biggest blunder ? How did it affect the conspirators ?
10. Discuss Antony' character under the following headings. (*a*) His practicality (*b*) his unscrupulousness (*c*) his cruelty, and (*d*) his selfishness.
11. "Cassius and Antony both are thoroughly practical and unprincipled yet Cassius is a better man." Discuss.